LOST VOICES
OF THE
EDWARDIANS

Also by Max Arthur

Above All, Courage: The Falklands Front Line: First-Hand Accounts

*Forgotten Voices of the Great War: A New History of WWI
in the Words of the Men and Women Who Were There*

*Forgotten Voices of the Second World War: A New History of the
Second World War in the words of the Men and Women
Who Were There*

Symbol of Courage: A Complete History of the Victoria Cross

*Lost Voices of the Royal Navy: Vivid Eyewitness Accounts of Life
in the Royal Navy from 1914–1945*

*Lost Voices of the Royal Air Force: Vivid Eyewitness Accounts of Life
in the Royal Air Force from 1918 to the Present Day*

The Last Post: The Final Word from our First World War Soldiers

LOST VOICES
OF THE
EDWARDIANS

MAX ARTHUR

Harper*Press*

An Imprint of HarperCollins*Publishers*

HarperCollins*Publishers*
77–85 Fulham Palace Road,
Hammersmith, London W6 8JB

www.harpercollins.co.uk

Published by HarperCollins*Publishers* 2006
1

A catalogue record for this book is
available from the British Library

ISBN–13 978–00–0–721613–0
ISBN–10 0–00–721613–0

Set in Minion by
Rowland Phototypesetting Ltd,
Bury St Edmunds, Suffolk

Printed and bound in Great Britain by
Clays Ltd, St Ives plc

CONTENTS

INTRODUCTION

In a world of high-speed travel and communications, advanced medical science and multi-media entertainment at the touch of a button, it is hard to conceive of a life where it was not unusual for country dwellers to pass a whole lifetime without leaving their native county. A great gulf separated the rich and the poor. For the wealthy, it was a life of comfort, with every whim attended to, while the poorest suffered almost unimaginable deprivation.

At the start of the twentieth century, life moved at a slower pace – the rich had carriages or, increasingly, cars. The poor went on foot, walking miles to work before a day in the factory, the mine, the mill or in the fields. The picture was the same throughout the country.

For country people the big excitement was the arrival of a travelling fair, or the annual one-day holiday for the works outing – perhaps to the seaside. In cities there were the raucous music halls, while the earliest cinemas were showing glamorous silent films. With no television, radio or recorded music, people were forced to make more of their own entertainment. The changing seasons brought traditional festivals and celebrations, while children displayed extraordinary ingenuity with their playground games.

Work – or the lack of it – was a key factor in the family's survival, and an industrial illness or injury to the breadwinner could be devastating. Children officially left school at the age of fourteen – often after a spell of working split days where they went to school in the morning and to work in the afternoon – but in big families, the oldest child would often have to start work even younger to support the growing numbers. For those with no family and no work, the spectre of the workhouse still loomed.

Working-class communities were close-knit – tenement dwellers in the cities and rural villagers alike – and in times of adversity or illness, neighbours rallied around. Where a doctor or midwife cost money that the family could ill afford, it was not unusual for a local woman to deliver babies, sit with the dying and lay out the bodies – often for no payment.

It has been my pleasure to meet a number of men and women who were born before and during the Edwardian period, the oldest being Henry Allingham, who is now 109. Their stories, along with those of many other ordinary people that have been recorded over the last forty years by a range of voluntary groups, archives and institutions, create a unique glimpse into an age which is now almost entirely beyond our reach. The length of the accounts I have chosen vary, some take many pages, whereas others simply select the most affecting moments. Most contributors appear only once, while others you will see several times. It has been a privilege to listen to the voices of these men and women, many now long dead, and to bring together their vivid memories. These are their words – I have been but a catalyst.

Max Arthur
London
January 2006

PROLOGUE
END OF AN ERA

Jim Davies
We lived in Windsor and I used to see Queen Victoria quite often on her terrace with her two Indian attendants. I suppose I was four years old. My father was a great patriot, but to me she was an old woman in a black bonnet.

Kitty Marion
On 22 January 1901, the manager of the Opera House, Cheltenham, announced to the audience the news of Queen Victoria's death. People listened and quietly dispersed. It seemed as if the world stood still and could never continue without the Queen. However, the following day King Edward VII was proclaimed King and life went on as usual.

Arthur Harding
It was the most extraordinary thing. Everybody – the children as well – wore black. Everyone was in mourning. Even poor little houses that faced onto the street put a board up and painted it black. All the shops had black shutters up and everyone felt as if they'd lost somebody. It was extraordinary that people who were starving for the best part of their lives should mourn the old Queen. I was a bit of a rebel and I couldn't really understand it.

1

Funeral of Queen Victoria, Windsor 1901, with her son
King Edward VII leading the procession.

Clement Williams

In 1901 I was in the Oxfordshire Light Infantry and I was present at Queen Victoria's funeral. The day was bitterly cold. It was snowing hard and we had to leave Oxford at five o'clock to get there in time. We caught the train, but there were no heated carriages in those days. When we arrived at Slough, seeing that we had plenty of time in hand, our commanding officer sent us on a twelve-mile march to warm us up. We marched into Windsor, where we were given a tin mug of beer and a pork pie. Then we stood about and waited until the ceremony began. We lined the route to St George's Chapel but we had nothing to do because the crowds weren't allowed there. It was very interesting to see Queen Alexandra, the Prince of Wales and the two little boys in sailor suits, as they arrived. Trouble began when the coffin arrived on the train. The coffin was supposed to be placed on a gun carriage to be pulled to the castle by horses. The train was late and the day was cold, but with the excitement of all the comings and goings, the horses simply wouldn't move. They didn't like it and were jumping and kicking about, and looked as if they were going to upset the whole thing, so they were taken out of their harnesses. The carriage was supposed to be followed by a Naval Guard of Honour, and a naval officer came forward and suggested that his men be put in place of the horses. The sailors were harnessed onto the gun carriage and they hauled the coffin up the hill right the way up to the castle. Of course, it took them a long time to pull the carriage all that way, and in the meantime, everyone was waiting.

We knew by the salute guns that the coffin must have arrived at Windsor, but it was taking a long time to reach the castle. Time went by and I saw Earl Clarendon, the chap in charge of the ceremony – he kept coming out and looking down the road, wondering why nobody came. You could hear a band in the distance but nothing was happening. Then Queen Alexandra came tearing out, looking this way and that way, before Clarendon persuaded her to go back into the Chapel. Finally, the carriage came along very slowly, hauled along by the Navy. After the ceremony, King Edward VII appeared on the steps of St George's Chapel. He stood with the Kaiser and we gave them the royal salute. They saluted us back. Then they went off and we packed up and went home.

Nina Halliday

We saw the procession from a stand which had been erected under the Guildhall. The seats were covered in black material and everyone wore black clothes, but I had a dress, coat and hat of a lovely mauve colour – I loved it. The streets were lined by Foot Guards and the pavements were packed tight with people all dressed in black. It was a long wait, as the train bringing the coffin and all the important people travelled very slowly from Paddington to Windsor – so that people at the stations which it passed could see it.

It was a wonderful procession, with the Life and Foot Guards playing the Dead March. The Guard of Honour led; then came the gun carriage covered by the Royal Standard. The new King, Edward VII, followed with many of the Queen's relations and Kings and Princes all in uniform. The finest was the Emperor of Germany in a beautiful white uniform and white helmet with lots of gold on it, and many Orders and decorations. Then came the chiefs of the Navy and Army and members of the Queen's Household, followed by members of the Queen's Court, including her daughters and other relations in royal carriages – all, of course, in black with long veils.

I seem to remember that a purple cushion was on the coffin with a small crown on it. The bands had muffled drums and as the procession came along, one could hear the slow booming of the guns. All very solemn, so much black and such a small coffin – but so much colour as well, with so many uniforms.

George Lappage

My chum and I led the procession into Windsor Castle. When that was over, we went back to barracks and that night three troopers and an officer were told to go up to Windsor Castle and do sentry over the Queen's body. I was posted just outside the Chapel door.

CHILDHOOD

Nicholas Swarbrick

I was born in Grimsargh, Lancashire. My mother died quite early of tuberculosis. In those days tuberculosis was incurable, and it was rampant. I was about four when she died, so I never really had a mother. I had one sister and a brother and my sister died of the same disease. She was in her late teens or early twenties. Of course, in those days, consumption used to establish itself, then it became infectious, but it was not infectious in the early stages. It became infectious in my mother when I was about two, and for that reason we had to be kept away from her, which was a dreadful situation. I can remember having to keep some distance away on account of her coughing. So I never had the sort of mother where you could fly into her arms. That was the very thing I was never allowed to do. I didn't know any different, though.

Alfred Anderson

My two older brothers, Dave and Jack, were born in Chicago, because my father had been one of many Dundee men who got recruited to go and help with the building of Chicago, and my mother followed him out there. They came back to Dundee before I was born in 1896. My father continued as a joiner and undertaker and my mother went to work in the jute mill – like her four sisters. I remember in those days we had gas lamps for light and coal fires at home – and we lived on a hill, so the horse-drawn carts had to struggle up and down. I used to play outdoors, and one day I saw

5

A tuppenny eel and meat pie was sometimes as much as
some children could expect to eat in a day.

two soldiers coming down the road – it was 1902 and they were returning from the Boer War. They were so glad to be back; they picked me up and carried me on their shoulders down the road.

Albert 'Smiler' Marshall

My father, James William Marshall, was a farm labourer, and he married a local girl, Ellen Skeet. When I was very small, my father put me onto a wooden cart pulled by a billy goat. When I was two and a half, he put me on the goat's back. The goat didn't like that at first and he bucked me off. My father picked me up and showed me that if I sat facing the tail and kept my arms round him, I could stay on. After that, I progressed to a pony and later to a horse. On most Sundays, my father took me to Colchester to see the soldiers' parade for church. Each regiment had its own particular marching music and I can still recall most of them. What excited me was their red coats. Many of the soldiers had just returned from the Boer War and they were wearing all their medals. At one of the parades, my father was approached by a sergeant of the Devonshire and Somerset Yeomanry who wanted me to become their mascot, but he said no.

Bessy Ruben

I remember arriving in this country. We came from a little village near Lvov, Ukraine, and our passage was booked through an agent. How on earth people arrived here intact, with their family and their few goods, I don't know. We went by train as far as Bremen. As soon as we got there, Mother got lost. She had three children with her, two boys and myself. My younger brother wasn't very strong, and she carried him over her arm. She was twenty-six or twenty-seven at this time. I remember my mother just standing there, waiting. Everybody ran to meet this agent, and Mother couldn't run with the children. My older brother, Sam, was acting like her husband. He looked after her on the journey. She said to him, 'We're lost. I've lost the people we're supposed to meet. What am I to do?' 'Well,' my brother said, 'go into that shop.' And I remember the girl in the shop was jerking some lemonade into a glass, and Mother could speak German, and she went in and she began to cry. This girl said, 'Just sit there for a while, and perhaps they'll come and look for you' – which they did! This agent was just as anxious to find us as we were to find him, and I remember that she was so overjoyed at meeting this man that she took his hands and kissed them.

We got on this cattle-boat – that's all I can describe it as. There were a lot of girls from Hungary going to America, and they took me under their wing. I remember they gave me a bit of chicken to eat. Mother asked me what I was eating and I didn't know what it was – this lady gave it to me. My mother said, 'Throw it away. It's *trefa* – it's not kosher.' Mother was seasick for the whole journey – she didn't eat anything at all, not anything. When we finally arrived in England, I didn't speak any English – only Yiddish. We lived above a shop and she sent me down with a penny farthing, to buy a pound of sugar. I went in and asked for a *fing* of *gemulenin sicha* in my best Yiddish. And everybody in there burst out laughing. I didn't know why. I was so confused. I was only five years old and I stamped my foot and started crying. '*Wo wus yachtielare?*' I shouted, which means 'Why are you laughing at me?' I walked slowly home to my mother with the money. 'Where's the sugar?' she asked. 'I don't know,' I said, 'they just laughed.'

William Roberts

My brother died when he was very young. I remember playing under a table with him. We put a cover across and played tents. We really enjoyed that. When he died, a horse and cab came and took him away. I remember him being carried into the cab through a door at the side. I wasn't supposed to see it – I was very young. They buried him on the edge of the old town.

Bob Rogers

My mother had sixteen children. She had diseased kidneys from too many births. My oldest brother died at twelve months. My second eldest died at ten months. Only me and one sister grew up. My mother had so many miscarriages. In the end, it killed her. She died at the age of forty-six.

Fred Lloyd

I was born on 23 February 1898 at Copwood in Uckfield. There were sixteen of us in our family – I had eight sisters and seven brothers. My parents really loved children. My mother died when she was forty-three – I learned from one of my sisters that she died in childbirth. My father died soon after and they said it was from a broken heart.

Edith Turner

When my brother was three days old, my mother had milk fever. That's when a baby can't suck the milk from the mother and the milk goes to the brain where it causes something like meningitis. It came from worry, anxiety and unemployment. My mother was unstable. She didn't know what she was doing. She smacked my brother's bottom till it was blue, and he kept crying. The more he cried, the more she smacked him, and she couldn't feed him because we hadn't any milk. My father went to the Board of Guardians in Dalston. They sent a doctor to the house and the doctor made an order that my mother should be taken to Homerton Infirmary. So my mother was taken away with my brother strapped to her side on a stretcher. At the same time, a nurse carried my youngest sister downstairs because she was found to have double pneumonia. That left the rest of us with my father.

Jack Banfield

In my family, there were seven children as well as Mum and Dad. Two of the children died as babies. That was very common. When you got over the age of about ten, you were past the post. Until then, there was measles, whooping cough, chicken pox, scarlet fever, so many diseases.

Florence Hannah Warn

When a tiny child died, the cost of a funeral was beyond the pocket of a poor family, so an arrangement was made to bury the infant at the same time as an adult's funeral. In front of the glass hearse there was a little glass compartment running the width of the hearse, and the little coffin was placed there, and so buried in the adult's grave. We had a little brother, Gilbert, who died of pneumonia, and this was the form his burial took. None of us attended the funeral, but I remember we had black sashes to wear on our Sunday dresses.

Don Murray

When I was at school, every class had at least two or three children who were knock-kneed, bow-legged or hump-backed. There was something wrong with at least three or four in each class.

John Wainwright

I had a little sister who died when she was eight. She was out one day, watching my elder brother play football at the local ground. She got a terrible drenching and she finished up with pneumonia. She died soon afterwards.

Edith Turner

I was undernourished and I developed ringworm and eczema. All of my head was covered with sores. I was taken to Homerton Infirmary where all my hair was cut off and my head was covered with a cap and bandages to cover the sores. I was in a proper ward but I was shut away because I was contagious. The treatment was free and supported by voluntary contributions. When I was better and able to come home, my parents were unable to take me. So I was put into the Cottage Homes, which was a place similar to Doctor Barnardo's, where children that they thought were unwanted were cared for until the parents could take them again. There was a matron but I didn't learn any school there. It was more like jobs around the house.

Rosamund Massy

I shall always remember staying in a Salvation Army hostel in a shipping town in the North. Inside that house, run by a remarkable woman, there were many little girls living there for safety, having all been criminally assaulted. These poor little children were between eight and ten years of age and their little old faces were heart-breaking. One of them told us that she had never had a toy in her life.

Florrie Passman

I was involved with a day nursery, and I used to visit the mothers who had young babies, in their homes. They used to take them to the nursery at about two weeks old, until they were four or five. The little girls were dressed in pink, and the little boys in blue, and when they went home, the clothes they'd worn in the daytime were put into tubs and washed, and they went home in their own things, which had been fumigated. This was because in the rooms of the places they came from there were bugs on the walls. They were difficult to get rid of because there were so many children living together.

I can remember a Rabbi telling me, 'Do you know, when I first came to England, I fell on my knees and I was kissing the earth. In Russia I was frightened to walk through a street in case I was going to be arrested – for doing nothing. But here you can walk about – you can laugh and talk – and no one's going to touch you here. What better place can you be in than in England?'

Mrs Landsman

I was in Petticoat Lane and I can remember seeing a child of about eight with no shoes and no stockings on, with his foot cut. A policeman picked the kid up and put him on his shoulder, and was carrying him to a hospital with blood pouring from his leg.

E. J. Dutch

I had appendicitis before the First World War. It used to be called congestion of the bowels, but then the King had it and they started calling it appendicitis.

Steve Tremeere

Mother had what they called a breakdown. She was taken queer and they took her straight over to the asylum, and she was there till she died at the age of fifty-four. Well, Father had been just an ordinary fisherman. He'd been brought up in the workhouse and he'd come out at thirteen and was apprentice to a trawlerman at Yarmouth. Well, he had to leave the sea and he went as a labourer. I was eighteen months old. There was my sister four years older than me and my brother Reggie in between. Aunt Maria, she wanted to take the girl, and Annie wanted to take Reggie, but Father said no. 'I'll bring them up all on my own,' he said.

Any rate, I went to school when I was three and a half. We wore petticoats then and we were left in another room, and we all played together. It wasn't supervised by a teacher. Sometimes older girls looked after you. Sometimes my sister came down there for an hour and looked after us.

I went to St Mary's School when I was six. Our teacher was an old spinster – a proper martinet, but she had a heart of gold. In her desk there was always an apple or orange or something which she cut up in little bits for us. Then we went up to the big school at eleven. You had exams then, and you had to get so many before you could go up into the next class. If you didn't get that, you stopped down there. I know some boys that stopped in number one till they left school at fourteen. We had one teacher who could take every-thing – every subject the whole of the year. Within a fortnight he knew every boy, and within one month he had you all weighed up. Them what could get on with their work used to go up the back of the class. All what were backward he had down in front of him. Always forty, forty-five boys in one class.

We were harum-scarums. It didn't matter about clothes – there was no school uniform then. As long as your hands and face were clean, that was it. You could go to school and you'd see some boys with a pair of trousers on and you wouldn't know what was the original cloth, it was patched so much. The only thing he looked at was your face and your neck and your hands. If he caught you, you went out to the wash-house. It was cold water – and you washed yourself, too. If you didn't wash he'd send a couple of older boys to wash you.

Elsie Beckwith

I remember holding my parents' hands as we walked into the hall, and we got seats downstairs. There was a sort of platform, and this boy was there. I thought his father was there – there was someone with him anyhow – but I was just a kid and I wasn't interested much. This boy said he was going to speak about salvation, and he took as his text 'How can we escape if we neglect so great a salvation?' I was only a kid, I was just listening, but I remember the text because my father wrote it down, he was an awful fellow for writing things down, he used to read them over and over again. I used to get it off, and mother said, 'Oh yes, that was the boy preacher. Hebrews 2.'

It was just a boy preaching, but everybody was talking about it at the time. It was at Howard Hall, a picture hall, I think, they had taken it over just for that Sunday evening. It was unusual, that's why people were so interested. They came from different chapels, Presbyterians, all kinds of things.

It was unusual to see a black person. If they came in on the boat they kept to where the boat was, the lower parts of North Shields, where the quay is. That's where they went into lodgings. As a child you weren't allowed to go there. Clive Street was terrible, the people living there would frighten you.

Steve Tremeere

Hard to believe, but poor or not, beggars an' all, we all went to Sunday school. It was a sprat to catch a mackerel. You had a stamped card. If you went to school on Sunday, the teacher would stamp it with a star. You had to have so many stars before you qualified to go to the school treat in the summer. Father used to give us whatever he could muster then – generally sixpence. We'd all go down there in Chitty and Mannering's carts, what they used to cart the flour about in. They used to fill them up with us kids and take us all the way up the town to where the mill is, along the river bank there. At the back was all fields, and that'd be where we had the treat – muffins and bits of bread and lumps of seed cake and one thing and another. Then there would be little sports as your ages went up. You got a little memento, and there were little stalls where you could spend your tanner. Farthing worth of dosh – toffee. It used to be wrapped up in newspaper. You could never get it off the paper once she'd wrapped it.

Anne Taylor

If you wanted a doctor you had to go round to one of these church people and get this form to fill in and take that down to the doctor's. Then he pleased himself whether he came or not. No welfare state then. If you hadn't got a ticket and you hadn't got half a crown, he wouldn't come in the house and look at you. The most dangerous things were diphtheria and scarlet fever when we were kids. Everybody had a dose of senna pods or brimstone and treacle every week. Kept you healthy – regular. For colds we used to have to go down to the chemist for two penn'orth of Friar's Balsam, penn'orth of aniseed and a penn'orth of sweet nitre. Father would get a spoonful of sugar and put three drops on it. Two drops for us kids, three for him. Your cold was cured. In the winter he'd get Russian tallow and he used to rub it on our chests, and since our clothes weren't thick, he'd wrap sheets of brown paper round us.

There were children, some was starved. You could see the poor little buggers – they come out with rickets – irons on their legs. Or you might be playing with this girl, same age, and when she got about twelve, you could see it coming, consumption. That was very rife amongst them. Any rate, most kids weren't so big as now, because they never had free milk or anything like that. Half of them never had dinners – but we always got one good one at the weekend.

Billy Brown

On a Saturday night that bedroom window was our look-out. The parents would think we were asleep, but we'd get up there and watch all the old women down there, all chin-wagging. If there was a fight we could watch it in the grand circle without anybody interfering with us. We often got up there in the middle of the night and had a look. There was a big lodging house out the back of us – Irish navvies in it, all sorts while they was building the breakwater. Irish navvies and their women. You should have heard the language of them! No wonder we learnt it when we was little. Drink – fight among theirselves. Then you'd see the old women popping down there every half-hour – sometimes less than that – penn'orth of porter. In the pub at the bottom or else the one over the other side of the road – The Cause Is Altered. They drunk more beer indoors than what the old man drunk outside. Then they used to shout at him because he'd been drinking!

Don Murray

My dad used to do everything wrong. He went with the choir one weekend to a cricket match. He only went as a spectator, but they were a man short so they decided he should keep wicket. He had no flannels and he decided not to take his bowler hat off. Well, the ball came to him and instead of using his hands, he stuck the hat out and the ball shot straight through it. When he came home that night, he stood in the doorway as drunk as he ever could be, with this little lid on top of his broken hat and a lot of sausages hanging out of his coat pocket down one side. He'd bought them for Mum as a gift offering to keep her sweet. She took one look at him and called him a damned fool. He looked at her. 'What have I done wrong now, my dear?' he asked. He was a very funny man. He was a very good singer, too. He used to sing in the pubs on the Saturday night. Mum would go down there to listen and when they came home they'd quarrel. I used to lay in my bed shivering, dreading them coming home and quarrelling.

Reece Elliott

In those days we were lucky if we had one pair of boots – no shoes, dear me. Many a time we walked with two odd uns. People who were well off would hoy them out over the wall, we used to get them and pick all the good uns out, you'd be maybe running about with a six and a seven, or maybe a seven and a nine.

My father cut my hair, and you know what he used to cut my hair with? Horse clippers. He was in with the horsekeeper at the pit, who used to give him big combs, when they were too bad for the horses. They had that many teeth broken, they used to give them to my father. You can imagine what that was like, sitting on the bloody cracket, getting your hair cut, all off, little bit top left, aye, the yakkers cut! Just a bit left on top. With the teeth being broken, he must have gone o'er the bugger umpteen times, like a bad cut in a cornfield! I used to be laughing when he was doing us. Sitting there squawking and scringing. My mother, not showing sympathy, would say, 'Be canny, you bugger, sit still!' Especially our Lance, he had a cowlick, Father says, 'I cannot do nowt with this bugger, it'll all have to come off!'

Bessy Ruben

My friend Dinah's mother had a cheese stall down Petticoat Lane every day except Saturdays. I used to go with Dinah to collect this cheese. One day, we dawdled along, taking our time, and we changed dresses, like children do. I put her dress on and she put mine on. Her mother was waiting for us to come back, and when we finally arrived, she mistook me for Dinah and clouted me. I said, 'I'm not Dinah!' and she said, 'Never mind, you're just as bad!'

Tom Kirk

In 1908, my father died. I went to the reception after his funeral, where I was reprimanded by Uncle Harold for kicking a football about the lawn. 'Tom, please, NOT at a time like this!' Sadly, I realise that I had seen so little of Father in the preceding year that his death meant little.

Jim Crow

When Mother died, Father got married again, and it was disastrous. She drank like a fish. I remember my father visiting my grandfather at his house in Lincolnshire and bringing the second wife with him. We were in the sitting room, having lunch, when my grandfather turned to my father and said, 'Jack, I don't think much of your choice.'

Jack Banfield

On the way home from school, one of the routines was to pick up what bits of wood you found along the wharves on the Thames, so that when you got indoors, Mum'd be able to light the fire. When I got in, Mum'd say 'Your dad's not been in, he must be working. Go round to the wharf and see.' So we went to where he was working and he'd say, 'Yes. We're working till seven o'clock. Fetch me a jug of tea.' So I'd take him a jug of tea and wait outside the back gate. When he'd finished the tea, he'd give me the jug back and there'd be some ripe bananas in it, off one of the ships, for us to have for our tea.

Freda Ruben

I didn't have any new clothes and I used to cry about it. My friends Fanny and Florrie used to go to Petticoat Lane to buy lovely dresses, and I wanted one. My mother said she'd got no money. I cried and cried – but I never got anything. If I wanted a farthing, I used to cry for it and not get it. I remember crying myself sick because I wanted one of those peppermints shaped like a walking stick. My mother wasn't impressed. 'All right,' she said, 'cut my throat.' 'I want a walking stick,' I wailed. 'Well,' she said, 'you can't have it.'

Ethel Barlow

Dad was an engine driver. He drove a steam train between Plaistow Station and Aldgate East. My brothers used to wait for him and he'd take one at a time on his engine for a little ride. When he came past our house on the goods train, he used to toot us up and my mother would come out to the garden and he'd thrown her a side of bacon and a huge lump of coal for our fire. That happened very often. There was a lot of pilfering like that. One day he came home and he had about ten pairs of new boots in his bag. We all had a pair. Another day, he came home with six bottles of whisky and gin. He hid them in the coal cupboard underneath the boards. He used to come home with all sorts of things: thirty bars of Fry's Chocolate Cream, a bag full of crabs and shrimps, all sorts. It helped us a lot – his wages was only £2.10 shillings. Every day of his life he went to work on bread and cheese and a can of tea. The railway police came to us once but they didn't find anything. My cousin Frank was also an engine driver and he lived round the back of us. The railway police went in his house and his wife tried to hide all the bottles but the police heard them clinking and they locked him up. He lost his job.

My mother was nearly always drunk, so I used to take my three brothers out of the house when I got home from school. One day, when my dad got home from work, he couldn't find my mother anywhere. We went out into the garden to see if she was there and we found her in the chicken shed on the ground, blind drunk, all the chickens running over her. So he picked her up, fetched her indoors, washed her and put her to bed nice and clean. He never said a word to her about it, not an angry word ever. He had the patience of a saint.

Arthur Harding

Every night, there were children in the pub all night long until the Liberal Party stopped it, and that was as late as 1911.

Mary Keen

On the Sabbath, I used to wake up with an awful feeling that something terrible had happened. There was just a feeling in the air. You daren't laugh and all your toys and books had to be put away. My father used to sit with a newspaper while we washed, tidied up the house and got ready for church. I had one special frock for Sunday and a top petticoat. In those days, I was bundled up from the top down to my boots. This petticoat had a starched top which used to cut into my neck. It was so painful that when it got to tea time, I would look at the clock, thinking, 'God, only another two hours before I go to bed.' I was so glad to take that thing off. At church, we sat in a pew and I would pass the plate, and if we were flush, one of us would put a ha'penny in, otherwise we put nothing in. I told a vicar once how I hated Sundays. I think I shocked him. After church, we had to go to Sunday school. In the evening, we were allowed out, but we were never allowed to 'hang about' as Father called it. We had to go for a walk and I used to like going to Kensal Green cemetery. I used to watch the people weeping and putting flowers on the graves and I used to think it must be lovely to be dead.

Ernest Hugh Haire

I can remember our Sundays. My parents were great church-goers. Father wore a frock coat and a tall hat and Mother wore leg-o'-mutton sleeves. We went to morning service and evening service and I went to Sunday school in between. People used to come to our house after church in the evening to have refreshments. We had cold meats, jellies and blancmange. Our friends brought music with them and we sang round the piano.

Ronald Chamberlain

I was brought up in a very strict environment. On one occasion, I went round to the home of a schoolfellow and he played some rather doubtful comic records on his gramophone. I went home and relayed these to my parents with great glee and was immediately

Boys and girls of St Joseph's and St Matthew's Schools,
Blackburn, 1905.

Children enjoying being filmed and waiting at the factory gates
to give their parents a packed lunch. Alfred Butterworth & Sons,
Glebe Mills, Hollinwood, 1901.

told that I must never go to that place again. There was great strictness about table manners. No elbows on the table. Don't put food in your mouth when it's already full. Don't speak while you're eating. We always said grace before and had to ask permission to leave the table. Similarly, there were very strict rules in regard to the treatment of ladies. We had to open doors for them, let them go before us and walk on the roadside when they were out with us. The way we were dressed as children was very restrictive. At the age of five or six I had a velvet suit with an elaborate lace collar, and I can remember how uncomfortable it was.

Albert 'Smiler' Marshall
Manners were very important in those days. If the boys didn't raise their caps and the girls curtsy to the gentry, then we were given a lesson in manners.

Mrs G. Edwards
There was a lot of crime going on in those days. I was always warned never to speak to anybody and never to take money or sweets from anybody I didn't know. I remember walking in Thornton Heath and a man came the other way, carrying a big bag of coal. As he passed me, he knocked my head and I started to cry. He offered me a penny but I wouldn't take it. That frightened me far more than the bump on the head.

Ella Grace Hunt
My mother used to keep a cane on the table, and if we didn't behave ourselves she said we would get 'Tickle Toby'. That's what she called the cane – 'Tickle Toby'. Well, for the most part we were very well behaved.

Thomas Henry Edmed
We lived in a millhouse on an estate owned by the chairman of the National Provincial Bank. Father was a labourer on the estate. He had been a colour sergeant in the Royal Welch Fusiliers. He was

paid eighteen bob a week, from which he had to pay four bob rent. That left mum with fourteen shillings, for seven children. She had a hell of a time making this money go round. We used to get wood from the estate. We had a big brick oven and mother used to get flour in by the sack and she baked all her own bread. For clothes and shoes, we were always on our uppers. Father had a pension from the Fusiliers. He got seven pound every three months, which would have helped, but the trouble was he used to spend most of it at the tavern.

Edith Turner

While my mother was in hospital with my brother and sister, my father had the opportunity of selling papers to earn himself a few coppers. When he was out doing this, I was locked in a room at home so that I couldn't come in contact with the landlord. The landlord would knock on the door, and when he got no answer he tried to open the door to get in. I used to lie on the floor and watch him to see when he went away.

Mrs G. Edwards

When we were little, my mother would fill the bath in the kitchen and bathe us in there. One day, she brought in a saucepan of boiling water and poured it into the bath, and when she went off to get some cold water, my younger sister fell backwards into the bath. My mother took her to the doctor straight away but he wouldn't have anything to do with it and told mother to take her to St Thomas's Hospital. We didn't think she was going to live. My father came home and when he heard, he was in an awful way and went straight to the hospital. After he left her, he was walking away when he heard her crying. He rushed back again and he found her in the ward with nobody with her and he made an awful fuss about it. He said he wouldn't leave her there. They told him that if he took her away, he'd be responsible for her death. So he left her in the end, but he told my older sister Nellie, who was about fourteen at the time, to go to the hospital to talk to the nurses to try and get them to take an interest in my little sister. She lived, but her back's been all scarred ever since.

Tom Kirk

In 1905 I remember a great adventure – a visit to London! I still remember the smell of leather seats and the swishing of the horses' tails as we went along Station Road. I remember Father's remarks on the train as we neared Peterborough. 'Look out on the right and you may see a red Midland and Great Northern train racing us!' The following day, we went to Brixton to pick up a tram into the City, but the electrical supply had somehow failed, and when the tram finally appeared it was pulled by a horse.

Dorothy Scorey

Mother said we all had to have a trade, because she was left a widow when she was in her forties and she said that if we were ever left like her, you have to have something you can put your hand to. She was so blooming strict with us. 'Any of my girls bring trouble home to me, the workhouse you'll go.' That's what she used to say. She wouldn't let us out after ten o'clock, and if we were talking to a boy, she'd come up and say, 'I don't thank you boys for keeping my girls out at night time!' I always used to say, 'We'll never get married, any of us!'

Ernest Hugh Haire

We had a servant who lived in. Her name was Bridget and we used to call her Biddy. She was a delightful Irish person who kept us in order as children. Her husband was a sailor with the Cunard Line. He lived with us too when he was home from sea, and did odd jobs for Father. He made all sorts of toys for us. They were marvellous people. We had another woman there for a time who was paid £8 a year.

Mary Keen

My father was a very hateful kind of man. None of us liked him. He ruled us with a rod of iron. We were afraid to speak or laugh. He thought we were a lot of dummies. He always rowed with my mother for no reason at all. We'd be sitting at the table, having our meal, and he'd glare at her, then he'd start swearing and cursing and he'd fling up the window and shout out, 'I'm going to let everyone know what you are! You're a so-and-so and a so-and-so!' His language was filthy. Then he'd go out for a walk and he'd come back and he'd be as right as rain. I think he was a bit mad. One morning we woke up and found that he was gone. We were rejoicing, but he'd only gone hop picking in Kent.

Jack Brahms

I was twelve when my mother died and after that I had to fathom for myself. Father couldn't do much for me. He used to make me go to the synagogue every morning and evening but apart from that he wasn't interested. He might have made a meal at the weekend but most of my meals were a ha'p'orth of chips from Phillips, the fish and chip shop in Brick Lane. I'd sit on my doorstep and eat it. Or else, I'd go to the soup kitchen to get a can of soup and a loaf of bread. I used to go to McCarthy's lodging house because they had a fire burning there and I'd have a warm-up. I had to bring myself up.

Daniel Davis

I had an aunt in Rothschild Buildings – Aunt Bessy, and she was very orthodox. Her eldest son was a cripple and he used to sit on a settee all day. He used to sleep there and eat there and everything. It was terrible to go into that place because he used to do his business in the room. You used to think twice about going up there.

William George Holbrook

On Saturdays I worked for my grandfather. He was a mean man. He was a greengrocer with a ginger beard and he used to pay me a shilling for the day. I had to walk to his house about four miles away through the fields. In those days there were no houses beyond Romford. So I spent Saturday making deliveries in his greengrocer's van to the people he knew in Romford. And when I went back to his house at night, he gave me a shilling. He used to keep his money in a bag that he kept in the scales. So I would say, 'Grandfather! A lady would like to see you!' and while he was gone, I used to pinch his money. He didn't know. When I got home, I shared it with my older brother and sister. Once, I bought fifteen shillings' worth of fireworks with it. When I left the job to start work on a farm, my younger brother took it on. When he came home the first Saturday, I said, 'Tom, he keeps his money in a bag in the scales.' 'Yes,' he said. 'I know.' Tom worked it out on the first day. I took a year to find out. The funny thing was, just before he died, I went to his shop in Romford and on his deathbed he gave me a gold watch. And I was the one who stole from him.

Bill Smartson

Every Saturday, before I started at the quarry, I used to go over to Ravensworth golf course caddying for the golfers. I got on caddying for a chap, Mr Nixon, he got me to wait every Saturday, and I carried his golf clubs, and I used to clean them after the match with emery paper. He would come out the golf house and say there's four shillings, take that home to your mother and there's sixpence for yourself. Well, out of that sixpence I could go to the pictures for tuppence, buy a bottle of pop for a penny, and get a three-ha'penny paper of fish and chips. I used to give my mother the four shillings on the Saturday. Many a time she was waiting on me coming back, and as soon as she got the money, she was away off to the butcher to get a bit of meat for the Sunday. There was about nine of a family, I was the eldest of nine. Hard days.

Harry Matthews

Pretty nigh every morning when we got to school, first thing the master used to say was, 'Come out the boys that have been on the breeze lumps' – picking over rubble for small pieces of coal to burn. There'd be about four or five from Oare and some from this way, and we used to go out and stand in front of him, and he used to send us home to have a wash and clean up, because we smelt so where you'd been on the breeze. Whether you'd been on it or not, when he said that, you went up, because that meant we never used to go back to the breeze till after dinner. Pretty nigh every morning, out we used to troop. I always used to be there.

I've been out here before it was daylight and I can remember raking the snow off once to get some breeze to have indoors for a fire. I've been out there and got that before breakfast of a morning, the firing what comes out of the breeze what they used to burn the bricks with. A policeman caught two of us getting this coke and we had to go up over the market in the court house – but we got off with it.

Kitty Marion

Strange how one learns the bad parts of a language most easily. I came home one day, having taken the baby for an airing, and cheerfully hailed my aunt with, 'You bloody bugger!' She was shocked and horrified. Where had I heard such dreadful language! I didn't know it was bad. I had passed two men in the street and one slapped the other on the shoulder laughing, using that expression. I thought it was something nice and friendly.

Ethel Barlow

I remember the Penny Bazaar. We called it the bazaar. There was nothing over a penny. You could get a lovely silver bracelet, a silver ring, earrings. When I bought a pair of the earrings, my dad used to say, 'Take them out your damned earholes and put one through your nose. You see! She ain't ours! She's come from the gypsies! They've changed her!' He always swore blind I came from the gypsies. I had long curly hair when I was small, but then I had concussion of the brain and they cut off all my hair.

Once my mum and dad were invited to a ball, because my dad

worked on the railway. My dad had to buy a rubber collar and a V-front that looked as if he was wearing a white shirt. My mother bought a straw boater that cost sixpence. She bought a black veil and a pair of gloves. Her blouse was years old with a collar of lovely lace. She had a lovely long feather boa round her shoulders. I don't think she had any pants on because she hadn't got any. None of us had. She curled her hair and she looked beautiful. All us kids were left behind that night with no food, so we raided the cupboard to look for all the dry crusts of bread. We found some sugar and we dipped the crusts in hot water and then dipped them in the sugar and we had a feed.

Helen Bowen Pease

On my eighteenth birthday, Mother walked out on us. It was pretty shattering. She was an odd person. She stuck to Father as long as she stuck to anyone. Father was only just forty and it was all excessively upsetting. I had six younger brothers and sisters and it was extremely difficult to explain to Father's friends that the last thing we wanted was to be handed over to our mother. Father was our principal protection. Mother was as hard as nails – or diamonds – because she had a certain brilliance. We had to fight it out in the law courts because she tried to take us children. I gave evidence, and it must have been quite a shock to the judge because Mother's father was a very famous judge.

Lillah Bonetti

My mother became a widow at twenty-three, leaving her with me. Then she married again. When I was fifteen, I decided that Southampton wasn't the town for me. I'd read about white slavery. I thought how lovely it would be, to be adopted or taken away or kidnapped. My mother was horrified when I said I wanted to go as a nursemaid to a family living in France. She tried to put me off, but being the rebel that I was – and red-headed – I decided I knew best. So I went over to France, resplendent in my nursemaid's uniform, thinking I was the cat's whiskers. I was there for two years.

I learned French, which has never done me much good. I was a rebel.

John Wilkinson

After my brother was born, my mother died, so my father was landed with two little boys. We had no other women in the family but our two aunts, so they offered a very happy solution, that we should go and live with them in South Shore, Blackpool. So I went in 1898, and we went to Raggett's kindergarten and then to Arnold School.

I remember a day's fishing trip in January 08. We'd been on our bikes to Garston, fishing in the river there, and I got the biggest fish I'd ever seen in my life. We wrapped it in some newspaper and I put it across my handlebars. Frank Raynor worked in the newsagent shop, so I asked him to weigh the fish for me. And it was five pounds! I was thrilled. Just as I was leaving, Frank said, 'Jack, have you seen this? It's a new book we've just got in.' It was called *Scouting For Boys* by Baden-Powell, and I thought, 'This is something new.'

I could hardly put it down and I read it through three times that night, and before the end of the evening I decided that I was going to get some lads together and join the Boy Scouts. There was no Army about it – never military – it was quite the reverse. It was the outdoor life, camping and cooking, birds and animals, and singing. I wrote out the first chapter that night, and put down a list of chaps I was going to ask to join. And when I'd finished with them, they were as enthusiastic as I was. I'd copied the chapter out and we made more copies from that over the weekend. We had a meeting every day that week, I got these chaps red-hot on scouting. It was out of this world. We formed our little patrol in the next six days. I had seven or eight people and I made myself the patrol leader. We picked on the name of Lions, as I thought it was a good sturdy animal, and in any case I couldn't make many animals' noises – but I could roar.

We sent fourpence for a dozen membership cards to the head office. Our first outing was the first weekend – we didn't waste any time – we were getting down to it. We were never short of things to do. We could walk up to the cliffs and all round was fields. Then sometimes if we were at my end of Blackpool, we could go down in the sandhills with the wildlife. We used to camp in the hills, not far from home, and we'd all got bicycles. We did all the usual things, and in the summer we went fishing and scouting and signalling and we collected cigarette cards and football cards.

We did all right for uniforms – we were in short trousers anyway, and we could always get short khaki or blue trousers, and a green shirt. My aunts made the shirts. When I went to Cheshire I made my own uniform – I got my tailor's badge for that.

Ernest Taylor

We used to watch the shrimpers bringing their long poles in, and one lot of them had a little shop where they would boil their shrimps and sell them. To get to their shop you'd go round in front of the fort and up the ladder. Sometimes you'd find a body washed up – and that used to put me off shrimps a bit. Of course the only thing to do was feel in his pockets to see if there was any money. You'd put your hand in his pocket and all these little things would run over you – they were shrimps, and you were eating these shrimps, and they were eating him. If you found a two-bob piece or a couple of coppers in his pockets, then you were well in. We would go back up the shore and tell the bobby on the dock gates there was a body down there. Then there would be a bit of a commotion, while we would walk around the docks and see what we could pinch. We only found two or three bodies, but they reckon there was one every day of the week.

Edward Slattery

I was born in Bacup, Lancashire, on 21 December 1891. It was a traditional valley mill town and cotton was still king. It was a world of cloth-capped men and women in shawls who wore wooden clogs with irons on the heels that clattered and sparked on the cobbled streets.

I was the first of thirteen children. Only six of us survived childhood. My mother, Maggie, was a short, stout woman – five feet tall and eighteen stone – of Scots and Irish descent. She had many friends among the neighbours, the doors of our house were always open and anyone in need always found solace from Maggie, either in money to lend, goods to pawn, or hunger and thirst to quench. It was there for the asking without any question.

At eight years of age I would look after my brothers and sisters whenever my parents went out. When they became ill, I often rocked them to sleep in the cradle through the long winter nights. They might have measles, scarlet fever or whooping cough. My mum and dad would stoke up the fire with coal and slack and make me comfortable in a large rocking chair, giving me instructions to wake them should my brothers or sisters get worse during the night. They then locked the doors and went to bed. As soon as they left I would tremble with fear – what frightened me was the expectation of a ghost coming from the dark passage near the stairway to the bedroom. Our house was built on the hillside underneath another building and the stairway, which was wet and dark, ran up behind the dining-room wall like a railway tunnel.

I shall never forget the sight of my twin brother and sister, James and Sarah, suffering with the croup. My mother got some stiff brown paper and covered it with goose grease, then heated it before the fire and placed it on their chests and necks, but they screamed more and more, and looked as if they were choking. When morning came, she sent me for the priest – she had more faith in his treatment than the doctor. Anyway, prayers or medicine, it made no difference, my brother and sister died just the same.

Six of my siblings died before they could walk – somebody seemed to come or die at our house every year when I was a boy. I was eleven when I first learned where babies came from. My mother was preparing to bake our weekly 20 lb of dough, when she started to scream for me to run and 'fetch Mary O'Donnell and tell her I am sick'. Mary lived a few doors away. She was not a certified midwife, but all the children around knew that she brought babies from somewhere. They loved her and thought she was an angel.

When she heard my message, she ran to my mother, and I followed. My mother lay on some papers spread out on the floor, which seemed to be covered with messy blood, and Mary was pulling a baby from her belly. She told me to go out and play for a while. I was reluctant – I thought my mother might die. However, I returned soon after and Mary had cleaned my mother up and put her in bed with the baby. She told me to put more coal on the fire and make the house warmer. She said, 'Your mother is asleep, and she has brought you another little sister.'

Harrison Robinson

I was born in 1892 in Burnley. I had four sisters and a brother, but my brother died of appendicitis when he was ten. My dad worked at the gasworks – he was a labouring type of chap from a farming family in Yorkshire. My mother never went out to work. My mother went into service at Kettlewell when she was eight years old. After that she never went back home on her holidays. She left service to get married.

I went to Alder Street School until I was twelve. Then I went in the mill half-time, mornings one week and afternoons the week after, with school the rest of the time. The doctor had to pass you as fit when you went, but it was a bit of a farce. He came to the mill – and everybody passed.

We weren't tired at school when we were working half-time and we had no homework. But we had tests we had to pass. I was very good at sums and arithmetic. I used to go to the corner of the class and teach the dunces how to do their sums. I left school when I was thirteen.

Bill Owen

In those days you only had to see a policeman and you'd run. You hadn't done nothing – but you still ran. You were terrified of the police, and there used to be some tough customers. In the coal yards by us there used to be some battles on Saturday nights. There were houses off Maynard Street and there were steps and railings – I've seen the police getting knocked over those railings.

Polly Oldham

My father was a labourer with Blackburn Corporation and my mother stayed at home. There were eight of us children – Harry, Jim, Jo, May, me, Frances, who died of diphtheria, Ethel, who died of TB, and Albert. There were two years between us all.

We lived in a two-up, two-down, in Hannah Street, Blackburn. We all lived there, but some got married and moved out. We were all very happy, although we weren't well off – Dad was a labourer, boiling the pitch all round Blackburn.

We had a wash boiler and Dad used to make broth in it. It tasted good. He used to put sheep's heads in, big lumps of beef, and vegetables and barley and dumplings. Then we'd go round the street giving out broth and sometimes patty cakes to the old girls.

Every child they had made it that much harder for my mother, because there was just the one wage coming in. Some of the children were at school when I was born, and within a fortnight she was back washing and so on. The older lads and my dad looked after the family for those weeks.

I started work when I was twelve – half a day at the mill, half a day at school, then I went full-time when I was thirteen. I had a bad arm, and I had to go to the infirmary every twelve months and have it scraped. They wanted to take my arm off, and my mother said, 'What chance has she if you don't?' 'Well, just as much chance as she has now.' So she said, 'Leave it on, then. We'll risk it.'

We used to play games with old buttons, and we used to have wooden hoops which you put round your neck or waist, and then swing them. Then we played tips – rounders. You'd hit the ball with your hand and run, and they'd try to hit you before you got to the next stop. We played in the street, and the organ-grinder used to come round once a week, and we'd go and dance on the flags to the music. The boys used to dance as well. Then a rag-and-bone man used to come round with a peep show. You'd give him rags, then he'd let you look through a little hole, while he was pulling a string to make these dolls dance.

We had a good wash before we went to bed. We had no bath, so we used a big bread mug. Mother used to bath us and Father used to wipe us – girls one night, lads another. We washed our hair every week in the sink, and then she'd put Rankin's ointment on – ooh it did stink! Our lads used to say, 'Is it sassafrass night? We're going out.' It smelled like sarsaparilla but very strong, it was to stop you getting nits. She wouldn't let us go to school with Rankin's ointment on, but she used to put it on Friday nights, then she'd wash our hair on Sunday before we went to school on Monday. She was a very clean woman – spotlessly clean. We had sand on the floor, but you could have eaten your dinner off it when she swept that sand up, and the bedroom boards were white – she used to struggle with bleach and water.

At Christmas we used to hang our stockings up, and we'd get a toffee pig, an apple and an orange, a bar of chocolate and a little toy – and you could buy a little doll then for tuppence, with a black head, and she'd give us girls bits of rags to make clothes for them. The boys would get a whistle or a flashlight – something like that, and a new penny. She'd make a rabbit pie with some beef in – I used to like the head. I used to like picking it over.

I had rheumatic fever when I was eleven and I was ill for a long time then. I went to Blackburn Infirmary and I got St Vitus Dance – they had to strap me down. You never hear of it any more.

When I was fourteen we moved to Providence Street next to the Co-Op – to a house with a bath! We wanted more room and it had three bedrooms. The toilet was outside, and downstairs we had the front room, a hallway and a kitchen.

Father was a great fellow – marvellous. He used to like a pint, but he'd do anything for his kids. When the fair came to Blackburn, the marketplace was full of horses that went up and down on a carousel. Then there was the cakewalk – all of it run by steam engines. There were huge swinging boats with each side holding fifty people. They were on big pulleys, and there were also swinging boats for two, where you had to pull yourself up, and on the ground there was hoop-la stalls. You could buy peanuts, hot chestnuts, popcorn and black peas. They used to sell lotus in the shop – you could chew it. It was like a big piece of root – like liquorice to chew on, but you'd spit it out – not swallow it.

Lena Burton

Our chief fun was dressing our father up – we used to dress him up in all sorts, and he used to sit there and let us. Proper silly games, but there was nothing else to do.

My father was bothered with gout a lot, and was off work, so I had to start working when I was thirteen. I felt awful in that mill, it was horrible. It was at Kinder's and I was with a woman by herself in the basement – she never used to talk to me. I used to cry every night. After six weeks my father said, 'You're not going there any more,' and he got me in at Bocking – and I was really happy there. I gave my mind to it – but I knew I could have done something better if I'd had the chance.

We used to look forward to the Christmas tea party, which was held at St Mary's School – each school had their own party. We used to make our own entertainment – dialogues and singing and recitation and dancing. And Whit Friday we used to get up at six o'clock in the morning to get ready, then we'd assemble at school and go on a walk, then come back at dinnertime for tea and buns. Then we had sports in the school field and then we came in for tea. The sports were running, racing, three-legged races, wheelbarrow races, skipping rope races and egg-and-spoon races.

We had a maypole, but not at school, at the band club. The band used to parade round the village with a horse and cart all dressed up – and once a year there was the bike parade, and the bicycles were dressed up with flowers. This was for May Day, and the May Queen and Princess would be on the parade too. They had to vote for the May Queen – and there was a lot of jealousy. I was never May Queen – I was on the retiring side – a bit shy.

We never sat down for a meal. My mother and father sat down, but we had to stand round the table – and we couldn't leave until we'd asked permission. And we hadn't to speak at the table – if we spoke he'd say, 'Let your meal stop your mouth – that's enough.' We never answered back. No matter how tired we were, we had to stand, and we went to bed at half past eight every night.

At Christmas we used to hang our stockings up on the mantelpiece and we would get an apple and an orange and a thruppenny bit, and one little toy – then it was filled up with carrots and things.

An aunty of mine bought me a doll, and as I was very fond of sewing I used to make this doll little clothes. I think my sister poked the doll's eyes out with a pin when she was a baby – and I cried.

When I was about twelve I helped out at school teaching the little ones ABCs and counting. There was a teacher there – I was just a helper. I'd wipe their noses and take them down to the lavatory, that sort of thing.

We used to have slates tied round our necks with two strings, and the school provided slate pencils. We'd sometimes say, 'Please sir, I can't write because my pencil wants sharpening,' and he had something to sharpen them. Then, when we were older, we started with copy books, and we had black lead pencils. When we got pen and ink, it was glorious, we made a lot of blotches, but we thought it was great. The ink was in inkwells set in a little hole in one corner of the desk. That was a great day in our lives when we got inkwells.

We always wore all sorts of clothes. First a vest, then a chemise over the top, then a liberty bodice, then a flannel petticoat and a cotton petticoat, then your frock, and a pinny over the top. And knickers – and woollen stockings that Mother knitted herself – she used to make all our frocks too. We kids were sweltered to death in those days. We had clogs and shoes for Sundays. I had to have buttoned-up boots and we had a button hook to fasten them. We had to take our Sunday boots off when we came back from Sunday school and put our clogs back on. You'd take your frock off while you played, and then change back to go to school in the afternoon.

My father used to dose us with castor oil every so often, whether we needed it or not. He would stand us in a row, the three of us, with a spoonful of jam in one hand and the castor oil bottle in the other. If your stomach was out of order Mother used to brew gentian root, wormwood and camomile flowers – and we used to have to have bitters – that put your stomach right. Every spring, we had a jar with black treacle and powdered sulphur in it, and we would have a spoonful of it every morning, whether we wanted it or not. That was to purify your blood. If we had a cold, it was black treacle, butter and linseed tea. We didn't go to the doctor's unless it was absolutely necessary, because we had to pay.

Mrs Clark

We lived close to the sea, and every morning, after my mother got the baby and me washed, we used to go onto the sands with a two-handled basket. She took one handle and I took the other – and of course she was carrying the baby. When we got to the seashore, my mother used to put a piece of cloth down for us to sit on, and I had to look after the baby. My mother then gathered sticks and coal to put on the fire. The wages were that small, you had to do something. So when my mother had got plenty of coal and sticks we used to come away. I would only be about three years old.

Polly Lee

I remember my mother having a small pail, and we used to go round the marketplace asking if people could spare us a little coal. My mother was a widow at the time, and when she remarried she got her coal, I think that was one of the things she got married for. She had to keep us.

Florence Hannah Warn

When I was about ten, I did some housework for a crippled lady, scrubbing cement paths with a long-handled broom bigger than I, then scrubbing a long passage of linoleum and polishing it afterwards, black-leading a huge old-fashioned fireplace, scrubbing the floor cloth in the living room, and then scrubbing the scullery floor.

It must have taken four or five hours. I was paid the princely sum of one shilling, but I had to hand it over to Mother, and received tu'pence for myself, but there was no feeling of resentment, as it was expected and quite usual.

Mr W. Cowburn

At times you just hadn't got a shoe to your foot. There were schemes where they sometimes used to send a pair of shoes, but they were nearly always much too big. You were either crippled with them or hoping your feet would grow. I remember me sister carrying me to school on her back. You were all right once you got into the classroom.

Mary Lawson

Great-grandfather was a wonderful old man. He was six foot three and about sixteen stone. On a Saturday he used to walk down the town, wearing a grey alpaca suit and his grey top hat and his stick, to the co-operative store. At the head office he'd pay the grocery bill and I would get a packet of boiled sweets, which used to last me all week. If he had pigs to sell they would already be in the market and he would meet his fellow cronies. They were all selling hens and chickens and what have you, and he would have a glass of whisky, thruppence a glass then. He would say to me, 'Now, if you sell a pig, I'll give you some pocket money.' I think I was only once lucky enough to sell one. Then we would walk back, strip off, have a meal, then he'd feed his family, feed the horses, the chickens, the pigs, and then I think perhaps he would get a sit down, because he liked to smoke and he smoked a clay pipe.

Mrs Linsley

I was born in Cornwall, where my father was a miner. But within a year he got a job working for an urban district council. He said, 'This bairn's brought us luck.' He built us a house, at West Kyo, ten miles south of Newcastle-upon-Tyne. In those days when you moved house it was on a horse and cart, with men with caps on. Mother was carrying me, trying to keep up with all our possessions, trying to get there with the key to let him in. She put me on the doorsteps to open the door. She opened the door and I walked along the passage – they didn't know I could walk. My father said, 'I told you that bairn was going to bring us luck.'

My mother's father had a stroke, and he lay there for five years. There weren't nurses, if you had a stroke you just lay there. He lost his speech, and he was paralysed. My grandmother couldn't manage, so my mother sent me to school at three, so she could walk from West Kyo to the Lizzie Pit every day to help her mother turn and bath and feed him. I think my father used a bit of influence with the headmaster, but at that age, I couldn't do a lot.

Mrs Carter

My father was very strict with us, we all had to be in by ten o'clock, even when we were engaged to be married. If we weren't in he went to the door and blew his whistle. Everybody heard his whistle, even if we were a long way off. 'It's after ten o'clock you know' – 'Well I've been . . .' 'It doesn't matter, ten o'clock's your time,' and that was it. Mother was a little bit sympathetic; she used to say, 'You should be in as you've promised.'

Polly Lee

We sometimes got on with our stepfather, but he never seemed to forget that we weren't his. I remember one night I wanted to go out. 'Has thee done tha homework?' 'Yes.' 'Has thee washed up?' 'Yes.' 'Has thee done the pit clothes?' 'Yes.' 'Well stop in.' If he was washing in front of the fire and you went between him and the fire, oh my! He had a song he used to sing when he was getting washed, 'She's in the aslyum now' – he meant asylum, but he got a hold of it the wrong way. I don't think he could spell asylum.

He was kind with the little uns though, when they were poorly. My mother had quite a few babies die very young, and he'd sit up all night with them. That was one good point he had, but of course they were his. She had eight to my stepfather, and just one lived.

Whilst boys played with soldiers, their fathers often served in
Africa, India, China, Burma and other far-flung places.

They were breastfed in those days, and her body wasn't nourished so she couldn't feed the children.

There were some awful houses, with no road out the back. Ashes had to be carried through the house. We used to have to put old matting down – there was no wash-away closet then – we had ash closets. Everything had to come through the bedroom and the kitchen on to the street. We had to ask the farmer when he could come and take it away, but then maybe something would happen and he couldn't get all ash and stuff out the closet. It would just be lying on the street, then the hens would come and have a feed. Then you'd eat their eggs! They kept the hens on the streets – there was nowhere else to keep them. My mother would never have an egg off anyone who'd got hens on the street, so there were very few eggs in our house.

William George Holbrook

I started school when I was four years old. We had to walk two miles to the school and on the way was this pub – The Good Intent. It was just a wooden building, but every morning, as we walked past before nine o'clock, there were two old boys with their billycock hats, sitting at a table in the yard, drinking beer.

Fred Lloyd

I was five years old when I started at Uckfield Holy Cross School. There were fifty children in the class. The school day started at nine and at twelve we had a break. Then we carried on until four. In the break, we played conkers, skipping, and football – except we used to kick a tennis ball because we didn't have a proper football. I was pretty good most of the time, but the headmaster, Mr Richards used the stick on me once. I let a firework off in the cloakroom and it went off right outside his window. When he gave you the stick, he liked hitting you on the tips of your fingers where it hurt most.

Albert 'Smiler' Marshall

My mother Molly Ellen was ill when I was young, so I started school when I was just two and a half years old, although I didn't go on the register until I was five. My brother drove me to school – he had an orange box on wheels, and I used to sit in it. I was four when my mother died – two days after Queen Victoria.

William George Holbrook

I attended a little one-roomed school of around thirty children. The headmistress, Miss Weedon, was an old devil. She lived in a house next door to the school and one afternoon, during a very heavy thunderstorm, her house was hit by lightning. They had to clear us out of the school and I can remember standing outside in the pouring rain singing, 'Oh Miss Weedon's house's on fire!' We were all clapping our hands as her house went up.

Emma Ford

Our school was very basic. It had rough whitewashed stone walls and it was very dusty. We had the old combustion stoves and the smell of the coke used to get on your chest. But the rooms were warm. We got out for quarter of an hour in the morning to play, and then ten minutes in the afternoon. In the yard, we didn't think of anything but skipping. The boys played with whips and tops. Sometimes I took my doll to school, but more often than not it was taken from me and I lost its frock or some of its hair. There were no toys in school to play with. We played with bits of paper and we drew. Our teacher, Miss Stephenson, used to wear a great big hat and her hair was all piled up. And her little waist was tight in and her bust stood right out. I don't know where they got their bustles from, but people's busts and behinds went right out.

Mary Allison

We used to use slates. They were horrid things – they used to scrape when you wrote on them. We had to bring in our own rag to clean them, but sometimes we used to spit to wipe the writing off. It wasn't a nice thing to spit, but in those days you just did it.

Jackie Geddes

Our teacher was Mr Rose. He lived at Chester-le-Street, and he used to come in on a little Douglas motorbike. He'd been in the Boer War. The slates we had were about twelve inches, bigger than the infants' slates, and you had to buy your own slate. And you used to have a string fastened on so you could put it on your back, or inside your satchel. You did your homework on that. When you came back though, it might be raining, and if you had put your slate under your coat, it used to get rubbed off. If you put it in your satchel it was just the same. So you couldn't protect it, it got rubbed or washed off, and when you got to school the next morning, it would be 'Where's your homework?', 'Sir, it was raining', 'It wasn't raining where I was,' and you got the cane. I thought that was very unfair.

Rebecca Bowman

When we got our photos taken, the teacher would get an exercise book and make a paper collar. You would never think they had a paper collar on when they got their photo took. They had bare feet, but still the teacher put a paper collar on.

We used to get a great big ball of thick wool on a Wednesday afternoon for knitting with and we used to have big long needles. And we used to knit a whole lump and then whoever had knitted the most got some marks for it. Then when we'd finished, it was pulled out and wrapped up and then put on the needles. The same ball of wool.

Emma Ford

In the summer, we all wore cheap straw hats with elastic underneath. In the winter, we wore woollen, hand-knitted hats. The boys always wore cloth caps. We would hang up our hats and then we went to wash our hands in the basin. There was one basin with a roller towel. When that was done, we went and sat in the classroom with our arms folded, waiting for the teacher to come in. When she came in we stood up and she would say, 'Good morning children.' And we had to nod our heads and say, 'Good morning Miss Johnston.' Then she came round and examined our hands, back and front. A lot of boys were sent to get their hands washed again.

Bessy Ruben

I remember there used to be a nurse who'd come and examine our hair. Those who were lousy dreaded her coming, but those who were clean she'd pass over, and we'd be very proud to know we were clean. We didn't have any nits. Well, quite a lot of children who were very nice children, really and truly had nits, and one of my friends was so self-conscious about it.

Edith Turner

I was put in the London County Council School. At that time, I had no shoes on my feet. There was a School Board man who used to visit if you didn't go to school and they used to threaten the parents that they would prosecute them if children didn't go to school. So I had to go to school. I went climbing up the stairs at school, with no shoes and socks. My headmistress, Miss McCrae, she was a proper bitch. No matter what illness the children had, she demanded that they went to school.

Joe Garroway

When I first started school it was just a room at the primitive chapel. I must have been a bad boy because I was put down into the cellar, and when dinnertime came they forgot I was there. Well it so happened my little sister, two years old, was buried that day. When I didn't turn up my uncle came to seek me. He came and shouted down to the cellar where I was crying. He said, 'I'll get you out, lad!' and he went and saw the caretaker. As I came up the steps to my uncle the teachers came back into the school, and he said, 'Who's put him down there?' My teacher was Miss Clark, and she said, 'I have.' He said, 'Take that' and whacked her and he walked out again.

Bessy Ruben

There was a lot of poverty. We had a girl in my class called Nelly – she was a Christian girl and I liked her very much. She used to come to school without shoes on her feet. I couldn't understand it – no shoes and stockings, and it was the middle of winter and raining. She used to sit next to me, and I said, ' Aren't you cold?' Her feet were so cold. I used to go home to her house for tea very often, and I could smell a very nice, welcoming smell – it was bacon. Although her mother offered it to me, I had an idea I mustn't eat it. I told my mother what had happened, and asked her, 'Why mustn't I eat it?' I couldn't have been more than nine at the time. And mother said, 'Because it's not very healthy.' And I said, 'But Nelly Conlan walks about with bare feet, and she's never had a cold in her life!'

Don Murray

We used to go round by the girls' school and watch them come out and make fun of them. But the girls had a way of joining together and instead of going home separately, they used to go home in groups, singing a song that's quite popular now, 'Strawberry Fair':

> As I was going to Strawberry Fair,
> Singing, singing, buttercups and daisies . . .

And they used to do a little dance and then they each branched off as they got to their homes.

Emma Ford

We all wore pinafores at school. They practically covered our dresses. And the boys wore what they called 'ganseys', which are jerseys. They were mostly handouts, and some of them would be too big and some of them too small.

Bessy Ruben

After the Russian pogroms, there was an influx of Jews to our area – the East End of London. There were a lot of children who had to go to school. Some were big girls, twelve or thirteen, and you couldn't put them in the infants' school, so a lot of them came to our school. The older girls like myself were given a class, just to teach them to speak English. I remember one girl – when I told her to say 'and' she couldn't. She said 'aernd' and she said 'royce' for 'rose'. This used to annoy me, and I did bully the poor girl a bit. One day, in the playground, she was standing in a corner, crying. I went over to her, and I said in Yiddish, 'Why are you crying?' and she said, in Yiddish, 'Everyone's laughing at me. You laugh at me. I can't say like you say the word in English. I can't say "rose" – I say "royce".' I said, 'But you've just said "rose"!' After that I became very friendly with her.

Florrie Passman

My sister and I went to the Aldersgate Ward School. It wasn't a Jewish school, and my sister and I were the only Jewish girls in our class. My mother, although she was very orthodox, was very broad-minded. Not like some people who said to their children, 'If they're going to have prayers, you must come out!' But luckily, my mother said, 'You must go to prayers and do everything, because when you get older, how will you know which is right and which is wrong? How will you go anywhere? What will you do if you don't know what they're talking about?' And do you know, I got the prize for the New Testament!

Bessy Ruben

I remember Miss Green. She had snaggle teeth. I was very fond of her. Then we had Miss Poole, who was a dear, and we had Mrs Cameron, who was a fiery Scot. And we had a Miss Jackson – she was so patriotic that she wore a Union Jack apron. After the Kishenev pogrom, there was an influx of Jews from Kishenev. A lot of the children came to our school and I remember distinctly this Miss Jackson saying, 'Now, all you foreigners who come from Russia, you should all go back to your own country.' And a girl sitting in the front – her name was Yetta Solomons – she was so incensed about it that she took out her inkwell and flung it at Miss Jackson, and smashed her glasses. Of course she was chastised for treating one of the staff in that fashion, but our headmistress was a very nice and a very clever woman. I met her many years later and I asked if she remembered the incident. 'Very well,' she said. 'We had that teacher dismissed, because she was in a Jewish area and she just didn't like foreigners.'

Richard Common

We had this one teacher, old Ramsay, and he was a tyrant. He used to have a stick. It wasn't a cane, it was like a very thin rolling pin, and if you did anything wrong he used to rap you with it. You held your hands out, palms upwards, but if you pulled your hands back, instead of bringing it down on you, he brought it up and hit you on the knuckles. One day old Ramsay went out, and one of the lads hid his stick behind the central heating pipes. He came back and he couldn't find it and he told us that when he did find it, we were all going to get it. He marked our names down on the blackboard with the number of smacks we were going to get. And my goodness, when he found it, we got it. He stood us all in line and he looked on the blackboard and walked up, saying, 'Ten for you! Six for you!' right up the line. The girls got the same. He hammered us all.

Nicholas Swarbrick

The Jesuits ran Stoneyhurst College in Preston and the Catholic College for Boys in Winkley Square was staffed by the same Jesuits as the College. These Jesuits were very much inclined to use the leather strap they called a ferula like the devil.

In my first two or three forms at the college I did very well academically. Each week we had a card which we took to our parents, which had four designations on it – the first was excellent, the next good, the next fair, and poor. In the first three forms I always had excellent – excellent on conduct and application. And I always got sixpence from my father for that. When I moved into the senior college there was one particular Jesuit priest, Father Ellison, and he was a devil with the ferula. On one particular occasion I had a lot of homework, I was given a lot of irregular verbs to parse – horrible things. I did my best, but Father Ellison hit me so hard and hurt me so badly that I refused to go back to school. My father more or less acquiesced, and my education was ruined. Although I was instinctively a studious person, that ruined my education. Nowadays, Father Ellison would have been jailed for what he did to us. If I'd had my way, I would have gone to the local Church of England grammar school where there was no ferula, but religious intolerance was fairly rampant, and I wouldn't have been allowed. After that incident I stayed at home and no one came in to teach me. I was fourteen when I left school.

Thomas Eustace Russell
When I was at Hatfield Road School in St Albans, we had a master named Cowley who was a brute of a man. A sadist. He broke a boy's wrist with the stick on one occasion. There was a great how-de-do about it.

John William Dorgan
In Choppington, there were two schools. One was the Church School with a grant from the County Council and the other was the Colliery School. My mother couldn't fit me out with decent clothes, so I couldn't go to the Church School. I went to the Colliery School. On Monday morning, every child in the school had to pay fourpence. That was an enormous amount of money in those days. Usually, I didn't have it, so I had to walk to the front of the class and put my hand out. I received four good straps on the hand. Girls who couldn't afford the fourpence got the same. About half the class used to get the strap every Monday morning because they couldn't pay.

Bessy Ruben
A lot of the children at our school didn't have birth certificates, so when they reached the age of fourteen, their parents would have to go and swear an affidavit at the solicitor's to say the child was

fourteen, and the child would have to swear too. At school one day, one of the girls said, 'I haven't got a birth certificate, and I've got to go and swear that I'm fourteen.' So Dinah, this friend of mine, said, 'Oh, you don't have to worry – all you have to do is, if you're a Christian, you stand up and say, "I swear by the Lord Jesus Christ", and if you're Jewish, you have to swear another way.' That's all she said, and she never meant anything derogatory against Jesus Christ.

The teacher was out of the room when this happened, but there were two Christian girls there. When we went out to play in the playground, I could see these two girls walking up and down talking, and pointing at Dinah and our little crowd. When we came back, the teacher of the class called Dinah out to the front of the class. 'How dare you stand up and make fun of Our Lord? We don't make fun of your Rabbis or your Gods!' and so on. And Dinah was weeping. 'I didn't mean anything,' she kept saying, and she didn't, but the teacher wouldn't even let her speak. She was sent out to the headmistress, and then she was sent to apologise to all the English staff of the whole school. She was sent to Coventry. The only one who used to speak to her was myself, and I used to meet her outside school. Sent to Coventry with a year's marks taken away from her.

Albert 'Smiler' Marshall

My headmaster was a wonderful man who took a great interest in me and all the pupils. He taught everything, including football and cricket, gardening – and he was also the scout master. The staff were a bit 'fishy' – a Miss Herring, a Miss Salmon, and the headmaster was Mr Whiting. They were all much loved by the pupils. Twice a week the rector visited for the first hour. We started with a hymn and were told about all the historical events which had taken place on that day. Any trouble, and you got the stick. None of the boys mentioned this to his parents, as he might well have been belted at home had he done so. Most boys had an orange-box on wheels, and when we were released from school, there was a rush down the hill to collect horse manure for the gardens.

Andrew Ruddick

My first school was run by a middle-aged woman called Minnie Turnbull. We used to pay thruppence a week, and the big school at Hallbankgate cost tuppence. Minnie Turnbull had ten pupils, five girls and five boys, so that was half a crown a week, and that was all she had to live on and she had a daughter and a father to support. When free education came into operation, after the summer term Minnie Turnbull had to close down, and we went to the big school.

Bessy Ruben

Commercial Street School was a lovely place. What attracted us very much at the time was the unseen heating. In the winter we had the warm air blown in and in the summer it was cool air blown in. We were told how lucky we were that this was our new school, and we were breathing clean, fresh air every day. The school had about 304 children, out of which about 300 were Jews and four were Christians. In consequence, we had all the holidays, both Jewish and Christian.

Harry Patch

I went to a Church of England school where the headmaster was a disciplinarian – so much so that he lost two teachers in three months. They couldn't stick him. But he was a good man. He gave up two nights a week, Tuesday and Thursday, for evening classes. His one condition was if you started, you had to stick at it. First hour on the Tuesday was English as it is spoken. The second hour was Latin. Anyway, we stuck it, and on Thursday the first hour was geometry, and the second hour was algebra. He asked us the shortest distance between two points, A and B, and of course the answer was a straight line. He told us to write down the definition of a curve. Well I couldn't think so I wrote 'straight line with a bend in it' and he gave me a rap across the knuckles.

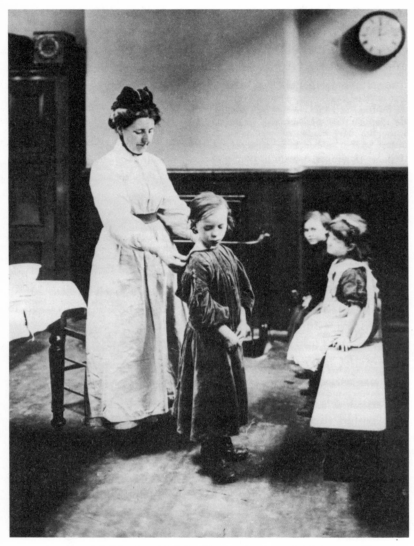

A schoolgirl is checked for lice and nits, which were rife
among poor children.

Henry Allingham

When we moved to Clapham, South London, my mother wanted to get me into a high-grade grammar school in South Lambeth Road. She went to see the head, who said, 'Send the boy up to me and if he can pass the school entrance, I may be able to find a place for him.' So I went to do the exam. He was a lovely man. He put me in the main school hall. He said, 'Now, make haste slowly!' and I did my best and answered all the questions on the paper. And I passed. It was a fantastic school, and they taught us French, science, woodwork, metalwork and art. The art master took us to the Tate Gallery. I used to spend Sunday afternoons at the Tate. I loved that school. I went there until I was almost sixteen.

Albert 'Smiler' Marshall

I was a bit of a fighter at school. A boy who had been expelled from another school started causing problems in our class. The master took me aside and told me to deal with him, so I met him outside where he was bullying some of the smaller ones and I gave him a good beating. He was as right as rain after that and he wanted to be my friend, but I wasn't having any of that.

Richard Common

The classroom had wooden ceilings, and when the teacher went out, we used to play darts with our pens. We threw the pens so that the nibs would stick in the ceiling. Then we would throw anything – hats or whatever we had – up to the ceiling to try and knock them down. One day, the teacher came in and we all had our pens except Billy Hurd, a Scotch lad who lived in Stanley Street. 'Where's your pen?' asked the teacher. There was one pen stuck in the ceiling. The teacher made Billy sit underneath it. 'You'll soon know when it comes down,' said the teacher, 'you just sit there.' And he made Billy sit underneath it all day.

Joseph Henry Yarwood

I went to the council school in Battersea, South London. I was poorly dressed and that made me a figure of ridicule. For a long time, I was known as 'mop' because I had long hair and we couldn't afford a haircut. Without being snobbish, I was an intellectual cut above these other kids and I could answer the teachers' questions. We had a sarcastic swine of a Scottish teacher who said, 'I wonder, Yarwood, how you can answer all these questions?' It was quite simple. I was always reading. My old grandmother used to say, 'He'll come to a bad end, that boy. He's always got a book stuck in his fist.'

Ruben Landsman

From school I put in for a thrift form. I was given a corduroy suit and a pair of boots, and I came home so proud of that suit. But when my father came home in the evening and saw it, he asked, 'Where d'you get that from?' 'From school,' I said. 'I signed the thrift form.' 'You can take it back.' Charity he wouldn't have. We had literally nothing to eat, but charity he wouldn't have.

Daniel Davis

I used to get clothes from the Free School. I got a corduroy jacket and trousers, and a pair of boots. I had difficulty lifting them. You could hear somebody walking in those boots a mile away. We got them once a year before Passover. We also got free dinner tickets – but they only gave a certain number of tickets to each class, so if you were lucky you got the meal, and if not you had to go home. And in the morning, if you came before time, you used to get a chunk of bread and an enamel cup with some milk in. At dinner I had to eat whatever Mother made. We had to be satisfied. It was a lousy life. During those years I was always very frail because I didn't get the nourishment needed.

Alfred Anderson

When I was ten I got a job before school, delivering milk from Denend Farm to people nearby. By the time I was twelve I'd saved up enough to buy a bike, and I used it to earn pocket money to do more milk deliveries. I used to have milk churns hanging off the handlebars.

Bessy Ruben

We used to do a school play at Christmas time. This particular year we did *Sleeping Beauty*. One of the older girls in the Seventh Standard chose the characters. She chose a girl named Annie Silverman for the Sleeping Beauty and I was Fairy Crocus. She showed the list to Miss Poole, who used to stay behind and rehearse us. She looked at the list and said, 'We can't have Annie Silverman for Sleeping Beauty. We'll have Betsy Schiffenbaum instead.' That was me. There was a feud between Annie Silverman and me for years. We put the play on in Toynbee Hall and it was a great thrill – it was wonderful.

John Wainwright

There was no thought of my going on to further education. When I got to the top class, X7, two of the older boys were studying for the Grammar School examination, but presumably their parents were better off than mine. I wasn't entered. In fact, when I was twelve and a half I was put in for the 'Labour Examination'. I went down to Wigan on a Saturday morning and I had to answer written questions and oral questions. I passed it and so I left school.

John William Dorgan

I owe a lot to the headmaster of the Colliery School, Mr Alcock. When I was supposed to be leaving school at thirteen, my mother went to see him and said that I was worth something better than going down the coal mine. She asked if I could stay on at school. The headmaster said yes. Another person stayed on at school – a girl called Mary Carr. We sat together at an old iron-framed desk made for two at the back of one of the classes. We didn't have a teacher so the headmaster gave us a book that he called a 'classic'. He told us to read the book and write an essay on it. Mr Alcock was very painstaking. He corrected our spelling and phrasing and then he would make us write the essay again. Sometimes I had to write it a third time. Mary Carr never had to. She was brighter than me.

Fred Lloyd

I stayed at the school until I was thirteen, and I was very good at writing and arithmetic – that was my thing. My writing was put up on the blackboard for other children to copy and when one of my brother's girls was at the same school twenty years after I'd left, she came to me one day and said, 'We've been looking at your writing, Uncle. It's on the blackboard.'

Don Murray

They had a scheme in those days called the 'Half-Time system'. You could work in the morning and go to school in the afternoon, and the following week it would be reversed. It didn't matter which way round you did it, you couldn't win because if you were at work in the morning, you fell asleep on your desk in the afternoon and got a clout from the teacher. If you went to school in the morning and went to work in the afternoon, you fell asleep at work and got a clout from the overlooker.

Jim Fox

Our headmaster was a strict disciplinarian. We called him 'Bossy' Read. He earned the name. If you met him on the Saturday morning and you were on the opposite side of the street and you didn't pitch your cap as you passed, he would bring you out on Monday morning and he would say, 'Look, Fox. I saw you on the other side of North Road on Saturday and you didn't touch your cap. Did you see me?' If he thought you had seen him, you got the cane.

Arthur Harding

I had a special pal called Peaky. His people were on the respectable side. The father was a collar-and-tie man working for the Port of London Authority. We were always together and always playing truant from school. Peaky couldn't read or write – he couldn't even sign his name. I did try once or twice to take him home and teach him the alphabet but it was hopeless. He didn't have any ambitions to be a scholar. So one day, we were in Brick Lane and they were playing a gambling game in the street. One boy there had a metal watch and chain on. So I said to Peaky, 'Let's have his watch.' I took it out of his pocket, it was quite simple. I put my hand up and swivelled it off. Just as I handed it to Peaky, the boy tumbled me. 'Give me my watch back!' he said. I laughed and Peaky walked away with it.

Well, the boy knew us, knew our names, and he did a thing I never thought he'd do. He went to the police. To cut a long story short, I got twenty months and Peaky got nine months. We became the first boys ever to be sent to Borstal. It was called Borstal because it was in the village of Borstal, near Chatham in Kent. We were the first guinea pigs in 1903. When we got there, they made two cells into one for us. There was a bit of a school there, where they had proper teachers. The governor, Mr Weston, wanted to make the new system a success. We were given library books and I read *Oliver Twist* – that was the first time I found out about Dickens. You weren't kept in a cell all the time and there was plenty of physical exercise outside. I also learnt a lot of woodwork in the carpenter's shop. Even though the more backward lads were taught to read and write, they couldn't teach Peaky nothing there. He did his nine months and when he came out, his parents had moved out of the East End to give him a fresh start. Not long after, he got a splinter in his hand and he died from blood poisoning.

Ernest Hugh Haire

I attended Tranmere Higher Grade School, Lancashire. It was a fee-paying school and the quarterly bills were sent to my father. I started as a small boy in the Infants and we used slates and pencils, which were marvellous because you could easily cheat. You just had to lick your answer out and copy what the person next to you had written. We had reading, writing and arithmetic. Spelling was a matter of repetition. I remember getting out early one day at the age of six because I was the only one who could spell the word 'yacht'. We were reading very fluently between six and seven. We sang our times tables. We had geography lessons, which were taught by rote at first. At seven, I remember reciting the rivers of England: 'Tyne, Wear, Tees . . .' all the way round. I didn't know where all these rivers were, but I knew the names and I could look them up on a map. As we moved on, we did geometry and algebra, and at the age of eleven we started Latin. It was a very wide syllabus and very well taught. The discipline was excellent. The boys played cricket and football and the girls played rounders. After that school, I went to the Liverpool Institute.

My brother and I used to take the half past eight Rock Ferry boat to Liverpool. It took twenty minutes. We would pass four or five big sailing ships – it was still the days of sail. We went across to the landing stage by the Liver Building, the Cunard Building and Mersey Docks Building. From there, we walked up Duke Street to the Institute.

The headmaster there was ruthless. When he arrived at the school, he came into our form room and set a history exam. During it, he spotted a history textbook under a desk, so he ordered us all into the school hall, where he stood us up on the platform and he sticked every one of us. 'I'll purge you lot!' he said. He was the only master who gave the stick. Usually, you went into his study and you were tapped down below to see that you didn't have an essay paper shoved down your trousers and then you received three strokes. Once, he spotted me running down the corridor and he sent me straight to his room and caned me. He wouldn't let me explain why I was running. The next day, he found out that I was running a message to a physics master, so he sent for me, apologised, and gave me two tickets for a Shakespeare play on the Saturday.

Tom Kirk

In September 1908, I went to a boarding school in Lytham run by an old family friend. He was determined that his boys should see life from as many angles as possible, so we had expeditions of all kinds. We took a cruise on the 'mud-hopper' up the Ribble to Preston and we watched Preston North End, the premier football team. The most exciting event was the first Air Display in 1909, where we watched Paul Chan sailing serenely above us in his Voisin biplane. The following year, Blériot arrived in his biplane, having just made the first crossing of the Channel.

We concentrated a lot on sport, which is common, I suppose, to all boarding schools. I think I fancied myself as a future county cricketer. On wet days, the headmaster would spend hours with us in the gym, bowling a tennis ball to the batsman or wielding a cricket stump – excellent practice for playing a straight bat. At soccer I played left back. We won many games against bigger schools, possibly due to the headmaster's dubious advice – 'Go for the man, never mind the ball!'

Jim Davies

I was at minor public schools. I learnt French, German and Latin, Mathematics, Algebra, History, Geography, English. I didn't do very well. I was too lazy. I got as far as lower fourth, but the fees weren't paid because my father went bankrupt and I never went back again.

Maurice Edward Laws

For a career in the services, my public school background was invaluable. It taught discipline, and the idea of working for a team and not just your miserable self. Also, you met others of your own type. Nine out of ten officers came from public schools. Discipline was good at Lancing. I got beaten at times, for my own good, no doubt. In fact, I made it possible to insure against the cane. Three of us started a system whereby the small boys could insure at the beginning of the term for a small premium and if they were caned, they received sixpence a stroke. Some boys, of course, were on the grey list and had to pay a higher premium and some were on a blacklist and we wouldn't insure them at all. These were the bad risks. The scheme went very well for a while and we were paying out, but unfortunately, towards the end of the term, the numbers of beatings went up. The boys were short of money and so they started misbehaving so that they could be beaten and subsequently claim on their insurance. The headmaster inquired into the situation and shortly afterwards, the scheme went into involuntary liquidation. I don't think the headmaster particularly applauded our initiative.

Norman Musgrave Dillon

I went to Haileybury College in 1910. It was originally the student college for the students of the East India Company. It had many associations with India, such as the names of the houses and the servants. It was a fairly primitive place. The dormitories had boards on the floor and the food was pretty primitive. It was not a luxury school. Many of the public schools were much the same – at Eton, the bathing facilities were even less adequate than our own. We were out of bed at seven o'clock in the morning and down for chapel at half past seven. At quarter to eight we had our first lesson. Breakfast was at half past eight. The second lesson started at quarter past nine and on we went until noon. At noon, there was a break for lunch until one o'clock. The afternoon was taken up by games or a seven-mile run until four o'clock. From four until six, there were more lessons, ending up with supper at half past six. Supper was left-over bread with cocoa. Then we had 'preparation' – homework – and we were in bed by nine-thirty with lights out by ten.

The lessons you had depended which side you were on. If you were on the classical side, you had the normal English lectures and subjects but you had Latin and Greek thrown in. If you were on the modern side, you had a much more modern approach, with Physics and Chemistry. I was on the modern side and I did a great deal of handicraft work in the workshops. I had no bent for the classical side. I was intensely practical and I liked using my hands. When I left, I passed out top of the engineering branch.

Discipline was pretty severe. Most of the discipline came from the prefects. Their word was law. If you were late in the dormitory, they beat you. I was beaten once when I arrived as the clock was striking ten. The prefects kept bullying down. You only got into trouble with your housemaster if your form master found you unbearable, and he would give you a note to carry to the house-master, who would give you the appropriate number of smacks with the stick. I would have thought that most boys passed through Haileybury with only two or three beatings.

The fagging system was in full force. An excellent system it was too. During the first three terms at the school, you were subject to this tyranny and you were liable to be a fag. Coming out from breakfast, you might hear a shout from across the quad: 'Fag! Fag!' Every boy had to run and the last one to arrive got the job, which might be to go down to the grub shop and buy something or collect some books or collect some boots from the bootmakers. If a prefect wanted a fag, he would call 'Fag!' in the dormitory and any boys liable to serve had to trot along quickly to his bed to see what he wanted. At Haileybury, each fag was at the beck and call of anybody senior.

Tom Kirk

I won a scholarship to Giggleswick – which relieved my mother of any further worry about school fees. What a joy after Seafield! A swim every morning in the cold swimming pool, Greek with dear old Hammond, Latin with Douglas, Maths with the genial Clark, French with Neumann – who took a fancy to me and gave me books until I was warned not to let him get too friendly. In those days nobody talked about homosexuality, bachelorship was a common occurrence. In fact, my final year at school was clouded by the 'Jepson Affair'. Douglas Jepson was a keen cricketer who used to practise with me in the nets. I also shared a study with him and he developed a sort of 'pash' on me. Stupidly, I did not nip it in the bud and he became jealous and possessive and estranged many of my friends. Hindsight tells me that this was homosexuality, but at the time I was bewildered. He used to say, 'Can I come and stay with you and perhaps marry one of your sisters?' He did come too, but my sisters would have nothing to do with him.

Norman Musgrave Dillon

Sport was very important at Haileybury. In fact, the main aspiration above work and a classical knowledge was to become a member of the rugby fifteen. I failed to make it because my nose was broken the day before a crucial match. Had it not been, I would undoubtedly have had my colours. We played rugby football over the winter, association football and hockey during the spring term and cricket during the summer term. There was tremendous competition between the Houses at sport. There was a cup for which the Houses used to compete with tremendous enthusiasm.

Gordon Frank Hyams

At thirteen, I started at Charterhouse. Straight away, we were given an exam by the house monitors, who asked us lots of questions about school institutions, the things you were allowed to do and the things you must never do. They also gave us awkward questions, such as having to name a monitor, and listing the colours he'd won. We had a system of fagging, whereby each monitor had a 'study fag' who had to look after his study and keep it neat. I was in a house called 'Robinites' and my housemaster was Oswald Latter, a well-known naturalist.

Being in a house meant you lived there, you slept there and you had your meals there. The house system was very strong and there was great competition between the houses over football and cricket. The dormitories were very good. They were divided up into enclosed cubicles, each one containing a bed, a chair and a hand basin. Our clothes were looked after by the matron, who cleaned and distributed them every week. The food was good, on the whole. We had porridge and a fried egg for breakfast, a main course and a sweet for lunch and tea at six o'clock, which was a big meal.

The forms at Charterhouse were sorted by ability, rather than age, so you had some older boys in the lower forms. I started in a form called the Upper Fourth. I was rather fortunate. It was a classical form and the master in charge was a man called Girdlestone. He was a very old man who used to waddle like a duck. He had founded his own house, and it became known by everybody, including the staff, as 'Duckites'. Girdlestone's method of teaching was very odd. When he gave Latin or Greek prep, you were supposed to look up any words which you didn't know and list them on a piece of paper. During the lesson, he called you up to read your prep and you handed your list in. If you stumbled over a word he'd say, 'I don't see this word on your list. Why isn't it?' and you answered, 'I thought I knew it, sir.' He was a dear old boy and we were very sorry to see him go.

Maurice Edward Laws

At the age of thirteen, I went up to the Admiralty for an interview to get into Osborne Naval College. The interview was designed, not to test your knowledge, but to see what kind of boy you were, and how you would react to an unexpected situation. I was asked all sorts of silly questions. The final question was asked over a blank map of Africa. One of the examiners, some old admiral, asked me what a particular river was. I said, 'That's the Congo.' He said, 'No, my boy. That's the Niger.' I said I was sure it was the Congo and someone else piped up and said he was sure it was the Niger. They went into a furious discussion and a porter brought in a proper map with the names on it and I took no further interest in the matter because my time was up. I never found out whether it was the Niger or the Congo. I didn't get into the Navy, but it was nothing to do with the interview. I failed on medical grounds.

Helen Bowen Pease

We were educated by a governess, Miss Cornish, who was the daughter of the headmaster of Eton. Our education was entirely literary, as girls' education usually was. It puzzles me, because Father was an engineer and the tradition in the family was in science and engineering, but they never took us to see a canal or a tunnel, we were taken to see Dr Johnson's house in Lichfield. They didn't show us Erasmus Darwin's house up the road. Sometimes, Mother taught us, and that was always rather unfortunate. Father took Maths sometimes and that was very entertaining. Father was a terrific historian and he used to ask us questions at dinner, like, 'When was the battle of Waterloo?' and if you said, '1815' he said, 'Silly! I didn't mean the year! What month?'

Dorothy Wright

I never went to school. I had governesses who taught me reading and writing and Mathematics and History. I got through an incredible number. Having a 'gov' wasn't like being in a classroom. The gov watches you day and night. I had other classes as well. A French class was got up for the children of the district. Monsieur Poiret came from Leeds University every week to teach us. We had dancing lessons in the Town Hall. It could be trying, because one was made to do the waltz or polka with some little boy that you couldn't bear. We had a drawing class taken by the headmaster of Leeds Art School. I had always been interested in drawing. My mother used to illustrate all her letters to me when I was at the sea with my nanny. And at Easter, she used to paint my Easter eggs. I wasn't particularly musical – I liked other things better. My mother bought me a violin in the hopes that I'd learn it. I did for a bit but I sold it to buy a pony. By the time I stopped lessons, I was leading a life of leisure and a great deal of enjoyment. I was learning how to live with older people and how to treat them.

Ernest Hugh Haire

Father decided to put me into teaching. In 1908, I went to St John's College in Battersea in London. We were affiliated to London University. The syllabus was very wide, and in the first year I did English, History, Geography, Science and Maths. The discipline was extremely strict. We had lectures every morning at seven o'clock and you had to be there on the dot. It was a bind – there was a competition to see how late you could stay in bed to get there for seven. Three mornings a week, the lecture was Chaucer, the other two it was Maths. Breakfast was at eight-thirty, then chapel at nine. We had lectures until twelve-fifteen, then lunch. We had splendid food and we were waited on hand and foot. In the afternoon, we had one lecture between two and three, but on Wednesday we were free all afternoon. We had another good meal at six, with beer provided at the table. I didn't drink at that time, but two prefects used to arrange to sit at a table with ten teetotallers each evening until it dawned on people that they were getting tight every night. After dinner, we had chapel at quarter to seven, and supervised private study between half past seven and half past nine.

I passed out of the college in 1910. I specialised in history teaching and I had to sit a paper on the letters and speeches of Oliver Cromwell. I did well on that, but I also had to do the school practice. That meant being assessed as you taught a class. The subject of the class was given by the tutor. I was hoping it would be a History or Geography lesson – in fact he made me give a grammar lesson on the ablative absolute: which was really a Latin thing. I took a class of forty-nine boys in a Chelsea school, in front of the class teacher, the headmaster, the tutor and the Inspector. For thirty-five minutes I taught the ablative absolute. I struggled. At the end, the Inspector came to me and said, 'My poor boy. You have my sympathy. Who the hell gave you that subject?' 'That gentleman over there,' I said, indicating the tutor. 'I wonder how he would have managed,' said the Inspector. The Inspector turned to the tutor. 'You are responsible for assessing the subjects and you gave this young man a lesson on the ablative absolute. He struggled manfully with it but he couldn't illustrate it. I'll bet a darn you couldn't have done it! What a ridiculous thing to do! And I'm going to give him an "A" mark!'

Bill Owen

I went to St Clement's School in Dove Street. We had a headmaster called Mr Campie – talk about discipline. Discipline was nothing when I went in the Marines, because this chap really was strict. Many times I didn't have a piece of bread to go to school with – there was nothing in the house – but had a polish on my shoes. I had one of those collars on, and that had to be washed and cleaned, and your hair cut. He had a cane, and he'd have your hand under the blackboard, and he'd bring it down on your fingers.

At school – talk about brainwashed – when we went out in the yard it was all 'Three Cheers for the Red, White and Blue'. I think that was the start of me joining up – having it drummed into me.

When I started school you had to pay a penny a week, and my old mother often didn't have the penny to give me for school. But while I was in the Infants, 1905–6, they came out with free education. Boots or clogs – we wore anything we could get. The old woman used to get a pair of old uppers off somebody and you used to get them 'clogged'. If they were good uppers, you'd get them clogged.

Tom Murray

I have good recollections of my school days at Tornaveen in Aberdeenshire. I went to school in 1906 with my sister Margaret, who was a year and a half younger than me. I was kept back a year before I went to school so that the two of us could go together. We had three teachers that I recall particularly. One of them was a drunk and was always in a bad temper. He used to thrash the children with a strap, mercilessly, because he would be sitting in the room and fall asleep while he was supposed to be teaching us. We were so incensed we decided – I must only have been eight or nine years of age – we would wait till he went away at night and pinch the strap and throw it away. And we did.

Edwardian classroom scenes – schoolgirls being
taught to prepare food.

At least one boy thinks he knows the answer.

James Lewis

Being a church school, there was a strong accent on religion, and the headmaster, Mr Weston, opened school with prayers in the morning, and closed school on Friday in the same way. We learned the Church of England Collects, the Apostles' Creed, and the Confession, and I enjoyed the Scripture lessons under Mr Allen. Our Geography lessons demonstrated the greatness of our empire, and our History lessons the greatness of our military and naval victories, and the prowess of our explorers. The portraits of King Edward and Queen Alexandra decorated the walls, and at the end of the hall was a large Union Jack with the caption 'For God, King and Country'.

Our misdemeanours were dealt with by being sent to Mr Weston, to be caned across the palm of the hand, which was quite painful, but not degrading or brutalising. We were usually proud to show our weals to our classmates and I never saw anybody taking it out on another boy. Mr Burgess, of Standard 5B, was the only teacher who didn't send us to the head for punishment. He administered it himself, with a hardwood blackboard pointer, which he referred to as his ash plant, but we liked him as well as respected him. My favourite teacher was Mr Birkbeck. He was the only teacher other than the head to wear his gown. Mr Birkbeck was a master of sarcasm and was quite cutting, but his wit brought humour to the lessons. He once told me that my writing looked as if a spider had come out of the inkwell and crawled across the page. Mr Birkbeck took Standard 6B, and he developed our musical knowledge. Up to this we had sung traditional songs such as 'The British Grenadiers', 'The Vicar of Bray' and 'The Lincolnshire Poacher' – but Mr Birkbeck taught us to sing treble and alto parts, and Schubert's 'Greeting' and Gounod's 'Nazareth'.

On one occasion the class was divided into two halves. One half was taken to visit the Cunard liner *Franconia*, while my half were taken to Hightown. We walked the five miles there through the countryside, and then we made tea on a fire in our billy cans on the sand hills at Hightown, then walked back along the shore.

H. Eccles

We'd have a week's holiday at Easter time. Before the school closed for Easter, the shops in the vicinity used to throw these biscuits into the crowd of schoolchildren, and there was a scramble for them.

They used to roll eggs down the hill in Preston. They used to come up to the park and sit on the guns that were captured in the Crimea, on the gun emplacement, and you could go in to those shops – the little cottages adjoining the Park Hotel. One of those used to sell little red cakes, and the cost was only a halfpenny, and you also got a halfpenny bottle of mineral water. That was the thing done among schoolchildren.

I went half-time at twelve, when I went in a grocer's shop as an errand boy. Then I went into the mill, where I started at six in the morning. You finished at noon and had to go to school in the afternoon. After that, when I became full-time at thirteen, I went to Bank Top evening school, and there I took up continuation studies in arithmetic, book-keeping and accounts, and general correspondence. From there I went to St Barnabas Preparatory Technical College – I was about fourteen. I was there two years, and then I went to the Technical College for commercial classes. I sat for the various examinations – London Chamber of Commerce, Lancashire and Cheshire Union of Institutes – and I joined up. I got work in a solicitor's office for about twelve months, and then a mill office, John Thompson's. John Thompson was a well-bearded man. He used to come up every day in his carriage and pair, and from the office I could hear the harness rattling.

Jackie Geddes

At playtime we used to run round chasing one another, and we often used to jump over a wall in the schoolyard, and there was a good drop on the other side. And I remember I had just got over this wall, when there was an explosion. And when I came back, they were carrying this boy out, and there was a rare commotion about it. He had had a detonator, you know, what they fire the shots with in the pit. He'd been poking it to fit it onto his pencil and it had gone off and burnt his hand off. Reddick was the manager of number six pit and it was his son that had somehow got these detonators. It was quite a shock that.

Mrs Colclough

When the twins were born, a little boy was a big thing – Granny Collins' family was mostly girls. Dad used to say if you go out with the twins take them up to see your gran, and of course they made a terrible fuss of Basil. Mother kept him smart, with a little walking stick and covered coat, beautiful dressed, but they never took any notice of Barbara. One day I went up the back street and I upset the pram. Aunty Kate came and picked up the little boy and took him away, but left the little girl and never looked at her. We soothed both of them, but they didn't take the bonnet off her.

When I went to see Granny Collins I was given a slice of cake and a glass of milk, Flora wasn't, she was put in Grandad's study and that was it. I used to be upset about that too because there was no need for it, but Flora wasn't like them to look at, and I was.

Mr Jordan

The girls were in separate compartments – they never intermixed with the boys. It was all silently, secretly done if you met a lass. You dare not let your parents know. They were kept apart – in churches and chapels the girls sat one side and the boys sat the other side. But we courted. You daren't tell your parents till you were about eighteen or nineteen and then you were more open with it.

Emma Ford

When I was three years old, I ran away. Mother came out and said, 'Has anyone seen a little girl?' Of course there was nobody about in those days. Although it was a town it was just like living in a village, because there was no traffic, there were no cars. All you saw were coal carts and horse traps. She looked round the street and someone told her a little girl was toddling into the schoolyard. And I'd toddled up and gone to Parliament Street and of course the headmistress kept me in. Mother came in and I was sitting on the floor with my head down. I wouldn't look up because I didn't want to go.

Mr Patten

We always set off in a gang. Farms in those days had more people and so more children on them, and there were no school buses, children walked. You were either in a happy gang or you were in a fighting gang – you know what children are, one day so-and-so was pals with them, the next day, not. It was a common sight in the nineteen hundreds to see the schoolchildren coming to school in gangs, some from Kimmerston, some from Hay Farm. And there would always be the odd one or two who didn't gang up.

You carried your bait – your bait was bread and dripping, bread and butter and a tin bottle full of tea. You gathered in the playground and had great fun until nine o'clock, when the schoolmaster blew a whistle and you ran into your classes. You cheated when it came to some of the difficult sums, if you could. You peered over the shoulders of the ones in front of you or something like that. You knew the good scholars and tried to get the answers from them. If it was a wet day, you went to school and you sat there damp the whole day. At noon, you broke up for dinner and you took your tin bottle. There were always stoves at the school and you popped your tin bottle on top of the stove to warm the tea up again. If you didn't slacken the cork, when it reached a certain temperature it blew the cork up into the air, which the teachers didn't like very much because tea was splashed over the stove and created fumes.

Mrs Wain

My maternal grandmother, Georgina Roberta Murray, born in 1850, was the thirteenth child, and was named after two older sons who had died in childhood. She often visited my parents, and urged us children to get up in the morning with 'Rise Cornelius, and put on thy pompeycrackers, and go and see a rye cockalorum go along the road with a high cockalorum on his tail'. We never knew what she was talking about, but any child would get up to dress in 'pompeycrackers'.

Albert Rowells

You had to go – if you had a brother in the school he had to come and make you go. If you didn't you'd be put in the Mickey book. You couldn't get off – old Corker was a stickler for discipline and attendance was his specialty. He held the best record in County Durham for attendance – if you were sick he would send for you to come and sit in front of the fire to keep you warm.

Tom Kirk

On my first birthday, I was presented by my uncles with a real steam engine of German make, with lots of lines. My earliest memory is of crawling after the engine, which was emitting a delicious smell of methylated spirit oil and steam. On succeeding birthdays Uncles Tom, Peter and Harold always presented me with additional lines, signals and points.

Henry Allingham

I lived with my grandparents until I was seven, and they rather spoiled me. My father's father was a jewel-case maker. He was merry fellow – he always wore a red Turkish fez with a black tassel. He used to tease me and play games. He'd pretend to pull my nose off and say, 'Eh, look, you've got your nose in my cup.'

Tom Kirk

When we were children, the Pierrots were terribly important to us. They used to come every year and put up a small stage with a piano amongst the sand dunes at Seaton Carew where we lived. At the end of each performance they would collect a few coppers from the children, in a bucket. They all called themselves 'uncle' and I remember their songs:

If I were Uncle Percy,
I would, I would, I would appear
On the end of the pier.
We all went to the shop to shelter from the rain,
We all had a lick of the raspberry stick,
And we all came out again.

Ethel Barlow

Every Easter there was a lovely big procession in the East End. I think they were collecting for the hospital. It was a mile and a half long. There was a cart with a barrel organ, and a cart with a big dancing bear, but the winner was always a yellow cart with yellow flowers from Colman's Mustard.

Sonia Keppel

Sometimes, King Edward, who I called Kingy, came to tea with Mamma, and was there when I appeared at six o'clock. On such occasions he and I devised a fascinating game. With a fine disregard for the good condition of his trouser, he would lend me his leg, on which I used to start two bits of bread and butter, butter-side down, side by side. Then, bets of a penny each were made, my bet provided by Mamma, and the winning piece of bread and butter depended, of course, on which was the more buttery. The excitement was intense while the contest was on. Sometimes he won, sometimes I did. Although the owner of a Derby winner, Kingy's enthusiasm seemed delightfully unaffected by the quality of his bets.

Edith Turner

As a child I used to play with my sister. We didn't have anything to play with so our enjoyment was plaiting our hair, rubbing our noses together, sitting on the table and trying to plait our fingers together. That kind of thing.

Thomas Henry Edmed

I used to collect nuts on the way to school in a park then throw
these nuts to the children in the playground. I've been known as
'Nutty' ever since.

Bob Rogers

We did a lot of scrumping in those days. In Dalston there were a
lot of fruit trees. There were orchards all round there.

Charles Watson

There were rows of small houses and we used to get a piece of string
and tie it round two front-door handles next to each other. Then
we'd knock on both doors and run across the road. One person
would come out and pull the door, then the other person next door
would pull their door. We were on the other side of the road laughing
at them. They'd shout 'We'll get you!' But they never did.

Mary Keen

We used to make up our own games. The boys had iron hoops and
the girls had wooden hoops. We had skipping ropes and we used to
have games where we'd form a great big ring with one of us in the
middle and we'd sing 'Poor Julia's a-weeping on a bright summer's
day'. About five o'clock on a Friday afternoon, a piano organ grinder
used to come round, but mostly we made our own amusements.

Reece Elliott

We would make dolls from an ordinary clothes peg. When it came
to the split in the clothes peg, that was the arms. For the feet it was
all wires. There were two parts to the feet and a little bit and the
clog, and you had a bit of string on the head. You sat on the edge
of the cracket, and you hung the doll over a board and somebody
would whistle a tune. It would be 'Oh Sally does tha like pease
pudding?' and so on. That's what used to go on. Uncle Lance was
the best of the lot, he could do owt with it. Get the feet go clack to
the tune.

Albert 'Smiler' Marshall

Both girls and boys played marbles. There were large glossy ones called 'alleys', while the girls played with smaller ones known as 'pimsells'. The girls enjoyed hopscotch, while the boys preferred 'fox and hounds'. We'd choose three or four to be foxes and they would run off with a four-minute head start and hide or keep moving around in a wood or field with long grass. The foxes had a piece of wool round their arm. After the foxes had gone the hounds had to find them and rip the wool off. This was supposed to be the end of their life. The foxes could blow the whistle or howl to give the hounds a hint. Then when all the foxes were caught the game ended. It could go on for hours.

Louis Dore

Marbles came in three kinds. Small ones were made of plaster or cement and were painted various colours. Larger ones, similarly made, were called 'bobsters' and the most prized of all were 'gallanis', made of glass with strands of coloured wire running through them. You would sit, legs outstretched against a wall, and place a bobster or gallani a few inches in front of you. The punters would then bowl marbles at this target and the pay-out would be two or three marbles per hit. Then there were 'peg tops'. These were rather top-heavy pear-shaped tops which were spun by first winding a length of string or cord around them and then throwing them hard to the ground. The tops had long iron pegs – hence the name – protruding from their bottoms and the object of the game was to throw your top at somebody else's so as to damage or split it. We also played with 'hoops' which were bowled along a road with a stick to guide them and keep them going.

Daniel Davis

In the courtyard at Rothschild Buildings, we used to play football with an India rubber ball, and if the porter got too near the ball he used to take it. He'd say, 'You mustn't play football.' That was because we used to smash the windows.

Louis Dore

This is rather horrible but a game among schoolboys was that of seeing who produced the best and biggest gob. An ordinary grey one earned few marks, a yellow one was a good 'un, but a green one was a winner. That is except in the case of a much rarer green one with red spots. Such a consumptive gob swept the board.

W. J. Barfoot

We collected cigarette cards of different pictures in sets of fifty. Marbles were played all the time, and when conkers were in season we would string them through the middle of the nut and knock each other out.

Charles Watson

My pocket money was a farthing a fortnight. We used to go to Mrs Mallion's little shop and she'd have a strip of liquorice and tear it down in strips – and if there were two of us, we'd tear it up and have half each. She used to make her own sweets and we got four if we had a halfpenny. She used to screw up a piece of paper with four sweets in.

Albert 'Smiler' Marshall

Boys were always out to make the odd penny. In summer, coaches taking tourists to the sea passed through the village, and the boys used to call out, 'Throw out your mouldy coppers.' Boys fought each other for tuppence. One day I was set upon by four boys. On my return home, my father said, 'Now you have met your Waterloo,' and he treated my swollen eyes with raw meat.

Bob Rogers

The only bath we used to get was a swim in the Regent's Canal. All the old chaps used to go down the canal and toss money up on a stick and gamble on whether it would come down heads or tails. A lot of that money used to end up in the canal, and when they were finished, we used to dive down for it. We also used to get on the barges as they came along and then dive off them. In Queen's Road, by the bridge, there was a big gas works, and in the winter we used to go in the water behind there and it was boiling hot. We never knew it was poisonous. To us it was marvellous. It was a hot bath.

Ruben Landsman

We used to go down the side of the Tower of London to the Thames and paddle our feet. Sometimes we went across the other side. Warm water used to come out from Hayes Wharf and run into the river. We used to paddle there but there was often trouble with the local boys, so we had to run quick. Oh yes, there were gangs. There was constant fighting between the gangs – between the Jews and the Christians.

Bessy Ruben

Bethnal Green was a Christian area and we avoided it because we were afraid of being beaten up. I remember a friend of my mother's coming up to us with his head all bashed in. He had been attacked at the end of Brick Lane going towards Bethnal Green. I remember somebody saying, 'Well, why did you go that way?' He should have gone another way to avoid Bethnal Green. But where we lived, there was security for us children. We came home from school and we knew the area and that our neighbours were our friends.

Louis Dore

In the streets, certain unwritten laws applied. Alone you could walk through someone else's territory without coming to too much harm. A few taunts and insults and the occasional stone might be thrown at you but you were rarely assaulted. But for a group of you to do so amounted to an invasion, and an opposing army would rapidly be formed. For a real street fight, a declaration of war would be made, and armed with broom handles and sticks, not to mention a pocket full of cobbles, the invader would advance slowly, chanting insults. 'Go home, your father wants his boots!', 'Get your hair cut!' or if names were known, little jingles like 'John, John, put your trousers on!' Except among a very few, certain words used freely today were taboo. 'Bleeding' was acceptable, as were 'sod' and 'bugger'.

Albert 'Smiler' Marshall

Guy Fawkes' Day was one of the highlights of the year. Boys leading a donkey, all dressed as guys, used to go round the village singing:

> Remember, remember, the fifth of November,
> The gunpowder treason and plot.
> I see no reason why gunpowder treason
> Should ever be forgot.
> With a dark lantern,
> With a light match,
> Holla, boys, holla, boys, make the bell ring.
> Holla, boys, holla, boys, God save the King.
> If you haven't got no money, give us some beer,
> Guy Fawkes comes only once a year,
> Bang, crash, wallop!

Then they let off fireworks with a cannon and real gunpowder.

Jack Banfield

We used to make our own fun. There was no television or radio, we used to all get round the piano and sing. Sunday was a day when you couldn't enjoy yourself in any way whatsoever. You couldn't sing unless it was a hymn. If you were whistling and you thoughtlessly whistled a song, you were reprimanded and told, 'Do you know what day it is?' There were no toys – nothing on a Sunday. It was a miserable day.

Dorothy Webb

Imber, on Salisbury Plain, was a paradise for children. We never had toys or books, but we were never bored, as there were so many exciting things going on outside. This was a purely agricultural village, growing acres of corn and tending large flocks of sheep. As the seasons came round there was sheep-shearing to watch, then the harvest when every hand was called on to help. We loved to go gleaning the ears of corn left after the rake had been round. What a feast for the hens when we came home, tired out and bitten all over by harvest bugs.

Rose Bishop

During the summer we roamed far and wide over the plain, with no restrictions of any kind and seeing no one but an occasional shepherd. In due season we went in search of peewit eggs to take home for breakfast, or to fill our baskets with mushrooms. The cry of the peewits and never-ending song of the larks, the beautiful little harebells, the rabbit warrens, the sudden start of a hare and, above all, the short, springy turf that was so pleasant to walk on. This is what Salisbury Plain means to me.

Dorothy Wright

I had a beloved Highland nanny who was the most wonderful naturalist. She knew the names of all the wild flowers. She knew where the various birds nested and she used to take me out carrying old leaking kettles that she found on rubbish heaps and she'd put one at the root of certain bushes and she'd say, 'You see! A robin will build in that!' And one almost invariably did.

William Keate

Butterflies. On a summer's day you could count twenty or thirty different species, and we would spend hours trying to catch them – and when we got tired, we would sit on the grass, dig out a square hole, put some twigs across the top and catch the grasshoppers – of which there were hundreds. What did not get out of the hole, you lifted out and set free while you went on to something else. We respected wildlife and flowers.

Henry Allingham

As a boy, I was friendly with the sons of Andrews the Chemist. They used to have a big house, and I used to go and play with their children. It was there that I sat in my first motor car. They had a lot of lovely swings and roundabouts in their playroom and they had a little lake in their garden with a boat on it. We used to be given a lovely peach melba in a long glass – and I wasn't used to that sort of thing. They were way ahead of us.

Joseph Henry Yarwood

We had Battersea Park nearby, and that was really marvellous. It had a boating lake and I used to go down there on a Saturday afternoon to read a book. They had a deer park and some wonderful cavern-like aviaries, full of owls. It was perfectly quiet. If I'd been on a gentleman's estate, I couldn't have had better surroundings.

George Perryman

We used to keep linnets, canaries and finches. There used to be a little pub opposite us in Canal Road called the Moulder's Arms that had competitions for the best singing birds, so we used to put our linnets and finches in little cages, and a black handkerchief over them, and take them over to the pub, where we'd hang up the cage with our name on it and they'd have the competition. When I was a youngster, I used to go on a bike to see my grandfather on a Sunday and he used to take me over to Hackney Marshes just beside the River Lea. He was a bird fancier, my grandfather. We used to set a trap. We put a linnet in a cage and put a trap next to it. We put food in the trap and attached a stick to the door and attached twine to the stick. We lay on the river bank and watched as all these linnets came down. They used to come down in droves. As soon as they got into the trap, we pulled the twine and the piece of wood came loose and the trap shut. We might catch two or three linnets at once. My grandfather used to sell them privately for two shillings or half a crown. The cock bird was the singer so he was more expensive.

Mr Lockey

My father didn't give me any pocket money so I had to make it in other ways. I had three long nets, a 100-yard, a 70-yard and a 33-yard, and I had a clever dog. I used to go out at night and set the 100-yard net up at the quarries while the dog lay in wait. Then I would send him round while I lay down. I would see the rabbits in the moonlight being herded towards the net as the dog ran back and forth. When he arrived at the net he would jump over it and come to me. Then I went to the net and took out the rabbits. At the time I was supplying fifty rabbits a week to the miners of Boldon colliery. The price was three shillings and sixpence a couple, but if they'd been shot, the price would only have been eighteen pence a couple, so it's clear why I was taking them alive. I was also a bit of a poacher, and when I was hard up, I would call hares. If the wind was the right way, I could call them from about a mile. Then I used to shoot them. I'd get five shillings a time. That kept me in pocket money.

Bessy Ruben

There was a barrel organ on a Saturday afternoon in Thrawl Street during the summer, and the children would dance in the street. We'd look forward to it. My mother didn't like it, but she'd let me go. I used to have my hapenny ready for him – his name was Percy. There was one little girl – a beautiful dancer – and we used to make a ring round her and clap while she danced.

Ted Harrison

I used to like the fairs on Hackney Marshes. I loved the joywheel. It was a flat wheel and it spun you round and we used to like it because you could see the girls' knees and their drawers. Or 'freetraders' as we called them. They were bloomers that came just above the knee. They were the latest thing. Another new thing was fancy garters. Some of the girls were daring – on the bottom of their petticoats they used to wear a little bit of lace that would show under the skirt. That was the enticement, you see. It used to get them a free drink at the pictures or a fish and chip supper. A little bit of lace showing.

Tom Kirk

On one occasion, when I was invited to Sunday dinner by the parents of a boy at school, we threw mud from behind a hedge at the girls of Lowther College who were coming out of church in a crocodile. We were spotted and soundly thrashed.

Arthur Harding

We used to go hop picking in Kent. Mostly it was people from South London. The farmer was called Hawthorn, and every year he sent a letter and paid for our fare down, otherwise we wouldn't have gone. He used to send the train tickets because he didn't trust us with the money. Because, frankly speaking, nobody was honest. When we got there, we all used to sleep with our clothes on in a great big barn – about thirty or forty of us. We children were a priceless asset because we were very quick at picking. We used to bung the whole lot in the bins, anything we could get hold of.

Albert 'Smiler' Marshall

We used to have a day's holiday from school for picking pears, and for lifting potatoes, the whole family taking part. Our only excursion was to an agricultural show at White City, and that involved a two-mile walk to the local station.

Sonia Keppel

Usually, Kingy, too, spent Easter at Biarritz, and gradually I came to realise that Tweedledum, Sir Ernest Cassel, was quite easily distinguishable from Kingy – Tweedledee. For one thing, Tweedledee laughed more easily and, as I already knew, he could enter into nursery games with unassumed enthusiasm. Always, he was accompanied by his dog, Caesar, who had a fine disregard for the villa's curtains and chair-legs.

Beach parties and parties with other children took up our time, and one Easter Sunday, Kingy, ourselves and a host of others set forth for a mammoth picnic. Kingy liked to think of these as impromptu parties, and little did he realise the hours of preliminary hard work they had entailed.

First, his car led the way, followed by others containing the rest of the party. Then the food, guarded by at least two footmen, brought up the rear. Kingy spied out the land for a suitable site and, at his given word, we all stopped, and the footmen set out the lunch. Chairs and a table appeared, linen table-cloths, plates, glasses, silver. Every variety of cold food was produced, spiced by iced cup in silver-plated containers. Everything was on a high level of excellence, except the site chosen. For some unfathomed reason, Kingy had a preference for picnicking by the side of the road. On Easter Day, inevitably, this was packed with carriages and the first motor cars, all covered with dust, and when we parked by the roadside, most of the traffic parked with us.

Ruben Landsman

The children used to do an annual trip to Crystal Palace, and all the boys lined up and the teacher gave you a brand-new sixpence each. And the monitor got one and sixpence. We marched to Aldgate Station or Liverpool Street Station. I remember the first time I saw the train.

Ellen Clark

We lived next door to an engineer, and every Christmas Eve he used to send his daughter round and she would ask my sister and I to their house. They would have 2 lb of the best raisins and they put them on a plate and they put some rum over them and they set light to them. The first time we saw this, we daren't touch them – we were frightened, so the other girls were eating them all. So the mother said, 'What's the matter with you Barbara and Mary Ellen?' And her daughter said, 'They're frightened to touch them'. 'Oh' she said, 'Get on with them – they'll not hurt you!' So we tried them and after that we didn't stop.

Tom Kirk

In 1908 I remember staying with the Robsons, a wealthy family in Stockton. I arrived at noon to hear that Sidney, the second son, had been locked in his bedroom with bread and water because he had tortured a cat. Meanwhile, Marjorie, Sidney's sister, was left alone with me. She suggested that we should change clothes. Not realising what this implied, I was starting to strip off, when her mother came in and marched me off to another room where she gave me a lecture on sex. Later that summer, when Sidney was again locked up for some misdemeanour, a game of hide and seek was organised and Marjorie disappeared. Some time later, she was found lying beside a haystack in the arms of a naked farmhand.

Arthur Harding

We used to do a trick – a bloody dangerous trick and all. We'd pin a sheet of paper on a bloke's back when he was in a crowd and we'd set light to the paper at the bottom. I had two pals – Wally Shepherd and Billy Warner. They both got knocked out in the First World War. Billy was a diddicoy – a gypsy who'd settled down – and the three of us were always up to bloody mischief.

Thomas Henry Edmed

A gang of us went into Windsor Park and we walked miles and found this hut. It was a carpenter's hut and inside it, there was everything; beautifully polished saws, choppers, axes, chisels and screwdrivers. It was the most elaborate place. What we did to that hut was really dreadful. We left the lot all piled in a heap in the middle. The police never found out who did it.

Sonia Keppel

At first, the Christmas holidays seemed to have a movable background. At the age of three, I spent them at Gopsall, where lived Lord and Lady Howe, and where I have no recollection of anything except of an enormous grown-up, fancy-dress dinner party on Christmas Eve. To this I was brought down, dressed up as an Admiral of the Fleet, impersonating my great-uncle, Sir Harry Keppel, whom I was said to resemble. My uniform was perfect in every detail, including the sword. But it was hot and smelt nasty, and my white, cotton-wool eyebrows and side-whiskers were gummed on, and were most painful to pull off. Violet was dressed as a Bacchante, and Mamma and Lord Herbert Vane-Tempest were got up as a pair of immense twins, pushed into the room in an enormous double perambulator by Papa, as a very hirsute nurse. I remember an alarming collection of Turks and Chinamen and Eastern houris and Watteau shepherdesses. I felt like Gulliver in Brobdingnag. And, the minute I sat down to dinner (as one Admiral to another), I fell asleep with my head in Lord Charles Beresford's lap.

The journey to Duntreath seemed to take nearly as long as that to Biarritz, but it had compensations. At Carlisle, we were allowed out of the train for ten precious minutes, dogged by my fear that the train might proceed without us. During this time we were allowed a change of magazine, and bottled sweets, at the bookstall. And here too, we took on a luncheon basket. 'Fee fi fo fum', we said, as we opened it, taking out mammoth rolls of bread containing sides of chicken. The meal tasted delicious, consisting also of the otherwise forbidden fruits of Cheddar cheese and unripe pears. And there was the fun of putting out the basket at the next station. Later, the inevitable pangs of indigestion were dulled by peppermints from Nannie's bag.

Nina Halliday

There were musical comedies in the London theatres, with lots of gay tunes. My sisters used to go and see them and buy the music and play and sing them for their own pleasure. There was one very special one called *The Geisha*, and for a while Japanese things were very popular. One shop sold them in Windsor. They had brightly coloured paper fans, and dolls of all sizes in crinkly paper, the small ones with arms and legs just stuck between the paper, and a soft paper body. There were coloured parasols of many sizes and they all had a lovely strange scent which seemed to come both from the wrappings and the clothes. I was given one lovely doll dressed in a green satin kimono, with a wide obi or sash, and a bisque china face, hands and feet, but she must have been made in this country – she had not the right scent. But the very best thing I had was the programme of the play – it was made of crinkly rice paper with a fully coloured picture of a Geisha on the cover, and a red silk cord and tassel, and it too had the same unusual attractive scent.

Joe Garroway

We had a circus every two years, Sanger's or Williamson's circus. They used to come to Consett, which was a busy place then. We would get up at six in the morning to see the elephants and antelopes and camels, it was the sight of a lifetime to see the circus come in. They had to get to Tow Law and put the tent up, and do the ring, and at one o'clock they had to give us a procession. The last procession I can remember had a lion on a steel chain and the keeper sitting beside him. They went up the reservoir and back, then performed at half two and half six. They were only here for one day, yet they had the show to put up, the procession to arrange, two perform-ances, and then to get ready to go to the next place the next day.

Albert Rowells

We used to play a lot of matches on the Moor at Newcastle on a Saturday. We had a brown paper parcel under our arms with our boots and such like, and we used to walk through the Fell, then get a penny car down to the High Level end, and then it was a halfpenny to walk over the bridge. And we used to walk from there onto the Moor. We went back into town and we would go into a café to get a tea, then maybe go to the Pavilion or the Empire or the Hippodrome.

Mr Spark

My uncle, Jack Cameron, knew that I had a sailor doll and nigger minstrel doll – when nigger wasn't a dirty word. The nigger minstrel stayed on the wall but I was allowed to play with the sailor doll. My

Easter parade for St Joseph's School, Blackburn.

father taught me how to spell nigger in letters. I wouldn't have been able to write those things but I had them memorised. Uncle Jack said, 'Spell nigger minstrel.' I said, 'N.I.G.G.E.R . . . nigger minstrel.' That was association of ideas.

Sometimes we used to get a pig's bladder and blow it up as a ball, and then smuggle that from one lad to another. That's all it was, it wasn't really running with it. We used to smuggle it from one to another and we either had to get it to the top of the schoolyard or the bottom of the schoolyard to score points. I was in my element if I was in the bottom of the scrum wrestling to get that bladder. And it didn't matter how you got it, you could push it up your jersey or put it inside your jacket pocket or under your arm. There was too much tackling, you were underneath a score of boys often, scratching around to get it. I was in my element doing that. That was probably why I went on to take up rugby.

Mr Powton

Each season used to have its game. There'd be marbles, and in springtime when the days were getting longer, we used to come down to the village with hoops. The boys used to have iron ones, but the girls had wooden ones, and we used to have the middle size, I think it used to cost fourpence with a stick. We'd come down the road before school – there was very little traffic then and it was just horse traffic – and then go up the road and come back again. And then there'd be ball games in the wintertime. Also in the winter my mother would dress up with my Aunt Lilly. She used to dress up as a man. She was slender, but Lilly was plumper, so she used to wear a black cap. It was just making fun amongst your own people.

Mrs Skinner

At Christmas, there was an advert in the paper for a nice big doll, and my mother said to me, 'Would you like it?' I said, 'Yes.' When I got up on Christmas morning, it was a big cloth doll filled with sawdust, but it was beautifully dressed – my mother had dressed it. We also had a Wooden Betty which my uncle had made out of wood. The eyes, nose, mouth and teeth were burnt in with a poker then painted. It went through five of us, and then it went in the oven to heat the Sunday dinner.

Fred Lightburn
We used to make firecrackers for the fifth of November with gun-powder from the store. The powder was in pellets and we used to roll it out into a fine powder with a rolling pin, then there was a certain way of filling it into folded paper. One or two of the old hands was well up to the job, and you used to get some hefty crackers, I can tell you.

Mary Maughan
For our one holiday a year we went to South Shields. There were shuggy boats and marquees, you could get a meal for sixpence and the village brass band would sit in a ring, and it was tuppence to have a dance to the band. It was with Sunday school, you got a bag of mixed buns, and mother would send teacakes and home-made pies.

Alwyn Lewis
There was a rugby field just outside our house and the girls used to play rugby with us. They used to wear clogs. There was one girl lived on this dirty old street called Becca Lewis. Becca Lewis was a great big rough girl – we used to think she was a woman, but she must have only been in her teens. She used to play rugby in her clogs and we were afraid to go near her.

Mr Patten
When you got home you maybe got a meal or you had to wait until the father came in from his job. If you didn't get a meal when you got in, you took off your school clothes, as you couldn't afford to soil those, and you went and played outside again. Well, there were apple trees, pear trees and plum trees in your district somewhere, and you would have to get them some way or another. Everything

like that was fair game, and it was always fair game to tease the keepers and those people who had apple trees and things. Even if we couldn't eat them, it was a question of being clever enough to steal them from the owners. Your status was improved if you were the one to steal the most.

Mr Harrison

I used to see fights at school and there was a fight in the streets every night as well. We used to play in the pit pond and it was full of dead ducks. You had to shove them to one side while you were swimming.

Polly Lee

We used to call in at the greengrocers and get straw ropes off orange boxes. We couldn't afford proper skippy ropes. If you saw anybody with skippy ropes with handles on you thought they had plenty of money. The straw skips didn't last very long though, they'd soon break. You sometimes used to sneak a bit off your mother's line, but when you were skipping double you needed a long rope.

Florence Hannah Warn

We did not have any pocket money, but sometimes we ran an errand for someone and received a halfpenny, so we would buy some sweets, and for a farthing there were lots of things one could buy. There was a strip of toffee called Everlasting, which it was not; a braid of liquorice which broke into strips and were called Shoe Strings; a slab of black toffee called Wiggle Waggle, which blackened the tongue and lips. Bull's eyes were marbles of sweet which could be eaten, but when rubbed on a rough wall, revealed a flat surface with rings of varying colour, hence bull's eyes. Sweet shrimps, white or pink fondant mice – we girls were a trifle squeamish about eating these – for a farthing you could get six pretty little boiled sweets called Rosebuds.

D. G. I. Lodge

My brother had diphtheria when he was two and my mother was expecting another baby, so I went to stay with my aunt and uncle, who was a doctor. They had no children but longed for a child. I stayed and I stayed, and then one day I said, 'I think one father and one mother and one little girl is best,' and from then on I stayed with them.

One night my uncle woke me up and put me in a dressing gown and carried me to the front door in his arms. It was a dark night. The clouds were low and misty. We couldn't see anything. Then we heard the migratory birds going over. It was the most wonderful sound I've ever heard. They were flying so low and seemed to go on for ever. It was amazing. Curlews and sandpipers, redshank, all piping and calling to one another. I know nothing to compare with that.

WORK

Ray Head

I went to work for the Post Office in the City of London. Hounslow was an agricultural town in those days, a little rural place. Most people living there worked on the land. Most people working in London still came from the area close to the City – I was an exception. Most of these people walked to work. There were thousands of houses in Lambeth, Southwark, Whitechapel and Dalston, and all the inhabitants used to walk to work in offices which were really clerical factories. Everything was so labour-intensive. Typewriters were only just beginning and the telephone was a luxury for the very, very few, so everything was written by hand. In the banks, all the ledgers were done by hand and there was a great deal of clerical work to do.

I used to wear a stiff collar, tie, trousers, heavy boots, a bowler hat and an umbrella. You needed heavy boots because they soon wore out with all the walking. The people higher up wore top hats. The atmosphere in the office was pretty formal. Contact between men and women was very limited. We were kept apart and we dined in separate dining rooms. There was no palliness with the bosses. We were very humble. In spite of all this, we were happy. It almost felt like a club.

Ronald Chamberlain

We lived in Canonbury in Islington. It was a very nice, lower middle-class area, populated by clerks, post office people, bankers and people who worked in shops. My own father was a clerk in the Post Office. He earned a modest income, about seven or eight pounds a week, and he brought up three children on that. He was always very particular to be well groomed and well dressed. He wore a bowler hat and never wore shabby clothes. He never worked in his shirt-sleeves and there were no Christian names used at work. They were very dignified in the office. He was a very modest man but he had a very high sense of propriety and conduct. All Post Office people had that attitude to their work. I remember being out with my father one evening and we saw a postman who had finished his work and he was slouching and rolling – he had obviously been drinking. My father was enraged by this. He went up to the postman and said, 'Pull yourself together, my man! You are a civil servant and so am I, and in the Post Office, you can't behave like this!' That shows the attitudes of the day. My father originally worked six days a week, but in 1906 or 1907 they gave him the Saturday afternoon concession and he was able to come home in the middle of the day.

Mildred Ransom

After a period of hovering, I decided to learn shorthand and type-writing. I went to a commercial school in the City and in intervals of hard work I sometimes contrasted the cold, gas-lit, smelly class-rooms with the scents and beauty of the Tropics. I don't know that I regretted them. I felt rather that I was satiated with sun and beauty and I wanted to stretch my brains and learn endlessly and make a path for myself through the clamour and hideousness all round me in this perfectly revolting school.

From this seat of learning I went to a copying office in Bedford Row and I am deeply grateful to it. It was the worst of offices and the clerks were habitually kept till 11 p.m. Payment was made by results, which meant that you were paid half the value of the work you did; naturally the two partners kept all the fat and gave out only the badly paid stuff to the clerks, and then generously handed out a meagre half of what the latter had earned to them each Saturday. I earned five shillings my first week. Later I rose to the amazing salary of fifteen shillings, and one day I meekly approached the junior partner and asked if she thought I should ever rise to £1 a week. She looked at me with utter contempt and said, 'Never,' and then turned to more practical matters.

Sometimes my fellow clerks and I sat in idleness when the partners were busy, working hard because there was not enough work for everyone, and the partners had to be overworked before they would hand out anything to the clerks. At such times I used to urge insurrection and try to get them to demand better conditions, but it was very little use. A more popular effort was the recitation of *Aesop's Fables Revised*. The favourite moral was 'You cannot pretty much most always tell how things are going to turn out sometimes'. But I was grateful to the office because I learnt from the point of view of the downtrodden junior what was bad and how not to treat a staff, and I learnt by experience how unspeakably bad long hours were for the health and that reasonable comfort had a money value in producing work.

Ernest Hugh Haire

Liverpool impressed us because it was so commercial. A boy coming out of Liverpool Institute, going into a job as an office boy or a junior clerk, would go to a shipping office, an insurance office, a bank or a cotton brokers. Shipping was a big business in Liverpool with Cunard and White Star. The cotton brokers were a tremendous part of Liverpool commerce. They bought the cotton and sold it to the spinners in Lancashire. Myself, when I left Liverpool Institute, I started work for a small private marine insurance company. My father chose it. He had a friend in the church who was a sailing ship owner who recommended me. At first, I was a junior clerk, relaying messages, but then I was sent to the Open Policy Department. There was a great trade between Liverpool and Chile. The ships went out round Cape Horn, taking out manufactured goods, then they brought back guano, bird shit, which was used as a fertiliser. I checked out the policies as each ship came in and I learnt a great deal of geography. But I only earned seven shillings a week.

Cecil Withers

I left school at thirteen and went to work for W. H. Smith and Sons, where I was a bookkeeper. I worked in the office of the General Manager, Mr William Smart, in Arundel House in the Strand, opposite the Law Courts. I had to wear a collar with studs and a tie. Every morning, I used to take the number 74 tram from Brockley, which only took twenty-five minutes to get to the office. Sometimes the tram would stop because a horse had gone down ahead. Sometimes a 'bloody horse' would slip on the cobbles and cause a stoppage. When that happened, sacks were laid all around so the horse could gain a footing on the road surface.

Mildred Ransom

Typewriters were by no means common in offices early in the Nineties, and copying work was still given out to stationers and printers who farmed it out to an army of out-of-elbow writers. When the many advantages of typing over writing dawned on businessmen, their documents were sent as an experiment to a copying office and copying by writing became a thing of the past. Finally, even lawyers gave way and said they had always been in favour of so excellent an invention. So women took premises and fitted them up with typewriters and were kept busy with every variety of work sent in from the aristocratic centres who, though obliged to drop the old-fashioned method of copying by hand, would not install machines of their own.

The old machines were very unlike those of today. The No. 2 Remington had a serrated bar running along its front, and many is the time I tore the back of my fingers on it while running back the carriage to begin a new line. Torn and bleeding fingers with dirt and oil liberally rubbed into the wounds were an ordinary accompaniment of the day's work till one became expert enough to avoid the snare, and no one ever dreamt of an iodine bottle and no harm ever came of it.

As years passed, firms everywhere began to fit up their offices with typewriters and to employ girl typists. Systems of filing were introduced, and instead of sending all copying work to be done out of the office, the work was organised so that it could be done inside by the normal staff. With this change, and particularly noting the rapidity with which it grew, it was plain that the period of prosperity in copying offices was passing, as work was only sent to them when the staff had too much to do and had no time to grapple with extra work. To those who could read the signs of the times it was plain that development was necessary. This was the origin of the secretarial schools and colleges. Girls had to be taught secretarial work, and even if every writer, MP and doctor had his own machine, he did not want to be always hammering at it. It paid him better to get a secretary and leave the hammering to her.

Schools were already in existence to teach shorthand, typing and bookkeeping, and sometimes modern languages, but their students aimed chiefly at clerical commercial work. The parents of girls from better-class schools disliked the milieu of the commercial schools and wished for a more suitable training. Gradually a demand grew and increased for a training which would be wider and better than a mere knowledge of shorthand and typewriting, and secretarial schools offered an educational scheme in which subjects were co-related, and where girls were taught to use in their new work the first-class education that most of them had received.

I took an engagement under the old London School Board, who appointed me to give a lecture at three evening schools every week. Two were most genteel and respectable and of unvarying dullness. Happy is the nation with no history, and more satisfactory still is the evening school which works hard and has no exciting incident of any kind. The third school made up for both the others in excitement. It had been closed down for a considerable time because of the perfectly awful incidents that occurred. I never could find out what these incidents were, and my inquiries were received with silence and large, circular eyes.

The school was reopened as an experiment and the entire staff was chosen primarily for their capacity to keep order and for their reputation as disciplinarians. I was deeply flattered when the head of the staff mentioned this, as I had no idea I possessed such a capacity, and it was not long before several of us wished we hadn't . . . The school was for girls only, which gave us a chance, and the staff was composed both of women and men. The responsible teacher was a woman. A more solidly loyal lot would be impossible to find.

My first opportunity to exercise discipline was on my first evening, when some of my class turned up unwashed, with hair unbrushed and wearing aprons spattered and soaked with blood. They had come straight from work in local slaughterhouses. None of the class had taken any trouble with their appearance, and the first thing to do was to teach them self-respect under the pretence of learning.

Success meant that somehow a teacher could hold the wild and wandering attention of his or her class and ultimately make them rule themselves. At first no dodge was omitted; girls pretended to be stone-deaf, to be unable to write – they left in a body if bored and invaded other classes. But they continued to attend.

One evening my class was tired of me and twenty-three out of twenty-five pupils had walked off to the arithmetic class. They informed the responsible teacher that their mothers absolutely insisted on this, so the unfortunate arithmetic master had a class of nearly fifty irresponsible rowdies instead of his normal trouble. I reported the exodus to the responsible teacher, who put the two Abdiels into the singing class. Thereupon, the singing master reported that he had no pianist and asked if I would play for him. Never have I forgotten that experience. My class promptly defied their mothers and deserted the arithmetic class and arrived, not out of loyalty to me, but to combine with the singing class in making the most appalling remarks that can be imagined. The mildest was that it was a put-up job between myself and the master to hang over the piano together.

We got over these little things; an extra teacher always patrolled the classes 'just to make sure' a teacher wasn't being devoured. Aprons came off, hair was brushed and faces and hands were washed. An immense improvement was noticeable and an inspector came round who was most complimentary. The school began to respect themselves and to modify their language. It was an uphill job, but after six months, when the school closed for the summer, it was a blazing success. Favourite teachers were escorted politely to their bus because 'the boys round 'ere are a rough lot.' Pretty manners were no longer greeted with derisive yells – we had progressed.

Before we closed down, the staff gave the school a party. We took them to Kensington Palace. We met at the Mansion House and went by tube to Queen's Road Station. That journey was a surprise to the officials and to the few passengers in our car. Very few of the girls had been west of the City in their lives, which had passed in a district of London full of slaughterhouses and factories; they were wildly excited. They told officials how silly they looked and criticised passengers' clothes in the freest of all free language. Luckily I had thought of bringing enough chocolate to keep them busy, and we burst out of the train at Queen's Road without serious mishap.

The traffic was then held up by us because a French poodle, tied up with scarlet ribbons, was crossing the road. A good deal of trouble ensued; the drivers were shouting; the girls were holding a debating society and the problem was the poodle. Was it a pig? Till they settled the point, they shouted and yelled to each other and ignored the traffic ... After this they seemed to have blown off steam and their behaviour was – nearly – exemplary. They were extremely shocked at a huge nude figure at the top of the staircase, and solemnly slapped her as a protest. We had tea, with our exemplary manners fixed firmly on, at the house of a friend of mine, and it was such a success that she asked why I had warned her that the girls were a rough lot.

Bill Taylor

I couldn't read or write, so when a firm gave me a delivery note, they would give me the orders at night for the following morning. I'd take the note home and try and work out the route which I was going to do, using a map. I'd look on the map for the names of places that were the same as those on my delivery note. I'd make a line right the way across the map, say from Holloway up to Barnet and on to the North Road to Darlington. Each big town I was going through, I'd mark on the map. So when I pulled up at that town, I'd get the map out and ask people which was the best way to the next town I'd marked. That was how I got on. I had to go from one town to another asking the way because I couldn't read any of the signs on the road. None of the guv'nors I worked for ever knew I couldn't read. If they did know someone couldn't read, they would fire them, saying, 'You're no good to me.' It had been easier when I'd been on the horses, because some of the horses knew where they were going. They helped a lot. But when it changed to motors, I had to do it all myself. I had a lot of tricks to get me through, though.

Driving was very different in those days. You had two half windscreens up the front and if the rain was coming down, you'd turn the top half up so you could see, but the rain would come through the gap and you'd get wet. We had a little hand-operated windscreen wiper which you could use every now and again. And you had nothing round the sides on the Model 'T' Ford, so if it rained you had sheeting that you could tie up so that you could see over the top, but your face still got wet.

The joy was the open road, going to different places, meeting different people. Of course you met so many up North who spoke different to you. And you were your own boss. You could do whatever you wanted. I used to have problems collecting my wages. I got into a lot of fights, making sure I got paid. There was one firm I always had trouble with. One day, the guv'nor gave me five shillings. I said, 'What's that? That's no good to me. You're thieving money off me,' and with that he thumped his fist through the window and hit me in the eye. Then the guv'nor's sons, big hefty blokes, came out to have a go at me, so I picked up a jack. I shouted, 'Come here! The first one hits me, I'll kill him with this bar!' Behind me was a brand-new Leyland car that belonged to the guv'nor and as I raised up the jack, the end of it went right through the windscreen. I had to run to get out of there.

As long as I was behind the wheel, driving, I was happy. When I used to go away on journey work, I'd perhaps be away a week at a time and we used to have to sleep rough in the lorry because often the guv'nor had no money. I've come home lousy, white lice running in my jersey. That's how bad it was in those days. You slept under canvas to keep you warm in the back of the lorry. And there used to be these 'lorry girls' in the cafés. They'd clean your lorry for a few bob and you'd take them from one town to another. Sometimes, they'd stop with you a whole week, sleep with you and keep you company. That's how they lived. You'd give them a lunch and kept them in grub and fags. When the wives found out about these lorry girls, a lot of marriages broke up.

Ernest Hugh Haire

After I qualified as a teacher, I was allotted a school to work at. I had no choice where I went. The school was St Anne's Church of England School, Birkenhead. I had a certain status because I'd been trained in London. I was met by the head teacher, who said, 'Right! I want none of your new-fangled ideas here!' He was a swine and he couldn't teach. There were four classes all being held in one room without even a dividing curtain between them. There was no lavatory, no tea, nowhere to hang your coat. On my first morning I was about to take my first class of thirteen-year-olds, when Wilkinson, the deputy head teacher, took me aside. 'I'll give you a bit of advice, my boy,' he said. 'You have a boy in your class who might give you a bit of trouble. His name is Harrison. Just clout him!' So after assembly, I went into the classroom and opened the register. As I started calling out the names, this tall boy stepped forward and said, 'Who the hell do you think you are?' I was flabbergasted. 'What?' I said. 'Who the hell do you think you are?' he repeated. I punched him under the jaw and he fell back and bumped his head.

The morning passed and later that day I saw a tall, well built man standing outside the school gate. 'Are you Mr Haire?' he asked. 'I am,' I replied. 'You hit my boy this morning!' 'Yes. I did. If your name's Harrison.' 'What did he do?' asked the man. So I told him and he looked at me and smiled. He put out his hand and said, 'I'll shake your hand, my boy! He's been asking for it for years! I'm a quartermaster on a ship and I'm away three and four months at a time to China and Japan and his mother ruins him. So you did the right thing. It's done him good!' After that, I played football with the boys in the playground, I took them to the baths, and I never looked back.

All the boys were from working-class backgrounds. There were boys who delivered papers in the morning and sold papers at night. One boy even had his own paper stand at Park Station and he was building up rather a good business. He was there every morning from seven o'clock and every night from half four till seven. The boys behaved. I very rarely had to use the cane, although I used to give the boys lines sometimes. I gave them very little homework but so long as they were reasonably intelligent, they mastered the three R's.

In those days, problems such as dyslexia weren't recognised. The boy would simply be considered backward. When I arrived at the school, you could find an eleven-year-old boy stuck in a class with eight-year-olds if he wasn't making any progress. He would just get left behind until he left school. I changed the system and started streaming them so they would stay within their age group. When I spotted a bright lad, I encouraged him. I gave him more work and helped him along so that he could reach college. The boys weren't ragged. They all had boots and were reasonably tidy. There was a police fund for children without boots and you could always draw on that. And we used to be able to distribute tickets for a meal of soup and brown bread and butter. But all of those boys were marvellous. And by 1916, most of them were dead.

Jane Banks

I became a pupil teacher. You sat for what was called a Preliminary Certificate of Education, and if you passed that you went as a pupil teacher in a school. I went back to the primary school I had been to, and I became a pupil teacher there. I was seventeen. I worked four days a week in the school and every Tuesday went back to the county school to keep up my book work, otherwise I would have let that go and would have lost half of it before I sat for my final teaching exam.

You weren't in charge of a class. You had to follow the teachers around to learn the procedure, and you had to work very hard as a pupil teacher. You were fully occupied the whole time. There was no slacking. You had to look after the stock room and cut up the necessary needlework for children, and you had to take classes occasionally.

I got ten shillings a month, which I had to go to the municipal buildings to collect. All the other teachers had their cheques sent to them, but as I was so young, I had to go and fetch it. Ten shillings a month! You see, little girls who went into service, they used to get ten shillings a month, but they also got a roof over their head, and they got their food given them. But when you were a pupil teacher, your ten shillings had to do everything. In the second year you got thirteen shillings and fourpence a month.

Elizabeth Lee

There was an advertisement for a special-subjects teacher – someone to teach and to help generally, at Rustington, a little town along the coast, where tuberculosis was very bad in those days. This was in a residential home for children in the particularly advanced stages of tuberculosis. Well, I applied for this job, to my surprise I got it. All they wanted me to do was to give the children that were bedridden little lessons, because they did have a school attached to the place and proper teachers. They wanted me to teach the ABC and reading, according to the age of the child, and then the special subjects to the older children – cookery, needlework, scouting and guiding, and country walks. They had their own private beach – and there was swimming. I was also allowed to take them in small groups into Littlehampton to shop occasionally.

My first lesson was disastrous. It was supposed to be Monday afternoon cookery, but there was nothing for me to cook – just two parsnips was all that could be found in the kitchen, and I had about six girls. I had to spend the whole afternoon with nothing but two parsnips, so it was more of a talk than a 'do' – but the kiddies enjoyed it – and it was somebody fresh.

A couple of days afterwards was sewing, and again there was nothing to sew. In those days girls used to wear a chemise – more likely we would call it a slip today. That was the undergarment, along with knitted woollen stockings, and the older girls were supposed to work on those, and I was supposed to help them. They also sewed pieces of old sheets and pillowcases to make handkerchiefs.

I thought that was extremely boring, so I took some pieces of coloured material and silks in and helped them to make dolls' clothes, and taught them to cross-stitch. The matron was delighted, because I got the children's interest – they didn't like the sewing. Then we did the same with the cookery. They were supposed to cook the rice puddings for next day's dinner, which were put in the big coal oven overnight, and it was lovely and creamy by the next day's dinner. We also did the vegetables for dinner but that wasn't very interesting.

Someone had a birthday coming up and we were allowed in the kitchen in the afternoon to go in for our special lesson. So I said, 'How would you like to make some biscuits or cakes for birthdays?' They all had a certain amount of pocket money, as did I, so I brought in the ingredients and we made some coconut pyramids with a little coconut and egg white. Then we used the yolks of the eggs to make little cakes – just plain rock cakes with currants in.

Matron was so kind to me, she thought I was keeping the children interested, which was more important than anything else, because it was such a dreary life. Bed early, afternoon rest, meals at set times, and always the same old food because there were things they could and couldn't have. The only recreation they had was on the beach. It was very limited and the doctor arranged when they could go in the water, and if the water was good, whether they could paddle.

Their play was limited because of their very poor health, but making these rock cakes – well, it's amazing how many people had imaginary birthdays, and how many dolls were sent from home and brought from home by their parents.

The children used to rush to the gate to meet me when I was there. 'Ma'am, ma'am – here comes ma'am,' and they'd escort me up to the school. They really enjoyed being taught and I enjoyed their company. It was a twelve-mile ride there from Bognor on a cycle in all weathers, but I thoroughly enjoyed it.

Then they changed matrons. This matron came in one afternoon when we were doing some sewing. The children were chattering and one thing and another, and she said, 'What's going on here, Miss Dowland? You're supposed to be teaching these children.' I said, 'They're learning to sew.' One had got some very pretty silk and was making a doll's skirt with several rows of ruching round – I remember that so well, because she cried so. Matron took it away. She said, 'You're supposed to be mending pillowslips, patching pillowslips – making your chemises and things.' She said, 'That sort of sewing's no good to the children. They're supposed to help in the house, and you must keep discipline.' I said, 'Well, the children are enjoying this sort of work, and they're learning to sew far more neatly and nicely than they would. They're also learning with coloured things, which is nice. And,' I said, 'the thing is, Matron approves of it.' 'Well,' she said, 'I do not approve of it.'

So the next thing I knew, there was a letter handed to me the following morning. 'We no longer need your services.' So that was the end of that. It might have gone on for quite a long time – it might have progressed – but the children were very ill, and it was very saddening. Of course, all the staff had to be regularly examined by the doctor, and it was so difficult to get and keep staff, partly for that reason, and partly because it was isolated. That was why the children were supposed to help, the ones that were well enough and old enough. So that was the end of that.

Spinning in Lancashire in 1901, while children seem very
interested in the newspaper.

Making deliveries for the brewery Nuttall & Co, Blackburn.

George Wray

My father died when I was thirteen and my mother decided I should be looking out for a job. I asked her to speak to an uncle who worked at a colliery. I wanted to go down the pit for one shift with him to see what it was like. Even in those days, people who weren't connected with the mines thought that it was a bit out of the order of things to want to do that. No one wanted to go down the mine when they left school. However, I went down for a shift with my uncle and I decided I wanted to work down the pit.

George Cole

I left school when I turned fourteen. I left at teatime, had a drink of tea with my dad, walked up to Seaham Colliery, signed on and started work the next morning. I was down the pit at ten minutes to five on the day after I finished school.

George Wray

My first job at the pit was working at the pit heap on the screens. I was looked upon as being a tender lad and I was once sent to the carpenter to collect a cap full of nail holes. I didn't know any better. But I was very interested in how the screens worked. I used to observe the coal coming up to the surface in tubs. It was then sent along a belt, where men who had been incapacitated through accident or ill health used to pick out the stones and rubbish. The coal then ran further along the belt onto a jigger, which divided it up so that the coal dust and the small pieces fell away, and the large coal ran along. At the end, it tipped over into the trucks. That's how they filled these ten- and fifteen-ton trucks of coal. I also learnt how they found out who had filled these particular tubs of coal. It was done by the man at the coal face using a token, put on the inside of the tub. There was an official weighman, who was the owner's rep. The men's rep was called a 'check weighman' and it was his job to see that the man who filled the tub got his rightful due.

John Wainwright

My father was a colliery weigh clerk. He worked in a small office on the surface of the mine at Worsley Mains Colliery near Wigan. In his office was a weighing machine, and as the tubs of coal came up the pit, they were taken from the cage on to a movable platform and were weighed by Father on behalf of the colliery owners. On the other side was a check weighman – he was an official appointed by the union to check up on the correct measurements and to see that my father's measurements were correct.

John William Dorgan

My first job was as a trapper boy. In the coalmine, there are two shafts – one shaft has a pump to pull the fresh air from the surface down into the workings. The fresh air is then pushed around the workings. The other shaft, called the 'upcast', has another pump that pumps the stale air out of the pit. The stale air is caused not just by the people down the mine, but by the fumes caused by shot firing. Powder was used to shoot the coal away from the coal face and to shoot the stone away from the roadways. So there was a lot of bad air travelling around the mine and ventilation was very important.

My job as a trapper boy was to sit in the dark with a rope in my hand and when anyone came along the roadway, I pulled the wooden door open to let them through. When they were through, I got up to shut the door again. There would be another trapper boy a hundred yards or so further along, doing the same. The idea was to trap the air, to regulate the circulation. When I opened my door, his door would be shut and vice versa. Although I was in the dark, I was given a candle which I could light at mealtimes. I had some bread and dripping wrapped in newspaper and a tin water bottle containing cold tea. I used to try and warm the tea under the candle. I never got lonely or bored. I've always been a person who's able to sit back and think. Meditate, you might say.

Jack Hepplestone

As a door trapper, you took your food when you wanted it. There was no lunch hour. The main item was bread and dripping. Because if you took bread and butter down, or meat, it used to go rancid with the gas. And we had cold tea or water in tin bottles called 'dudleys'.

John William Dorgan

After being a trapper boy, I became a pony driver. In the mine there was a complicated system of getting coal away from the coalface. First, you had the coal miner who filled his coal into an iron tub. The tub was then pulled clear by a pony controlled by a 'putter'. The putters were older boys, aged about sixteen to twenty, who brought the coal along a roadway of short-length rails to a landing. From there, the younger boys, like myself, collected the tubs and pulled them several hundred yards by pony to the rope haulage roadways. The tubs were then hauled away by engine power. Then, I had to collect empty tubs from the endless rope and return them to the landings, where they were taken by the putters into the workings, where they were filled by the miners and the whole process began again.

I was paid by the number of full tubs I brought back from the coalface. It was all counted by the score. If I got forty-three tubs out a day, that was two score and three and I was doing very well. Your coal tub was the size of a kitchen table and your pony had a leather and wooden harness. You attached the limbers of the harness to the tub. The putter sat between the pony and the tub and you had to bend forward so your back didn't scrape the roof. For all the years I worked there my spine was just a succession of scars and scabs. When I got married, my wife was astounded when she looked at my back. Every two inches, there was a scar.

But I was a big strong lad and I always made decent money. As a putter, you only worked in a certain district for three months. There was a quarterly draw where the places were put into one drum and the names put into another and your name was pulled out alongside

A lunch of Cornish pasties at Dalcoath Tin Mines, Cornwall 1906.

a working place. That was your spot for the next three months. At some of these working places you could make good money, but some of them were bad. The roof conditions were wet, and all you could do was groan and accept it, but I was usually lucky. At eighteen and nineteen, I was making a lot of money.

Jack Hepplestone

I started as a pony driver. There was no training. The pony was taken out and limbered up and I just started. I took the empty wooden tubs into the coalface and then I brought the full ones out, three or four at a time. Each tub carried fifteen hundredweight to a ton of coal. They were pulled by ponies and they ran on rails. The pony pulled several tubs in what we called a 'tail chain'. I used to sit on the bumper of the tub with my lamp and the pony used to know his way. The rails were in six-foot sections with a wooden sleeper underneath, and then they were bolted together with a fish-plate. Tubs used to derail quite often. If you could get the tub back on yourself, you did. You'd put your back to one end of the tub and lift it back on to the rail and then do the same with the other end. If it was too much for you, you fetched one of the fillers from the coalface to give you a hand.

The ponies were little things – Welsh ponies and Shetlands. They used to come out of the pit for a week's holiday when they could run around the fields. After that, they'd be brought back down to start work again on the Monday. They were looked after by an ostler who kept them in pretty good shape. The ostler cleaned them, bedded them down and fed them. I always had the same pony. I used to give him a carrot or a bit of spice. He loved a bit of spice.

I got seven and sixpence a week. That was considered fair. Labourers' wages at the time on top were only a guinea a week and they used to work seventy-two hours. We were only on eight-hour shifts, five days a week. The shift was either from six in the morning until two in the afternoon or from two in the afternoon until ten at night. Overnight, repairs were carried out. The rails were attended to and the roofs were repaired.

If I was on mornings, I used to get up at about half past four and set off to walk to the pit to get there by six. I walked to the stables, took my pony out and started the day's work. Unless you had some bad roading and you kept having to lift the tub on and off the rails, the job was pretty routine. If your Davy lamp went out, you had to wait while a deputy came round so that he could light it with an electric affair, because you weren't allowed to use matches down the mine. That was a strict rule. You couldn't smoke, and that's why miners always used to chew tobacco. You had to be very careful with the Davy lamps. They were hand-held, and if you shook them, they went out. They weren't attached to your hats like later on.

Down the pit, you provided your own clothes. You wore wooden-bottomed clogs with an iron rim round them, corduroy trousers and a woollen shirt. You were filthy but there were no pithead showers. As you came out of the pit, that's how you went home, then when you got home, your mother and sisters washed your back down while you swilled all the coal off.

Alwyn Kerr

There was a strike when we were in Cumberland, which wasn't surprising as my father, the pit manager, was at loggerheads with everybody. They brought all the ponies out of the pit and took them to a field quite a distance away. And when the strike was over we boys were told to get the ponies and ride them back to the pit and see them in. To get the ponies up and down the pit, as they were too big to get into a cage they used to fasten a very strong net under the bottom of the cage and you walked the pony into the net and then they took the cage up. Then the reverse happened when it got down to the bottom.

George Wray

I had an accident while I was driving a pony with two tubs down a steep incline. At the top of the incline, there was a siding where the man with his pony brought his tubs. On this occasion, he didn't put a sprag in the wheel, he just unloosed his pony and left it. The tub ran away down the incline and dashed into my tubs. I was pinned between the shafts of the pony and the tub. I couldn't move and I was there for about half an hour in the pitch black because my lamp had gone out. Fortunately for me, some men who were changing their shift saw what had happened and they came along and set me loose. It took them a quarter of an hour, and it will show you how small I was, that one of them carried me in his arms down to the bottom of the shaft. They put me in a tub, pulled me out of the pit, stuck me into a coal cart and took me home. There was no question of receiving any medical treatment in those days. I was just taken home. My mother accepted it as part and parcel of the job, and she went to fetch a doctor who reckoned all I wanted was a good stay in bed. So I was off a month and then went back to work in the same pit.

Jack Hepplestone

After pony driving, I became a filler for a collier called Tom Moore. As he got the coal down, I filled the tubs with a shovel. It could be hard work or it could be easy. Sometimes the distance between the top of the tub and the roof could be only five or six inches, so I had to lift the tub off the road at one end to lower it. Then I shovelled the coal in before lifting it back on the line. That was hard. Sometimes the distance between the top of the tub and the roof was large and it was easier to pop it in. If there was no coal for you to shovel in, you used to pick up a tool and get some down yourself. Tinsley Park was a wet pit. There were two seams. One seam had a steep gradient, and the further it went down, the wetter it got. One day, I got a job filling for a collier down there and I was up to my knees in water. When I came home, my father-in-law said, 'Are you working in the water?' 'Aye,' I said. 'Would you have a job out of the pit if I got you one?' 'Yes,' I said. So he took me to see the gaffer at Vickers Maxim. They had been working on twelve-hour shifts and they were going over to three shifts of eight hours, so they wanted another set of men. The gaffer said, 'Are you used to a shovel?' I laughed. 'I ought to be. I've been working in the pit for

Workers leaving Pendlebury Colliery after their shift.

Women working with a recent catch: North Shields 1901.

years.' The job was emptying coal from wagons into a bunker. The pay was fifteen and eightpence a shift. I was only getting seven and sixpence down the pit so I accepted the job.

George Wray

After pony driving, I started 'run riding'. It was one of the most dangerous jobs in the pit. I had to meet a set of tubs that were hauled from the shaft on the rope. I used to jump on the rope attached to the last tub and go right in to the district where the tubs were going. If any of these tubs got off the way, it was my job to drop off and work the overhead wires that were fixed to the roof, in order to notify the man at the shaft bottom to stop the tubs. I had to put the points in their proper order or else there would have been a real smash-up. It was a dangerous job but it was very interesting. I even had a telephone down there. After a while, the man in charge in the back shift said that in future I would have to walk and not ride on the tubs, as it was too dangerous. That put a damper on things, but when he wasn't there, I used to sneak a ride.

Jack Hepplestone

Dinnington was a very hot pit. It was a deep pit but the gradient of the coal seam wasn't very steep. Seams run in gradients, and usually the further the seam runs down, the wetter it gets. Dinnington was more on a level, so it was very hot. It could be dangerous because they were still using wooden props. There was a standing order that when you were abandoning an area of the mine that had been worked out, all the wooden props had to be brought out. You had to go in and put a chain around the props. The chain was attached to a long bar with a spike that was stuck into the floor. Then you pulled it and the prop came away. Normally, the roof dropped, so it was dangerous. The pit I'd worked before had been a wet pit. That was a different problem. There was a pump working all the time, pumping water out. I heard that at some pits, water formed at the back of the coal, forming a lake, and when it broke you had to get out sharp, but that never happened while I was working.

John William Dorgan

My father worked in the mine, but instead of working on the coal side, he was a 'stone man'. When the coal was taken from the seam, the mine had to be developed further. So the stone men took the roof down to make a roadway about ten to twelve feet high. He started work at four in the afternoon and finished at two in the morning. There were no electric cutters. He had to drill holes into the stone. That brought out the stone dust, and it gave him chest trouble and he lost a lot of work that way.

Jack Hepplestone

There were a lot of accidents at Dinnington from roof falls. Sometimes they happened once a week, sometimes more. Roof falls were caused by top weight coming down and crushing the props, or if a collier accidentally knocked a prop away. If a collier was buried, two or three men would go down and dig him out and take him clear. If there was a fatality in the morning, a buzzer used to go and you didn't work in the afternoon. But when you weren't working, you didn't get paid. You only got paid for what you did. Danger was accepted by people working in the pit. It was a natural thing. It was a living and no one knew aught else. It was a family tradition to send each son down pit. There was no other industry knocking about.

There was a Deputy for each district, who ran the job. They used to come round every shift and do safety checks. They'd visit every place and they'd tap the props and they did the shot firing. The collier would drill a hole in the coal and put a shot in and when the Deputy came round, he'd fasten his cables up to it, set off the charges and blow the coals down. The Deputies used to test for gas as well. If gas were accumulating, they'd draw it out. When I was door trapping, the Deputy used to come up to me and ask if I were getting on all right. He'd sit down and ask what I had to eat and he'd offer me a bit of his food. It was all very pally. Beneath the Deputy was a 'dogger'. He looked after the ponies and he relaid the tracks. If there was a pile-up, he'd straighten it out.

John Wainwright

There were always a lot of minor accidents in the mines. The only accident I had was when I was pushing a tub of coal and I caught my finger on a jagged edge. The cut went septic and gave me blood poisoning. I was off a week. When I was off, I received workman's compensation. I think the maximum was thirty shillings a week. There was also a voluntary association – The Miners' Permanent Relief Society – which was run jointly by the mine owners and the workmen. The workmen paid a contribution of thruppence a week and the owners put the same amount in. So if you were off, you got the normal compensation by Act of Parliament, and then you got a few shillings a week on top. When there was a fatality, there was something for the family. Whenever you saw a collier, he always had bruises on his hands and face. Little blue marks where he'd been struck by coal.

Dick Morris

It was a custom among miners to take their sons with them in the school holidays. I was down maybe a dozen times with my dad over the school holidays, just to get acclimatised to the inevitable way of life. But it wasn't the same as the first day by myself. The other times I could grab hold of his hand. Nobody will ever know what I felt like on that pit heap that morning when I went on my own. I'd been to see the gaffer, he gave us a note for the lamp man, to get a lamp, and as I climbed up that wooden staircase under the pit heap I was terrified. The lads went into the cage first, then men last. At the bottom, as you stepped out you put the lamp up for the overman to see if it was locked safely. He said, 'Dick Morris, go along with that lad there, he'll show you how to gan on.'

Jim Fox

I was at Wingate at the time of the colliery explosion. I remember it very distinctly. I remember going up to the colliery yard and seeing the bodies being brought out on stretchers. There were twenty-four killed in that explosion. It left a huge mark on the community. In fact it was national news – it brought home the dangers of working in the collieries.

Dick Morris

When the West Stanley Colliery known as the Burns Pit disaster occurred, on 16 February 1909, I was living at Pelton Fell. I got home from the pit at four o'clock in the afternoon and bathed – because my dad insisted we had a bath before a meal. So I was on my hands and knees bathing in front of the fire, when Mrs Porter, our neighbour, shouted across, 'The Burns Pit's gone off, you can see the smoke coming out the shaft.' We could see it from the front window. My dad said, 'Come on!, hurry up! There's nothing for it but to get there!'

When we got there, there were quite a few people. Our gaffer, Wilson, was there and he was going round asking for volunteers for rescue parties. We stood underneath the screens, watching the shaft. Smoke was still pouring out of it. By the time we'd been there half an hour, I couldn't see anything, so my father put me up his shoulder so I could see. The police were trying to keep a gangway open for the rescue people. The first job was to get the shaft clear. It took three quarters of an hour before they got the first cage to the bottom and then hosepipes were laid down the shaft to put the fires out.

After another half-hour, the first rescue people began to explore the shaft. There were a lot of women crying, knowing their men were down in the pit. It took from about half seven, when we got there, till eleven before they brought anybody out. But it was just one or two survivors. By now it was dark, and people were walking home.

On the Wednesday, we heard that there had been a few survivors, but there were no definite figures, just a lot of rumours. On the Sunday, they buried the dead in two long trenches outside the churchyard door. I've never seen so many people in all my life as that Sunday, people from all over the North of England. There were bands and banners from every colliery and lodge. People were walking up and down the street, going into the houses and looking into the coffins. I said to my father, 'Why don't they kick them out Dad? It's like these people are ghouls, out of one house and into the next one, just peering into the coffins.' 'It's curiosity,' he said. 'I suppose they've never seen anything like this before.' We tried to get into the churchyard but it was impossible – we couldn't get anywhere near, so we stood on the road leading down to it. We watched the coffins being carried into the churchyard and they didn't have enough time to bury them all because by the end of the day, half of them were still stretched back up the street. But by the following Sunday, the trench was filled in.

Alwyn Kerr

My father went to South Pelaw to be under-manager and while he was there the Burns Pit fired. He said that it was the most pitiful thing. He was well known from being at Beamish, and he said when he got to the pithead at Stanley, where the Burns Pit was, people he knew – especially women – were asking, 'Have you seen any sign of our so-and-so?'

When a gas pit fired there were parts of the pit they couldn't get to on account of the pockets of gas, and so later they would come across dead people who were still sitting in the same posture as they had been when the thing fired, getting their food and this type of thing.

Mr Lumley

I didn't know there had been an explosion till I got home and my sister said there had been a chap sitting in the bar who should have gone down the pit at four o'clock but he'd been sent home. He'd been sitting with his head in his hands – whether he was pleased he hadn't been in it, or whether he was thinking about his pals that were in it, who knows. Everyone had a family member involved in it. Hundreds of families. 168 men and boys had died that day. My uncle was a check weighman and he had to go round all these families with a book. He died a fortnight afterwards. He had been right on the scene, he ran to the shaft when he heard the explosion, his moustache was all singed, and people said he got some of the black damp. But I think what killed him was going round all the families

Eliza Brown

A few weeks after the Burns Pit fired, I used to go across the fields and see wild flowers. I couldn't afford good flowers, so I put a few wild flowers on those poor lads' graves where there were no flowers on. My mother used to say, 'What are you putting them things on for?' 'Mother, I knew some of the young men and all. They would speak to us as they were going to work.' She said, 'Well I see your point, if we can afford them some time we'll get a few good flowers for them.' But we never got round to that.

Alwyn Kerr

I had an experience at New Brancepeth that shook me, even as a child. I was playing in the street when a horse-drawn ambulance drew up and out got six lads, still black – there was no pithead baths – and they had their hoggers on, their little shorts. They carried a dead body from the ambulance into a house, and there were two elderly ladies standing at the doorway in jet black and with starched aprons, waiting to receive the body. The young widow was standing just a little bit further back.

Andrew Ruddick

I was in bed at the time of the explosion at Coxlodge, Jubilee Pit, when Jimmy came home and told me what had happened. I went to the pithead but the under-manager said we should go home and get pit clothes on. We were there at midnight on Tuesday, emptying slush on the bank, eight hours on, eight hours off, eight hours on, right through to Friday night, then they gave up hope. Putting this slush in tubs and sending the tubs away. We had to give up in the end. It was pitiful. Deputy Robert Patterson died; he had a wife and young family. Matthew Hilliard was married too, he had a grown son. James Wharton lived with his mother and aunt. It was a terrible death. Matt Hilliard should've had the VC. When he went down into the pit, the bank of slush was coming. He went in and the others were saying, 'You're committing suicide,' but he said, 'I can't help it, it is my duty.' He never came back up.

Mrs Short

In 1910 the colliery bought a big old hearse. If a family was very hard up, they allowed them this hearse for nothing. It was the most frightful thing you ever saw – it had eight great big dollies, made of feathers. As a child, the whistling of the wind in these feathers was terrifying. It had glass sides, and it was drawn by horses, and the whistling as it came down Beamish Road made us run away.

Jack Hepplestone

Everyone joined the union as soon as they started. A man came around and you'd pay him fourpence every week and that kept your book in order. When it came to any raises, you'd have a committee meeting at a pub. I went now and again. The union was very important to us, seeing that rules and regulations were kept, but we never had a strike in my four years in the pit. Every so often, there was a parade and a miners' meeting. People were proud of being miners. There was a Miners' Institute and people went down there on a Saturday night and a Sunday for a pint and a singsong.

John William Dorgan

I was a member of the Miners' Union Committee for a while. At the end of the three months, the coal company used to give every putter a shilling. It was just a custom – a shilling was nothing to us because we were making decent money, but we used to draw the shilling from the colliery office and hand it over to one of the pony drivers – the younger lads who took the coal to the 'endless rope'.

One Saturday morning at the end of a quarter, we went to the colliery office for our usual shilling and we were told that there weren't any. The management had decided that the shillings would be on our pay check at the end of the week, to save the pay department from coming in on a Saturday morning. That didn't suit us! We wanted that shilling to give to our driver boy! I was one of the big cheeky lads so I went in to see the colliery manager. He told us we'd have to accept it. 'It's no use talking like that!' I said. 'We've come for our shilling and we're going to have it! The driver boys are not going to be disappointed!' So the colliery manager sent down to the bank for the shillings and we were paid. But I asked the manager, 'Why have you done this without telling us?' 'We informed the union,' he said. Well, the union had never bothered telling us and we never went to union meetings. So about eight of us went to the next union meeting. There were only a few others at the meeting so I told my fellows to move me for the committee and I was voted on. But it didn't suit me. The union committee met once a week and they never finished their business. The members were paid for every meeting they went to, and at the end of the meeting, they adjourned to next night so they'd get extra money. I went along for the quarter and then I resigned. That was my only acquaintance with the unions.

John Wainwright

As an incentive to get the youth to go to union meetings, we were given a packet of Woodbines. The men were given a pint at the local pub. The union representative was usually the check weighman. He would arrange the prices for the piece workers – the colliers and contractors. He looked after the interests of the miners and he would see the management for the men. The unions were very strong. During the railway strike of 1911, we just came out as a matter of course. The strike was on and it was an order and we all came out.

William George Holbrook

I was on strike duty during the coal strike in Lancashire. They threatened to throw the manager down the pit, so they sent for the troops. I went to Leigh and we guarded the pits. Before we got there, our colonel said, 'If there's any trouble from the strikers, a little jab in the behind with the point of the bayonet will stop it!' but it never came to that. The strikers were very friendly with us and things quickly quietened down.

Then there was another coal strike in Lichfield and we were sent there. The third strike we dealt with was the railway strike at Liverpool Street in London. Porters and ticket collectors were on strike, so it was my job to take tickets. I did it for three nights and then the strike fizzled out and they came back. It's strange, but in all three strikes the strikers were friendly to us. They didn't shout abuse and there was never any trouble. We never had to use any violence. But we didn't feel guilty about breaking the strikes. We felt we were doing our duty and that was that.

John Wainwright

While I was working down the mine, I joined a Saturday afternoon course at the Mining and Technical College in Wigan. I worked until two o'clock on a Saturday afternoon, went home, had a quick bath and went down to Wigan for half past three to attend my Colliery Manager's course. It was a four-year course. I think I was a bit exceptional down the mine. I was sent to all sorts of jobs; I was sent with men timbering, sent with contractors, sent to the coalface. I had to work hard on these but the management was giving me the chance to experience all these jobs. I was aiming at being a manager. I was the only ordinary miner in the colliery studying for a manager's certificate. There was an examination to become a Deputy but I was aiming higher than that. Before you could sit the Colliery Manager's exam, you had to obtain the Deputy's Certificate, and a first aid certificate, and you had to have a certificate that you'd done five years down the mine, including two years at the coalface. I was ready to pass the course when the Great War broke out.

Albert Tattersall

I was born just outside Rochdale. We were a family of twelve without a mother, and the day I made thirteen, I went into the pits with my father at Stecksteads. We used to start at seven o'clock in the morning, so we had to get up at five and walk four miles to it – there were no buses or trams. I went in as a 'drawer' – fetching the full tubs from the miners, and taking the empties out. You brought the full tubs to a chain that ran them down to the roadway, where there were loading bays. There were ups and downs all the way, and you had to push the tubs along with your head. You'd have a pair of old stockings in a cap on your head, doubled up. They used to call it a boaster. That would give you a bald patch.

I started work in the pit on eleven shillings a week, from seven in the morning to three in the afternoon. We worked on Saturday from seven o'clock to one o'clock. We wore just a cap and these boasters, one shirt and a pair of camiknickers. In the upper mountain mine you kept your clogs and stockings on, but in the mountain mine you worked in your bare feet. The other drawers wouldn't work with you if you went in with your clogs on, because if one dropped off, you might cut a foot on it – but the passage had been worn smooth with their feet.

The lowest height I've worked in was eighteen inches – it wasn't a problem. You got used to it – it was a way of working. You kept warm by working – you had almost nothing on. If you wanted to go to the toilet there was what they called a gob, which was where they put all their waste dirt. You took your dinner wrapped up in newspaper and you used that as toilet paper. You could smoke in the pit if you liked, there wasn't any gas there. Some used to chew tobacco or smoke a pipe – and some smoked Woodbines at a penny a packet. You didn't smoke while you were working – you took five minutes' rest if you wished to. You could have as much time as you wanted – but while you were stopped you were not earning. I took jam sandwiches to eat, and a bottle of cold tea – which I kept in a tin box – mostly an Oxo box. You didn't wrap it in a handkerchief because if you put it on a prop on the side, the rats would have it. Rats were every where down the pit.

Richard Hodgkiss

I was at the ropeworks at Teckavent and it was coming up for breakfast time. We felt this shudder, and that must have been the explosion at the mine. This was at ten to eight, and eight o'clock came, the buzzer went and I grabbed my coat to run home – I'd only half an hour to get home, have my breakfast and be back for half past eight. I set off running and got to the top of Branker Street when I met Billie Hayes – he looked frantic. He said, 'The pit's exploded' but I didn't really understand what he meant by that. I said, 'Just what do you mean?' He said, 'Pretoria – blown up.' I said, 'Good heavens. Which one is it?' He said, 'It's the yard mine.' I said, 'Me dad's down there, and our Lewis, and Uncle Jim and Uncle Stanley.'

I ran to the pit. When I got about 200 yards from the shafts, there were three or four policemen, and one put his hand on my shoulder and said, 'Just a minute, young fellow. Where are you going?' I said, 'I'm going looking for me dad.' 'Is he in there?' I said, 'Yes – my brother Lewis, and my Uncle Stanley and Uncle Jim' – they were my dad's brothers. He said, 'You'll have to stay here.' So I stayed there, and then more people began to come, and we waited and waited. Dinnertime came and no sign of anyone, only people passing to and fro from the pit. Then came teatime, and no better off, and one or two cine camera men came, and they took pictures of us. I saw myself in one of those films in Grant's Show on the Town Hall Square – the fair used to be there. It was called Grant's Magic Bioscope.

When the pithead went up my father was blown back and killed outright. The damage was pretty extensive, and there was an obstruction which stopped the engine from getting the cage up or down. It came dark, and I came back home. Mother had heard by then, I'd been there all day. I said, 'There's no one come out of the pit, Mum.' Well, I could see she was really worried, and she was expecting a baby. This baby was born exactly a week later, on the first day of the New Year, 1911. He was born two months premature, but he was a perfect baby except for that he had no nails on his fingers or toes. But his heart was split in two, and he only lived till the 27th of January, and then he died. So we were in a world shattered, and there was no hope. We got word there was no hope of anyone being alive, and my dad, who was a colliery deputy, was found on the fifth day. He was only about a hundred yards from the pit bottom. He was on his way round the return airway – and he'd one clog missing, so we assumed after that he'd had a foot blown off.

They brought him to the front door, and my brother and I went to see him buried at West Orton. Three weeks went by, and there was no sign of my brother, although three hundred and forty-two had been accounted for. Then Dr Hatton, who was the officiating doctor for the colliery, came and said to my mother, 'Lizzie, I'm afraid we'll have to accept that your son Lewis is in the unidentified grave in the churchyard at West Orton.' He'd hardly said these words when one of my dad's brothers came running in the back way. He said, 'Do you recognise these, Mum?' and he had two pads of cotton wool, and inside was a piece of green mindle stocking – it was a funny colour, really. Mother was in bed, and she said, 'Yes, that's our Lewis's stocking.' 'Well, they've found him.' So she turned to Dr Hatton and said, 'Would you go and see our Lewis – you know, he has a tooth missing which he had out the night before the explosion.' So Dr Hatton went there and then, and he looked in our Lewis's mouth, and there was the cavity, and that was the only identification of him. He was found in the sump – that's the bottom of the shaft. There were two floating in the water there. So they brought him out, and all the bodies and coffins were all soaked in eucalyptus oil, because the stench of some of them was terrible.

They brought our Lewis to the door and my brother Tom and I went with him. It was about a fortnight after that the new baby was buried. We called him Lewis, too, so there are three Lewises in the cemetery on the stone.

The villagers of West Orton were left shattered. It was a common sight to see twenty, thirty hearses lined up, and a coffin put in each one. All the coffins were more or less one length – apart from my Uncle Jim's coffin, which was a thick oak one with a beautiful inlaid purple material in the lid. That happened every day for the best part of three weeks.

It came to assessment for compensation, and there was about £145,000 collected nationwide, and from foreign parts too. Then came the assessment court at Bolton. We got £300 for my father, who ranked for the top grade, and £20 was awarded for my brother, who was a fifteen-year-old boy. So Mr Hodgkinson, who was my mother's solicitor, went to see her and said, 'You see what they've awarded you for Lewis?' She said, 'Yes.' 'Well,' he said, 'don't accept it, Mrs Hodgkiss. Because to be awarded £20 for a fifteen year-old boy is a scandal. I'm going to appeal.' And he did, and she was awarded £75 for Lewis. That made it £375 which was paid into the court, and we were allowed a pound a month from that. But if either me or my brother wanted clothes, we appealed to the court for £5 so we could be rigged out. We had to face the judge, and he looked us over saying, 'This could be mended here. This could be mended there.' We never got the £5. So we had £1, not from the court, but from the colliery office, and we had five shillings and threepence rent to pay out of that, and that left us with fourteen shillings and ninepence a week to live on.

After the explosion, I went to see the owner at the works where I was, and told him that I'd come to give my job up. 'How come's that, Richard?' he said, 'Well, I'm allowed four shillings a week from the explosion fund, but from here I only get three.' 'I see,' he said. 'My advice to you is to give up working and get the four shillings from the colliery.' That was our life then. Mother broke down and it was a terrible job with her.

Robert Anderson

In 1900 my father was manager of Elswick Collieries. Once when we children were having breakfast in the kitchen, we noticed a strong smell of carbolic acid coming from some sheets on the clothes lines near the ceiling. We asked Mother, 'What on earth are those?' She explained, rather tactfully, that there had been a bad accident at Elswick Colliery and that our father had asked her to get these sheets ready to wrap up the bodies of the miners who had been killed.

Not long after that, I remember my father showing me a small round cylindrical box made of tin, about an inch and a half in diameter and six inches long. He explained that there had been some miners trapped by a fall of stone at Elswick and that they were having a job to clear the fall and rescue them. What they had done was to drill a borehole to where the trapped men were caught, and to pass food and drink through to them in this box.

Tom Tinkler

Miners would live in the mine for a week carrying their own food. We had beds but it was a rough sort of a life. We used to carry a basin and a tablespoon – the basin was so you could make a 'crowdy'. You put in some oatmeal and hot water, stir until its stiff, then add a bit of butter and sugar and eat it like that. There wasn't any milk. They weren't very popular, crowdys, but old men lived on them a lot. We carried various things, all homemade.

Raynor Taylor

I worked at the Urban Twist Cotton Mill. The cotton used to arrive in England in bales from America. American cotton was middle grade – Egyptian cotton was better but that was only used for specialist jobs. The compressed bales were opened and put into a machine which broke the raw cotton up. It churned it all up on rollers. From there, it went to another machine which lengthened it until it was taken to the spinning machine, which turned it into thread.

When you had the cotton threads on bobbins, they were taken to weaving sheds. My job as a 'piecer' was at the end of the drawing-out process, when it was being put onto the bobbins. As a piecer, I was the lowest form of spinner. I started at twelve, working half-time. You were allowed to leave school for half a day to work. One week you'd work in the mornings, the next week you'd work in the afternoons and reverse it the next week. When the machine was producing cotton thread, if a thread broke, it was my job to piece it back. The machines drew the thread out and wound it onto the bobbin. When a thread broke, it used to wrap around the top of the spindle, which went round at a terrific speed. You put the thread on your finger until it caught and pieced itself up.

I started work at six o'clock. Our area had its own 'Private Watch'. Families paid coppers a week, and every morning a man came round at the time you wanted to be woken and he came along with a long pole with pieces of wire on the end and he knocked on the bedroom window and he kept on knocking until you got up and looked through the blinds. And then he shouted the time and what sort of a day it was – 'It's half past four and it's a cold morning!' That was before anybody had an alarm clock. I worked until eight in the morning and then took half an hour for breakfast. Then I worked till half past twelve and I went to school in the afternoon. When I left school at thirteen I loved the feeling of being grown up – I thought I was a hell of a man.

I moved to the Durban Cotton Mill in Hollinwood, where my wage was two and ninepence. I gave the money to Mother right away. For every shilling I gave her, she gave me back three ha'pence. She called that 'odd money'. I spent my odd money on sweets. You could get two ounces for a ha'penny. The Durban Cotton Mill was a very modern mill. It was built in 1906. The factory had a maple floor and everyone in the spinning room worked in their bare feet. It was very warm and humid. You wore a shirt and a pair of overalls. In the weaving section it was so loud that people became adept at lip-reading because they couldn't hear anything being said. Certain branches of the preparation were so dusty that after many years, a disease was identified that affected the lungs. It affected mine, in fact.

If you weren't in the mill before six o'clock, they closed the gates and you weren't allowed in until after breakfast. You didn't get paid for those two hours and that was called being 'quartered'. For breakfast, you had bread and jam or a banana. At dinnertime, the factory provided an oven where you could warm up your dinner. You just ate your dinner where you worked. At the end of each room was a set of toilets. At the Twist Mill, the toilets were cans, but the Durban was so modern, it had flush toilets. No smoking was allowed in the factory. Everything was saturated with oil and they were terrified of fires. There were buckets everywhere. Woe betide anyone who was caught smoking!

We had a very strong union, known as the Cotton Spinners Union, and everybody had to be a member. The union was involved in all sorts of disputes. If the threads kept breaking because the cotton that was being used wasn't up to standard, then they'd bring the union in to complain about it. I paid fourpence a week for the union. I went on strike when the owners wanted to reduce our wages. The strike lasted a long time, but my father was working so it didn't make so much difference to us as a family. There were no pickets because there was no question of anyone going in to work. Like all strikes, it finished up with a compromise.

I never found the work monotonous because I didn't know any other life. In those days, no one left the mill until they died, so when someone died, you moved up the scale and someone took your place and that's how promotion came in the cotton mills.

Joe Armstrong

When I was fourteen, I went to work at the same cotton factory as my mother, in Brindle, Lancashire. I worked as a weaver from six o'clock in the morning until half past five in the afternoon for four and sixpence a week. I didn't like it much and I only did it for a few weeks before moving on to spinning. As a spinner, I was on seven and sixpence a week. I was only a lad and it was my job to put a full bobbin in when the bobbins were empty. When you were spinning, you wore a shirt, a pair of white trousers and no shoes, because it was so warm. It was very noisy. We used to get a week's holiday in August but you weren't paid for that week. You didn't get paid for Christmas Day, Boxing Day, Easter or Whitsuntide. You got the holiday but no pay.

I was there until I was sixteen. One day, I bought a packet of Gold Flake during the dinner hour. It was thruppence for ten, sixpence for twenty. I climbed on to the top of the factory roof to have a smoke and when I came down, the manager was waiting at the bottom of the ladder. 'You've been smoking!' he said and he sacked me. Smoking wasn't allowed.

Olive Whitehead

There were four children, and at twelve I was the oldest when my father had an accident. We needed some more money coming in because his tripe shop wasn't keeping us – and he'd scalded his leg so he had to keep it rested up. My mother knew the wife of the boss at Collinge's, and that's how I got started at their mill. I could only go part-time, and I got ten bob a week.

At first we had to learn to tie weavers' knots, and sucking shuttles up – you spent quite a lot of time learning these knots, and the weavers didn't like learners because while they were showing us, they were losing money. Their money stopped if their looms stopped. They'd have four looms and they stood in the middle and you had to be able to tie knots before you could do anything. Then you had to learn to suck the cotton through the shuttle – this was velvet weaving. It tended to make your teeth go bad, as the cotton rotted your teeth when you sucked it – kissing the shuttle, they called it.

The stuff they wove was called tabby, and nearly everyone who worked there bought it. They made pillow slips of it, and it used to last for ever, because it was uncut velvet.

I don't remember being tired. I used to have to work hard because my mother didn't have such good health, so when I came home, she used to go to bed and I had to look after the shop. We used to be open till eleven, on Abbey Hills Road. There was a chip shop over the road, and people used to buy chips and then come and have some tripe put on it.

At the mill you had to clean the machines every Saturday morning, ready for Monday. You had to get a hand brush on the wheel while it was turning and let it go round while you were sweeping all the floss off. It was dangerous, but we were brought up with it, and you got into it slowly. If you wanted to talk to anybody, you had to learn to lip-read because you couldn't be heard above the noise. It was very, very noisy, and if you were talking to the woman in the mill gate where you were, you had to go straight to her ear and shout. If you were in the midst of four looms, it was even noisier.

Harrison Robinson

When a four-loom weaver had to leave, they'd move a three-loom weaver up into her place, and a two-loom weaver up – and a tenter up to a two-loom, and then we'd get into tenting. Tenting means helping a six-loom weaver, as a way of being introduced.

When you were a tenter you spent most of your time stetting looms on, and putting the shuttle in and putting cops on, and taking odd ends up. They wouldn't let you do so much or they wouldn't earn enough.

My wife's sister worked at the mill, and had a shuttle fly out and hit her in the eye – she'd only one eye then. On the sleigh boards they had a wire to protect you in case the shuttle flew out – it would hit the wire.

The children who went from school to the mill did much the same thing. There were odd ones who would go in the warehouse, or go reaching in for a loomer – a loomer has to put the reels through one at a time, and the reacher-in has to hook them on. The Burnley weaving was all plain stuff – it went to India, most of it. Nelson was the fancy weaving – and they said that Nelson was the wealthiest working-class town in the country – they earned more money than we did in Burnley. At the mill where I was you'd average twenty-six shillings a week on four looms. But in some places they wouldn't average more than a guinea a week. You're only rich or poor according to everybody else, and we didn't know we were poor. We didn't feel poor because we were like everyone else.

In the warehouse there would be perhaps a dozen people standing there waiting for sick work – and if you were too late, they'd fetch one of them. The tattler was very important, in that he was the overseer for the looms, and he used to go and pick one out of the queue and fetch them in.

We wore worsted trousers and an ordinary waistcoat. Women used to wear a fent, which was a piece of cloth with a belt round to put the scissors and stuff in. We wore clogs on our feet, and the women wore big shawls – a good thing for a cold day. But it was never cold in the mill – there was steam blowing out all the time – it used to be a humid atmosphere, it worked better that way. In summertime they used to go round when you stopped for a moment with a degging can – a watering can – and put water up every alley, all over the mill. But there wasn't anywhere in the mill where you could wash your hands – there was just one cold water tap. And you didn't use the toilets unless you really had to.

You had to pay tuppence a week to brew your tea if you stayed at the mill for your breakfast or dinner. Some had to stay who lived a long way off. You'd get tickets, and every time you brewed your tea you got a ticket. At Christmas some mills used to carry on – there might be a bit of jollity but not a lot. You were just keen to earn your money. They had a holiday on Christmas Day, but we never got paid for holidays. When you got married, everyone in the mill would pay a penny and they'd buy a present.

There were a thousand and ten looms in our shed – but there were some with fifteen hundred in one building – and all driven by steam. It was the tattler who came and put the new beam on and set it up. He was in charge of about 120 looms, and he'd to put your new beams in, and if anything went wrong, he had to put it right. Because while the loom was off, you weren't earning. The tattler was paid according to what his weavers earned, so it was to his advantage to keep them going. Your wages weren't the same every week, because you were only paid for what you finished that week.

Alfred West

I wanted to learn a trade, so I went to the Lysarts Steel Works in Newport and I put myself down for five years apprenticeship in the rolling mills. The steel sheets were rolled out flat and sent by boat to another firm in Bristol to be galvanised and corrugated. Motor

Work is finished for the day at North Street Mill, Chorley, 1901.

cars were just coming in and we were making flat sheets for the body work.

The heat was terrific in the mill – there were furnaces everywhere. We used to wear clogs, moleskin trousers, a vest, a towel thing around your neck and one end of it in your mouth just to keep your mouth moist. After eight hours of that, you were sagging. My job was 'scaling'. The iron bars would come out of the furnace and they'd be stretched out to about three feet, but by that time they were getting cold so they were put back into the furnace. Then they were rolled out until they were six feet long and then they were doubled over. Then they were returned to the furnace until they were really red hot and rolled out again until they were twelve foot long and very thin. That's how we made the sheets, but there used to be so much metal wasted in this process that the management ran a prize for the team who produced the least amount of waste. There were eight of us in my team and we won the prize three months running – £20 to be split between us each month. I had a good eye to match the different sheets up. If one sheet was three or four inches longer than the others, then when the guillotine came down later on, it had to go to the edge of the shortest one and that produced waste. So it was important to keep the sheets to within half an inch of each other each time. That's why my eye was important. We used to get booed because we were always winning the prize.

Jackie Geddes

We used to take meals for my uncles, grandfather and father twice a day – cooked dinners, because they were working long hours – right down in the works. There was a little locomotive, loaded with red-hot ingots, running inside the steel works, and there were a lot of accidents. A fair number of kids were killed before they set up little stations, all railed off, and when you came with the dinners, that was where you had to stop. They were numbered, station 1, station 2, and whichever part your uncles or grandfather was working at, they came out, and took the meals from you. It was all in proper strong tin containers. We would go in at about ten o'clock, and then again around three, because they worked twelve hours, six of a morning till six at night. Then there was towels to take in, because they sweated a lot you know, so there were towels to bring back too.

Harry Berry

I joined the messenger boy service in the London and India Dock Company in 1908. I joined because of a lodger we had who used to work in the docks. My uniform was a jacket with embroidery on it and a cap with 'L and I D' – the London and India Dock Company – on it. I used to deliver letters to merchants all round the city – Cheapside, Wood Street, Cannon Street, the Tower, St Paul's. Soon afterwards, the Port of London Authority took over and they carried on the same way. After three years as a messenger, I was transferred to the Albert Dock as an assistant to the foreman. I became a kind of tally clerk to keep a record of all goods that were brought in for export.

I had to get up at half past five in the morning. I couldn't afford the fare so I paid a shilling a week to hire a bicycle from Roffrey's in Holborn and I bicycled every morning from Bethnal Green to the Albert Dock. I got into work by seven. In the evening, there was always a ring of trucks to be unloaded and I had to wait until they were all done so that I could keep a tally of them and mark the measurements and numbers. I had a three-foot rod with a little knob at the end and I used to measure the cases with it, and weigh them on a scale. After that, they were stored in a large shed. The cargoes were all manner of things for export.

When the dock strike was on, I was transferred to the London and St Catherine's Dock. The strike was for the labourers. They were only getting eighteen shillings a week in those days. Afterwards, it went up to twenty-four shillings a week. I was transferred because it was too far for me to travel. I was getting up at five-thirty and finishing work at eight at night and then I had to ride all the way home on my bicycle. It got too much for me. So I went back to the

London and St Catherine's Dock. There, I dealt with the importation of goods – tea and silks. They used to unload the ships at Tilbury Dock and the goods would come on the railway to the Commercial Road. The goods were all under bond, under Customs lock, and I kept a tally of all the weights and measures before they were placed into locked vans and transferred to Cutler Street bonded ware-houses. So, for example, the tea arrived in tea chests and I would take a note of the mark and numbers and the grade of the tea before it was transferred to Cutler Street.

At Cutler Street, the tea was taken to the showroom, where it was inspected by all the various tea merchants who came and took samples. The tea came from all the various gardens in India, China and Java and it was laid out for the merchants – nests of tea chests weighing a hundred and forty pounds were laid out with the number of the boat inscribed on the side. After that, I worked on silks. When the silk arrived at Cutler Street, it was in bales wrapped in straw inside cases. The silks came in various thicknesses. A sample of each thickness would be laid out on tables for the Customs officers to examine. Different thicknesses and weights of silk attracted different rates of duty. After the silk was examined, it was stored away in the bonded rooms. Then, when we received a delivery note, showing that duty had been paid, we'd deliver it to the silk merchants. They were mostly in Wood Street in Cheapside. I had a wonderful memory for where the various goods were stored so that when the labourers came to pick up the silk for delivery, I could say, 'These are on the second floor on the third alley.'

Jack Banfield

During the dock strike, Price's Bakery had a horse van that came round. It was a single-pony van on two wheels with a flap at the back. Once it stopped in the street and the driver got off and let the back down so that the loaves of bread fell out, and people just helped themselves while he stood watching. He probably went back to the shop and told the guv'nor that people had pinched all his bread. That shows the community feeling.

Minnie Lane

There was a man who lived in Rothschild Buildings, who worked on the docks. When the dock strike was on, my brother was working on the docks as a blackleg. This other man used to watch him and one night, he was there waiting to give my brother a good hiding. My brother knew he was looking for him and he avoided him. The thing was, never mind the danger, my brother was glad of the job.

Jack Banfield

The main source of work in Wapping was casual dock and riverside work. Men used to get to a particular berth or wharf where a ship had arrived by six o'clock in the morning. Some of them would get the job, but the pay was by the hour, so even though they might get a job at six o'clock, they might be paid off at eight o'clock. The most anyone could hope for was half a day's money, up to twelve o'clock. Very often they'd go out at six, but daren't come home in case there was a call at seven or eight, and that might go right through the day. By the end of the week, they'd only worked one or two days but they'd been there all week.

E. J. Dutch

My father got me into the docks. I worked in a warehouse in Cutler Street. My first job was as a marking boy. After the strike, the men had all gone back to work and were made permanent men. I must have been a good worker because I was made a permanent man. The wages was twenty-four shillings a week. They started me off in the ostrich feather department. In those days it was a flourishing trade. It was all foreigners – Italians and French who used to come over and buy them. The feathers came from South Africa in these big cases and they all had to be opened and sorted out. Every month or six weeks, they had a sale. In those days, ostrich plumes were the thing. The highest price paid was £100 for a pound of plumes. The feathers were brought from the docks to the warehouse in a horse-drawn cart. They were put in the lift by the general gang downstairs to take them up to the top floor. When it arrived on the top floor, everything was done by the men in our department. The work was separated out. The carpet section, full of Persian carpets, was on the floor below and the curio department was on the floor below that. There was a drug department and the tea warehouses were all around.

Jack Banfield

Brewer's Quay used to have the General Steam Navigation boats that ran to Rotterdam and Amsterdam. They used to fetch Dutch produce: butter, cheese and eggs. Opposite Brewer's Quay was a coffee shop, so if a man was fortunate enough to get work in Brewer's Quay, he would slip half a dozen eggs into his pockets and cross over to the coffee shop, where he'd give them to the proprietor. In return, he'd get a rasher of bacon, one of the eggs, some tea and two slices of bread. It was tit for tat.

E. J. Dutch

I'd had enough of working in the warehouse. I wanted to go on proper ship work. I went to Poplar, to the East India Docks. There I started unloading with the proper dockers. I was a greenhorn and they used to put me down at first. It took me two years to learn the trade. I would be working down in the ship's hold, putting the stuff into slings or on to boards. The stuff was hauled ashore either by a crane or by winches. It was a hard job. When you were working on a ship, you didn't stop. I unloaded the *Cutty Sark* twice. Once it had tin, the next time it went into Millwall Dock and had wool. I used to unload the Jamaica banana boats.

Sometimes half the cargo was rotten when it got here and they used to put it all into barges and throw it away. The bananas used to come out on elevators, running them right around to the vans. I remember the rum quay. They used to blend the rum them-selves with these barrels and we did the bottling there and when no one was looking we used to have a drop. The man that did the coopering, who used to mend the barrels, he was never sober. You had to be careful, though. You had to watch out for the foreman because once you got caught pilfering, you wouldn't be on that job any more.

Philip Harrington

On one or two occasions the bananas being unloaded were yellow and ripe for eating. The inspector condemned them because by the time they'd gone through the Market, they'd have been rotten. So the foreman brought a whole bunch in and we all tucked in. They used to say that you can eat as much as you like, but you mustn't take anything out of the dock. Another thing we used to eat was the dates. The people loading them would drop a crate and we'd take a handful and eat them. I also remember this French frozen meat company that used to come in and they always had a lot of these naughty photos. They asked youngsters like me onboard to look at the pictures.

Jack Banfield

After Christmas you used to see kiddies with whacking great teddy bears bigger than themselves, or three-wheeler bicycles, and you knew that these toys had been smuggled out the back door off St Bride's Wharf.

Jack Gearing

In 1907 I became an apprentice waterman and lighterman to my father, who, like his father and grandfather before him, worked on the Thames. I signed the same indentures that my grandfather had – they stated that an apprentice had to 'faithfully his master serve, his secrets keep, not waste his goods, nor commit fornication, contract matrimony, not play at cards, dice, tables, nor haunt taverns or playhouses or absent himself from his Master's service, day or night'. We used to sail up from Faversham to London in our barge, *Mayflower*, with bricks, hay and building materials. On the return journey, we carried horse manure from the streets and stables of London for the farmers to spread on their fields. Later I went up to

Waterman's Hall in London to get my licence entitling me to take a
fifty-ton barge on the Thames single-handed.

Albert 'Smiler' Marshall

If you were an apprentice, or you had a job to go to, you could leave
school at thirteen, but if not, you had to stay until you were fourteen.
After that, you had to leave whether you had a job or not. I was
apprenticed to the nearest shipyard, so I left school at thirteen. I
changed from knickerbockers into trousers. At the shipyard, I was
working with a Yorkshireman who was making all these beautiful
doors. All I was doing was handing him the screwdrivers and saws
and different tools while he was doing the work. In other words, I
was a first-class-carpenter's labourer. At the end of my first week's
work, I got two shillings and fourpence and felt quite rich.

Harrison Robinson

Wherries were the best way to see the river – they were so slow.
Road transport did for them, but before that there were hundreds,
you couldn't move for them sometimes, they carried everything.
The cargoes of pitch were a terrible load. If it was warm and windy
you'd get blinded with the stuff.

Harry Matthews

In the brickfield, they did little else than drink beer. I must have
been only about eight or nine when I used to go to and fro to all
the pubs to fetch beer. I used to be outside the Willow Tap waiting
for him to open at six o'clock. I would go through the brickfield
past Davington School out to Oare, a pint in a bottle. Well, generally
I used to get three – a pint of ale and beer, and two pints of beer
for the three men that were working in the shed. Then I had to go
to the Windmill, get three more pints. That would be about seven
o'clock. It was tuppence a pint and I'd bring them all one back.
Then back home. But my father did drink beer! He was a temperer
over there, and one fellow told me that my father would nip over
the Windmill and have a pint and come back again while they was

making a couple of barrowloads. They never used to pay for it till the end of the week. It was always Shepherd Neames' beer. They used to go and square up Saturday, then start putting it on the slate again.

If you hadn't got any work and you wanted something, you had to put your appearance in over the workhouse Friday afternoon and state your case. Then, if they were going to give you anything, they'd give you perhaps half a quid's worth of tickets. You could go to the store and get a bit of grocery, flour and bread, which they used to bake over there. It was called Parish bread and it was about the length of two ordinary loaves put together. You couldn't buy cigarettes or bacca with the tickets they gave you – you could only go to certain shops, and it would be so many for cheese or whatever. If you could never get any work they used to give you a ton of granite to break. You had to crack it up to be put on the roads, and if you broke a ton, they used to pay you fifteen bob for it.

A lot of old brickies finished up over there. That became their home then. We always called it 'the Spike'. When they got too old for other work they used to go over there and make ha'penny bundles of wood. They got all the old hop poles from the farmers, cut them up, and then you'd see perhaps five or six of these old men making small bundles of wood and tying them up. Then two of them would take them round the little shops in town and sell them.

William George Holbrook

I started work at a farm across the road from us. It was still dark in February and I used to start at six in the morning. At nine o'clock, I had a bit of bread and cheese. We worked on till midday then had another piece of bread and cheese and then worked until six in the evening. We worked six days a week – all day Saturday – and we got six shillings. I used to give my mother five and sixpence, so I had sixpence to spend. So, once a week, I went to the swimming baths at East Ham. That cost me thruppence for train fare and thruppence for the baths.

Bill Stone

I was born in the hamlet of Ledstone, two miles north of Kingsbridge, South Devon. This was before electricity or gas, so the house was lit with candles and oil lamps. My father rode a pony and trap around the farms. He used to do everything himself – he even killed pigs. My father always said you mustn't just have one pig; you must have two, as they see who can eat the most and get fat quicker. He would sell the two pigs and keep the heads, or half of the pig. We had fowls and chickens as well, so we had eggs and chicken as well as pork. We used to eat rabbits too.

I went to work on a farm when I was thirteen, for half a crown a week – with Farmer Giles on Sherford Down Farm. I lived on the farm with two others, about three miles away from home.

Norman Halkett

I was still a child when I learned how to groom a horse, how to harness it and how to walk up and down the long rigs alongside your favourite ploughman, listening to his songs and watching his work with the horses. The great art was to make a pair of horses plough with no reins at all, to finish the rig, turn the horses and commence another rig – still with no reins. When evening came, or rather when 'lousing-time' came – lousing time was when the day's work was over and the horses were loosened from the yoke – they were then more or less handed over to us children. We were placed on top of the leading beast; and our job was to bring them home by words only, no reins to be used. They turned this way and that to 'hie' or 'wheesh' or 'tcht tcht' or 'whoa'; and of course, I have no doubt the horses were so tired they would have found their way home anyway. But we children thought we were master horsemen.

The love and affection which these ploughmen had for their animals was extraordinary. They groomed them; they fed them; they looked after them in every way as a mother would look after her son. I have seen them at the midday rest hour come into the stable, shake up the straw in the stall of his leading beast and lie down there and sleep. I've seen the man's face actually resting on the foot of the horse; but never at any time did the horse stand on him, tramp on him or damage him in any way. Such was the bond between them that nothing of the kind ever happened.

Albert Love

I once went to a big ploughing match in the Norwich area, and there were a lot of Welshmen ploughing. And, of course, their work was altogether different from ours. When they were ridging the land up, the horse walked on top of the ridge, and the men using them would just call the horse on to the top and it would go straight away. When they had done so much flat ploughing, the ploughing was all levelled off, as smooth as the top of a table. And it looked to me as if the Welshmen took all the prizes; and I thought it was a very good turn-out indeed. A lot of them up there of course, they'd got these big old, rough Shire horses. But the man's control of his horse was different altogether from ours in Norfolk. He never spoke to his horse: the horse knew what he'd got to do.

John Harding

There was lots of superstition which influenced our lives – Wales is full of superstition. For instance, Sunday was a complete holiday. It was a terrific sin to use an edge tool on Sunday – particularly an edge tool. Yes, seeds should always be sown when the moon is growing – otherwise they will grow downhill. Some seeds you could plant in any month, of course, but some seeds – and particularly cuttings from flowering shrubs – you mustn't plant when there's an 'r' in the month.

Percy Barnes

I don't think it was more difficult with bullocks than with horses. For one thing, they were more obedient. Horses, sometimes, are very self-willed, I've had horses almost like human beings, they seemed to know pretty much as near as you knew yourself. But a bullock, if you treated him right – you didn't dare be unkind to him or make him nervous – I always thought he was more obedient than a horse. Then of course they knew their place. They knew their names. You always worked two together, and the off-bullock never had only one syllable in his name, hence Winch and Winder, Pink and Piny, and such names as that. You always used to say 'Yea' to them to make them come to you, and that off-bullock, he'd always be the first one to come to you, and his mate, he knew, might be back there amongst all the others, but he'd find his way up there. They were mates together and that was how they always worked.

They're very easily subdued. Sometimes we've had them sulk and lay down. We used to put a few drops of water in their ear, and they'd soon jump up. They didn't like that. And when we broke them in we had a stick, about five feet long, with a little spike in the end of it. When you said, 'Yea', you gave the bullock a prick in the shoulder. That used to make him shoot forward. That's how they learnt. They never forgot that either. When we'd been harvesting sometimes, we used to stick the whip in the back of the wagon and carry on picking up the sheaves, and if you wanted them to start up, you just pulled a straw out of the sheaf and you could guide them with that straw, just as if you'd got a whip or a goad. They never forgot that spike.

They used to get pretty tired by the time of night. If they got too out of breath they would hang their tongue out. We would have to turn them round towards the wind and let them stand there a while. Then you put them in the yard at night and went away and left them. You didn't have to go back or anything. You just gave them some roots ground up and hay, and straw. You never had to groom them like horses. There was a lot of work with a team of horses, it was an easier life with oxen. I never remember them being shod, but they used to nail little plates to the outside of the hoof. You never wanted to join the claws together, because when they walked they moved those claws. My father said that the oxen got used to it. They were like little fish plates, three little holes round the outside.

When I was a boy at Cranbrook they told me one day to carry some hop poles down to the baker, Mr Dadson. I loaded these hop poles up on the cart, and sauntered down Stone Street with these old oxen. I had to carry all the hop poles round into the bakehouse an armful at a time, and it took me a long time. The old oxen, they just stood out in the street chewing their cud. They didn't seem to worry about anything. Everybody was afraid of them because they had such great big horns, but they wouldn't hurt anybody. They were faithful old things, I always liked them.

George Hewins

I was never out of work in the summer. It was sixpence an hour for a good bricklayer then, and we worked fifty-six hours and a half when the weather was fine, from six in the morning to half-past five o' nights. The only summer holidays we had was when it rained and you went in the shed to dry. We had no holidays with pay, nor tea breaks. If you had a bit of food you ate it as you went along. Saturday was pay day. We didn't get our money before one o'clock, and if the job was in Stratford, the gaffer would likely keep you waiting at his house. Sometimes we had to wait an hour or so while he finished his dinner. We didn't get paid for that!

John Harding

In the month of April, depending on the weather, the shepherd received the sheep under the hills, and then he became responsible for those until they went back down in autumn. His work was to see that the sheep were all on their own grazing patch. The mountains were allocated and, to some extent, fenced, and he had to keep the sheep on their own plot and also take care of their health. He had about two thousand sheep.

First in the spring was 'the strike' – some disease which caused the dead sheep to swell up. That usually happened on a fertile spring, when they were eating too much or doing too well. Then there came the difficulty of sheep lying down and rolling on their backs. If they were not got up the same day, they usually died. They won't live on their backs long. That was not at all easy, because you had to see every sheep in two thousand every day – so that kept the shepherd busy. The only disease which was really troublesome was foot-rot. By dipping twice a year they kept sheep-scab under control.

The dipping was mostly done by hand then, in a wooden tub, and the sheep were caught and handed to the man who dipped them. They were put in the dipping tub on their backs, catching hold of their legs, and then just rolled over and lifted out on to a draining board, and then rubbed back and forth on the draining board. They were dipped in two kinds of powder. One was manufactured by McDougall's, and that was a reddish colour. The other one was brown – Cooper's sheep dip had a brownish tint.

In autumn there were the sheep sales, where the surplus sheep were sold off. The male lambs, the unsuitable ewes and the old ewes that were getting too old for breeding – they were sold off, and the rest of the stock were kept on the fields and sometimes fed hay and corn.

In winter they were rounded up with dogs. You rounded up every farmer's sheep separately, and in time the sheep got trained so that you only need blow a whistle and they'd collect at a certain spot. Of course, the sheep dogs were almost human – they would gather the sheep to that particular spot, then you were able to count them and see that they were all right.

It takes a lot of experience to be able to count sheep, because they run past you in two, three, fours and fives, and it's like the people selling greengrocery calculating the value of a certain weight – you have to be able to count, not in twos or in threes, but in four, six and seven. Some of the old shepherds were masterpieces and they counted in twenties.

I knew of one instance when twenty sheep were missing when they were taken down to the shearing. After taking them down to the farm, my old uncle thought, 'There must be some of these sheep short – we'll count 'em again.' I had a piece of slate and put a stroke down for every twenty that he shouted. And we were twenty sheep short – so we had to go back and fetch them.

If the sheep were lying down, you didn't attempt to count 'em. You blew the whistle and sent the dog round to form them in a column. The dogs were so well trained that they'd make the sheep walk past you in a column which you were able to count – not in ones and twos, but four, five or six abreast.

The sheep were brought in and put under shelter if possible. If it was fine weather, of course, it didn't matter and they were left in the field, but if it was likely to rain, they were packed into all sorts of buildings where they kept dry overnight. The next morning, the shearing barn would be laid out with sacking to keep the wool off the dirty floor – with benches all round the walls. The shearers took their places round the wall and two men – or maybe three, according to the number of sheep – would carry the sheep to the shearers.

When the sheep had been sheared, they were driven into the yard to wait for the pitching. For this they had an old round pot with pitch in, and they dipped the iron pitch mark in the pot and just stuck it on the side of the sheep, or sometimes on the shoulder. Different flocks were pitched in a different way. Some were pitched on the back, just above the tail, so that the pitch mark would be seen when the sheep were running away from you. It was usually the name of the farmer – or his initials – and this same mark would go on every sheep owned by that man.

Then there were fences. Wherever the fences were in a bad state, the shepherd would be employed in the winter to carry out repairs, also a certain amount of ditching, where a patch of ground had become waterlogged. The fences were mostly oak posts and wire – five or six strands of plain wire. The chief work was making the end post secure, and that was a craft, almost. A hole was dug about four feet deep, and where possible, flat stones were wedged around it so tight that it couldn't possibly move. Then a strut was put to the second wire, from the top into the ground to take the strain. A flat stone was usually placed behind that as well, and then the wire was drawn tight with a screw. The end was attached to a screw, and you just kept turning until the wire was absolutely tight.

There was a lot of trouble in Montgomeryshire – thousands of sheep died from liver fluke. It was a sort of slug which grew on grass in damp places. I'm not a vet, but I know when a sheep died of fluke, and you cut the liver, the fluke was the same shape and colour

as the plaice fish, or the lemon sole. It was about an inch across –
they grew so much bigger inside the sheep. That happened when
the sheep were taken off the hills and on to damp, flat land, which
was not suitable for sheep.

There were shepherding superstitions too. You should never turn
the sheep onto the hill until the vilfriw had grown. Then, according
to the shepherd, the sheep would live on the hill. If you turned them
before this particular shrub grew, they would just wither and die
away. The vilfriw was not necessarily eaten by the sheep, but it
happened to be a plant which grew under certain conditions. When
the vilfriw was growing, there was grass for the sheep to eat.

Jack Larkin

When I started work on the wagons, I used to go to Selling Station
to pick up the hop pickers and their luggage, or if they came from
Folkestone and Dover to Chilham Station. But when the Londoners
came down, when we got back after unloading them, our mothers
wouldn't have us indoors until we'd changed all our garments outside. We used to be as lousy as cuckoos. They used to bring all their
dirty bedding down. All their dirty, filthy, stinking bedding, to put
in the huts. And bugs! Oh Lord, bedbugs! Our mother used to make
us hang our garments up and give them a good shake, and then she
disinfected them with some powder and she wouldn't have them
indoors.

Then, going back, they used to leave all their stinking bedding
behind. And the farmer wouldn't have the straw back in his yards,
because of his animals getting the fleas and the lice. We used to
burn the lot away from the huts for safety. We used to look forward
to taking the hoppers back again, because outside Chilham Station
was a pub, and us chaps with the horses always used to get a drink.
Then some would give us a bob, some a tanner. It was about dahlia
time at the end of hop-picking, and we used to put dahlias and
Michaelmas daisies all round the wagon – dress them up and make
a proper gala day of it.

John Harding

My uncle was a game warden – which meant first of all destroying varmints – carrion crows, weasels, stoats – sometimes foxes and other birds that were inclined to destroy the eggs of the game birds. He had to shoot them. Even one carrion crow could kill dozens of lambs – rob dozens of nests, grouse, partridge – we didn't have any pheasants on the hill – and other valuable birds such as woodcock. Keeping vermin under control is very, very important. Of course he had to keep an eye on the poachers, too. But this wasn't a big problem on the hills. That was a bigger problem for the gamekeeper where pheasants were bred. Most of the poaching we had on the hill was the odd small farmer shooting a rabbit or a hare for his family dinner. He was not interested in the game birds. They weren't after the money – they were after the food.

With poachers, my uncle usually had a talk with them. If it happened to be a very poor man who wanted a rabbit, he advised him where he could shoot one, and he let him. Of course, rabbits and hares are ground game – they belong to the tenant – so the person who had the game rights had nothing to say about a farmer taking a rabbit.

Jack Larkin

There were just three of us – the Wagoner, myself as mate and the stock boy – who lived in. We had our meals in the farmhouse and there was a bit of an old cottage attached to it and we slept in there. The farmer always had a barrel of beer in and we had small beer for breakfast, ale for dinner and small beer for tea. The only time we had hot tea to drink was on a Sunday. Breakfast in the morning was a darn great lump of fat pork, half a loaf of bread and, if they'd got plenty of milk, a jolly great bowl of milk. That was something to go to work on! After I left that last farm, when I joined the service at nineteen, I weighed twelve stone four pound. I hadn't been in the service three months and I went down to less than ten stone.

I lived on fat pork for twelve months. And sometimes it wasn't done properly and when the knife went through it you could hear it sort of crunch. Pork fat not done properly is awful. The Wagoner used to go down to the stable at four, come home at five, have his breakfast and back again at five-thirty. We used to have to be out in the stable at six with the horses to go out in the field ploughing and stay there till two. That was eight hours without a bit to eat or drink. The farmer's wife used to get nine shillings a week for my board and lodging and she had the lot. But it was only for one year, because the Wagoner left and another one came, and I boarded with him. His wife used to bring us tea and a piece of bread and cheese when we were down on the farm. I was in clover!

There were three pairs of horses, the Wagoner's and mine, and what they called the 'allworks'. Well, the farmer was a bit of a market gardener as well and in the summer time the allworks used to go to Dover market every week. Sometimes they'd have two loads to go, and they wanted an extra trace horse, well that used to be me. I started at eleven o'clock at night and would get back about four-thirty or five o'clock in the morning. Do you know what I used to get for that? A pint of beer and a piece of pork and bread. No extra money, it was just that £12 a year flat. I used to get home and go to bed, but I had to be back at work at nine in the morning.

Harry Gambrill

We had nine or ten men with each threshing machine. They would carry the straw and chaff and caving, look after the stack, cut bonds, stack the straw and work on the ricks, pitching the sheaves to the thresher. The farmer paid for their labour and they got three and a half pence an hour, ten hours a day, but we used to draw the working men's money off the farmers when we'd finished and pay them. The men always used to look to us drivers to pay them. Sometimes the farmers might give us a tip for taking the money and paying them, keeping count of their hours every day.

We started at some farms at six o'clock in the morning, and every Monday you had to go and light a fresh fire. Someone would be detailed to go, perhaps at 3.30 a.m., because it took a couple of hours to get enough steam up because of the dead coal. On ordinary

Another long day at Parkgate Ironworks, Rotherham, 1905.
One man is showing his feelings about being filmed!

mornings, if you'd been working the day before, the flue tubes were clean and it wasn't so long, about three quarters of an hour, before you had enough steam to turn the wheels. Sometimes they used to bank them up, chuck in a lot of fire, put a drop of water in the ash pan and wet sack over the top of the chimney. Most times all you had to do then was lift your ash-pan lid up for draught, take your wet sack off, and pike the fire up. It used to draw up like that.

Farmers used to give the men a pint of beer at nine o'clock and a pint of beer at three in the afternoon. If they had to work after six they used to give them a sandwich or two and another drink to encourage them to finish a stack so we could get away, otherwise it meant two hours the next day and no more work. We didn't get any lost-time money, and all we got extra to our wage was a shilling shifting from one farm to another. If it was here to Margate we only got a shilling and if it was only across the road we got a shilling. There was no wet-weather money. If it rained we used to hang about, but once three o'clock came we'd shut the engine down, put the top on the chimney and that was the end of it. We'd go and have a warm-up beside the fire, and a bit of food, then get into the barn and have a rest.

Lots of the old thatched barns were infested with fleas. You were lucky if you didn't get some. You were itching, scratching, scrubbing all day long. If you hung a jacket up, a coat you were wearing to work in the morning, and you weren't careful where you hung it, you'd find some mice in it. Some of the farms had lots of cats, but they never done away with the mice because they used to live and breed in the ricks. God, there used to be thousands! They'd get in your clothes and many of the men used to get them in their trousers, so they used to tie the bottom of their trouser legs up. Dirty little devils, they were. One night, I had a wash, turned my shirt collar up and sat down at the table. It was a nice beef pudding with a bit of kidney in it, lovely it was, with a drop of gravy. I felt something prick my collar, so I put my fingers down there and out jumped a mouse on the table.

You'd catch as many as eighty rats a day out of the rick. Some farmers put wire netting six or seven feet away from the stack, then get the thatch off. Ever so many would jump out and the chaps used to be in there with sticks hitting them and chucking them out. They used to put faggots down on the ground and the rick on them so when we'd got the stack nearly finished, down to the last sheaf or two, some of the farmers would say, 'Your time will still go on, boys. Pick them faggots up and make a long bundle the other side of the fence.' As you picked them up there was little ones and big ones. Oh, it was a regular game! The farmer always used to give them perhaps some extra beer, or if they were teetotal farmers an extra copper or two.

At Bockholt Farm in Waltham they lost some little Southdown sheep one time, which died of disease, and they just chucked them in the barn and stacked corn on them. Anyway, we didn't know about it until we got down to the last row of sheaves and found the rotten carcasses of these sheep.

Rats! You've never seen anything like it in your life. There were hundreds. We killed a tremendous lot of them. A bloke said, 'There's a hole in that tall door post and there's rats in there.' The bailiff bored a hole quite a way up, then he got some hot water out of the engine and poured it down, and they got eighteen of the biggest rats you ever saw out of that hollow post. They were squeaking and hollering and some of the chaps gave them a clout – because they're filthy things. Most of them will go for dogs and bite them. Some of them are very big old sandy things, all sores up their tails. Cor, I used to hate the sight of them.

George Hewins

You could always tell when it was pea-picking time – the roadsters turned up. Gyppos, Irish, tramps, they had a round, see, they knew where they could drop into work. They went to the same farmers every year – the farmers knew the roadsters would be there, they relied on them coming. And folks like us. We all went pea-picking. One June, I was bricklaying for a farmer up Tiddington Road, and he gave me and Tommy a whole field to pick!

Mostly, picking started at five o'clock. The Stratford women wouldn't come till breakfast time, when they'd seen the kiddies off to school. If they were hard-up the kiddies came too – the school never troubled at pea-picking time – it was more hands to pick. They were alright at picking till they started to eat the peas. The missus took the old wooden pram up Loxley Lane, a mile and a half with the little 'uns. They paid you as you picked them. She'd drag a pot o' peas up to be weighed, about forty pounds, and if she'd got any left over the bloke'd take them out and give them to her to put in her apron for the next pot. If they were wet from the dew or rain, they weighed more.

The roadsters had no home to go back to. I felt sorry for them. They'd go to the one farmer, set up their tents, finish his peas, then he'd throw them off his land, he wouldn't let them stop once they'd finished, even for a night. They'd move on towards Evesham or Alcester, fruit-picking for another farmer.

Frank Kemsley

We had a lot of horses from London. They only lasted two years in London. They used to put two ton behind one big horse, and that took so much out of horses' legs, the front legs used to go over, bent. So we used to buy them. They used to come back on the farm and they used to recover. They were only six or seven years old. We used to get them used to farm work and then sell them to farmers around about. There were chaps up there at the London mart used to bring them down for us, and for other buyers too. They'd walk perhaps a dozen old horses out of London, stopping at every pub. By the time they got down here they were pretty near boozed!

Gypsies used to come in and ask if they could stop for a day or two on our land, especially when the fairs were on. We didn't mind them. There were some bad gypsies and some good gypsies. We had one lot, name of Collins, used to come and see my dad, and if they'd got a decent pony they used to bring it and sell it to him. One day they sold him an old grey horse starved of life. He could hardly walk. Father gave him a fiver and we nursed him up and got him into a good condition. We sold him to Earl Sondes. Three years afterwards, father had a letter from a woman named Baker-White and she had this grey horse. She was going to Germany and she wanted Lord Sondes to have this horse back, as she didn't want to sell him. She wanted him to have a good home all his life.

Earl Sondes said, 'No, I don't want him. You send him to Ted Kemsley. He saved his life. He'd like to have him.' So she wrote to my father. We went over there to see her in the pony cart. 'Now,' she said, 'I'm going to give you that horse on the condition that you never sell him. You keep him till he dies or have him put down. You can have his cart and the harness and everything with him.'

She told her groom to put the horse in the cart and put all the tackle in it. I brought it home and we kept that horse eleven year. He was a beautiful horse. That's the old horse we used to drive people to the weddings with when I got older. When he got too weak to work, he got very lame, and winter was coming. 'Don't like doing it,' my father said, 'but we shall have to put old Buller down.' I couldn't go and see him killed.

They used to have horse sales at Romney Marsh fair. It was a great game that was, but you had to watch what you were doing. Oh yes, they were very sharp. Of course it's like everything else, if they're selling a thing they don't cry stinking meat. My father, he was very keen, he knew what a horse was. For one thing he'd look in his mouth and see how old he was. Then he'd feel his legs and tendons, to see that he'd got no bog spavins and that sort of thing. Then he'd get a man to trot him up and down and my father used to stand and watch them. If he showed even a slight limp, he knew he was a bad egg. They used to fire some of the horses if they'd got weak tendons and were a bit lame. They'd get like a red-hot poker and run it up and down their leg to burn it and strengthen the tendon so they could sell them. After you'd bought one and he'd gone lame, you hadn't got a leg to stand on! Some of these fairly decent, straightforward dealers would say, well, have him on trial. Then of course you'd got to pay for it, have him on trial and if it was all right, well, naturally you'd buy it.

Charles Hancy

There were ten cow-keepers round here in Broad Street, Bungay. My father had several cows and at six o'clock every morning we used to go on the common and get the cows up. You couldn't get them up before six, that was when the bailiff used to come down and unlock the gate. We used to come home with the cows, shove a tin of corn into the manger for them, tie them up and set a-milking. Me and my two sisters, we used to milk eight cows before we went to school. After we'd finished milking we'd go indoors, have a wash; then we used to take a big can of milk up the street and leave it against the public house, The Swan. Then my mother used to go round the town with the milk: she'd take two big cans and measure it out at your door; some just had half a pint for a ha'penny. She took two cans that she carried herself, and then pick up the third from The Swan, so she didn't have to come home until after the round. And then I turned the cows out again and swept up all the droppings in the yard before I went to school. And I used to take half a dozen cans of milk to customers on my way to school, then bring the empties home at dinnertime.

When you got home at dinnertime it was a full-time job again feeding the cows. We had to clean the beet first, grind them, and then mix them up with the chaff. We shoved a bushel of food in the manger for each cow, then it was off to school again. Then when four o'clock came it was the same routine. Then you had to start cutting chaff for next day. It was all done by hand – the old beet-grinder used to shred the beets. You'd fill the old machine up and then turn the handle, and then it'd come out shredded.

When I was about ten, the other boys wouldn't sit beside me at school. I used to stink of cows, so they reckoned. I used to get into rare trouble over that.

Here in Bungay there's been a lot of nonsense about 'common-owners'. Well, there isn't such a thing as a common-owner. All people owned was a piece of paper entitling them to feed two head of stock from the beginning of May to the end of October. Some of these papers used to go with the cottages and whoever hired the cottage had the right and privilege to turn two head of cattle on there – one commonage, that represented two head o' cattle. Those that didn't own commonages had to hire them. So many beasts were allowed on the common and they were always let on the Thursday before 12 May. That was the day they opened what they called The Lows, which was one side of the common that's more or less fenced off. The other side they called The Haycroft. The centre of the common, that was called The Hards.

We'd book our cows at the end of October. That gave us the privilege to turn the cows on the common all winter, from the end of October right through to May. That was for the centre of the common – The Hards. That was for exercise and water, really, although there was enough grass there to half keep them.

There were no taps round here, and there wasn't any water laid on in Bungay. Only pumps. There were three pumps in this street. One in the yard supplied eight to ten houses round here. There was another one that stood near The Groom, and another down the bottom of the hill. Those with cows down there had to cart all that water for them right from the bottom of that hill when it got so bad they had to keep their cows in. So they kept them out as long as they could. If it wasn't too bad, they'd go down and break the ice in one of the dykes for them, rather than cart the water all that way up, because a cow can really drink some water!

Ernest Stanger

The hopping season used to be good for shop business if you could stop the stuff from being pinched. You had to be careful where you left stuff laying about the shop, otherwise you'd lose it.

My uncle had a shop at the top of the hill, and one morning when he'd just had some of these big cheeses delivered, someone put his head in and shouted, 'Mr Walters, come and look after your cheese.' When he went out, some Londoners had put one of these cheeses on end and it was rolling away down the hill while they trotted behind it. They were all Londoners. All sorts of tricks they got up to.

Freda Vidgen

From January the London hop-pickers had been writing postcards to book hopper huts and bins for the coming year. So in the winter evenings we children used to address the return postcards and put 'Hop-picking will commence . . .' Then we had to get these couple of hundred postcards sent off to London and book the hopping train. Then the farm wagons used to be got out, and the horses were dressed with ribbons, and brasses, and they went three miles to Marden Station with us country children running behind them all the way. Two vans went for luggage, and a dung cart went for old people. They had a bushel basket that they used to pick apples in and they would throw it up in. Most of the old ladies weighed twelve, fourteen, sixteen stone because all the porter they used to drink in London made them so stout. So the Wagoner would put the basket down, put his shoulder under their bottoms and heave them up into the dung cart. The children would sit up on top of the luggage. Then, coming down Pattenden Lane, the horses would stop and the families would undo bags and tip out two or three children. They put children into sacks so they shouldn't have to pay the fare down, took them out on the train, and then put them back into the sacks to get off.

Then they had their huts, and they all renewed acquaintanceships with children from last year. We got all the huts ready. The farmer would get stones, faggots and straw for their beds, and we would whitewash the huts. Then the Wagoner went round every day and put two faggots outside each hut for firing and so that nobody would pinch them. The children would be sent home early to put them in the huts and get the fires going to boil their kettles and billy cans. They did all their washing and that was draped along the hedges. They never did any ironing because there wasn't anywhere to heat irons.

They were real characters, these Londoners. My father, he was in the Territorials, and he had a bugle and used to come into my bedroom, open the window and blow this bugle for the people to start work. Then in the afternoon he would shout, 'Pull no more bines,' but everybody in the hop garden pulled another bine because they wanted to get some hops in their bin to start in the morning! And paying-off day was a marvellous day. Most cottage people had an extra allotment where they grew potatoes and dahlias to sell to the hop-pickers. And the farmer would put boxes of apples in his farmyard with one of the farmworkers to share them out because he knew that if he didn't give them apples they would pinch them anyway. They then used to come to the door and say, 'Ha'porth of apples and penn'orth of taters.' They wanted the bigger potatoes and the small apples. We made quite a lot of money.

Every dinnertime when we came home from the hop garden, my mother would put a piece of white sheeting on her lap and we would kneel in front of her and she would have a comb, a double-edged, very fine comb, and she would scrape it through our hair to get these nits off the strands of hair and shake them on to a newspaper and burn them. That was done morning, noon and night so that you shouldn't get these nits and have to have your head shaved. Your greatest shame was to go to school after hop-picking with your head shaved.

Evelina Goddard

My father took up the hay business. He took to it like a duck to water, and I think he was considered a fine judge of hay. Most of the hay went to London. They kept the horses there! Each big house had its carriage and pair, and of course they had to have hay. Cows were also kept in London then. But the cows had second-class hay – horses had the first-class hay. Upland, that's the best hay – should be cut before the longest day. And you mustn't have rain on it if you can help it. The marsh hay which went to the cows – you could cut that in July – any time you jolly well like! But Newmarket was terribly particular; my father sent a lot of hay to Newmarket; and they wouldn't have it string-baled. It had to be hand-tied with what our men called a bind or bond. They made the bonds out of straw. If the string that bound a truss of hay got into the manger by mischance, the animals often ate it with fatal results. But if a straw bond got among the fodder, the animal could digest it without difficulty.

We had one man who could cut a truss of hay almost to a pound. You see, hay varies so. Some of it is very light and some of it is heavy. My father was very keen on stover, which is really clover hay. Well, it must smell a bit. My father passing a stack would say, 'That's all right! I can smell it.'

My father also had a hay-iron. You would push it in the stack, twist it round and pull it out, then smell the hay that came out on its end. You could measure with it as well. The iron was in two parts which you could screw together. He had a little leather case to put it in. I should think it measured two yards. I've been with my father when he measured up the stack. You measured round the stack; and the thing was, some of the hay was heavy and some was light. My father gauged that by this iron – from feeling its weight – how it went into the stack.

When Father made up the trusses of hay for Newmarket and London he used a machine. Three men worked it. There was the foreman who did the cutting; the others made the binds, and so on. The art was in cutting the truss out of the stack – if it was a stack of heavy hay, you wouldn't want so much in size because it would have weight. But if it was light – which was never so good – you'd make up a rather bulky truss. I believe they weighed about four stone and a half, and I think they always allowed a pound or two for wastage. Then my father used to send a press and three men to Havergate Island near Orford. It was a difficult job to get it across the river there on a flat-bottomed ferry affair.

Charles Hancy

My job was to deliver the hay. You got used to the old hay-carts. They'd rock you to sleep. I've seen the mail-cart come towards me at Brooke in the morning, and it ain't been a hundred yards away from me – and I never see it pass me. I've been asleep afore it got to me. He has been asleep too! He rode into me one morning. Yes, he'd been asleep. There's one run into me one morning at Gladstone.

It was the second hill at Galveston; and the post-office used to have an old cart like a box-cart; and there'd be an iron rail on the top to hold the parcels on. That hooked in with my rope, and that turned him over. He was sound asleep – so was I!

Our only trouble was with the police. We weren't very old, and they were always standing about waiting for us to be asleep in the wagons. I got summonsed seven times in one year for being asleep in charge of horses. Yes – I've been up at Bungay and Buckles – I've been up at every police court round this country for being asleep in charge of horses.

Albert Love

We used to load up all the day before and draw out of the stockyard at the farms between two-thirty and three o'clock in the morning. We had a journey of about six miles from Aburgh to Dasburg village on the Norwich road. We'd pull up at a public house named Tasburgh Bird in Hand and have our breakfast. We'd stop there roughly an hour to give the horses a little spell, then proceed from there to Norwich. We'd have tea or coffee, or we'd have a drop of liquor if we could see our way clear. Sometimes you could just manage a thruppenny drop o' liquor, because we got half a crown journey money. That was our fee. We took the horses' bait with us.

Approaching Norwich, we'd keep watching the time, perhaps edging on to be getting there a little bit quicker, because as soon as you were drawing into Norwich, police used to be standing out there, and if you weren't there by ten o'clock in the morning they wouldn't let you in. Then you had to stop somewhere and put up till the next day. At ten o'clock they stopped all the traffic loading up and down the town and you were not allowed through with loads of hay or straw or anything. They'd send you back. I've known men drag the wagons of hay on to the side of the road and leave them there, and then go back to them the next day after putting the horses up somewhere.

James Thrower

I became a feeder, feeding the corn into the thrashing drum. It was a bit of a risky job. I got a fork stuck through my hand more than once. I got several tips off here and little stabs and one thing and another. There was one man I worked with – I did seven seasons with him – and there wasn't so much as an angry word or 'dammit' passed between us. Of course, we had to walk to work. We walked 108 miles one week, and we earned eightpence each for that week! That was about 1907 or 8. We walked from Little Thornham to Shimpling and we walked there for a week. We went there with a new cloth on the drum, as near as could be, and when we come away there wasn't a piece of it any bigger than your hand. Wind! Wet! I got wet and then I got dry! And we couldn't do this job because of the weather. And there were oak trees stood up there, and it snapped three of 'em off just like snapping a match. That was a rum wind!

Harold Smart

I knew one poacher, he poached all his life and never did get caught. He'd go into one wood, perhaps Easter Wood, then perhaps into Chedgrave the next night. Another night he'd be on the Marquis of Bristol's estate, then he'd go to the Saxham estate. He covered a wide area. He used to shoot the birds with a muzzle-loader gun – he'd load up with shot and powder and ram it. I've known him shoot fourteen in a night.

Another particular poacher used to fill a hamper and take it into Bury St Edmunds to sell. He would have a spy – the carrier perhaps, because there was a carrier in all villages with a horse and cart – and he'd get him just to walk down and see if there was a farmer, or any authority, in that particular place where he'd brought the birds. And if there was anybody there, he'd keep back. If there wasn't anybody there, the buyer and the chap would take the hamper out of sight and unpack it. Then he used to go back and fetch the money. The cock birds used to make half a crown, and the hen birds two shillings, and a hare would make half a crown. That was the time when wages for a farm worker were ten or twelve shillings a week. He'd make a good week's work in one night. There was plenty of money in that job if you could do it without getting copped.

Before the First World War, the farmers they'd got real people under them. My son had to go to work alongside of me – and if I tried to get him another job in a trade or anything, the farmer would have turned me out of the house and sacked me. They used to more or less claim the sons to go to work with the fathers. That's how it worked. My son started up there with me on the farm, but he couldn't get on. The foreman always kept on at him – and he was a good lad. He was a good worker. Well, when he left, that was the first thing the foreman flung at me. He said, 'He'll sack you!' and I said, 'I don't mind if he do!' My son was not more than sixteen. He left and went over to Stradishall – building Stradishall aerodrome. But the master, he wouldn't part with me. He told the foreman, 'That's the last thing I should think of doing.' And I stayed with him until he retired. But generally, they used to claim the sons to go for about three shillings a week – sixpence a day – from six to six.

Mr Bailey

The farmers wouldn't work as hard as their wives, though. It was a hard life for women in the country – and in the town too, where they used to go into the factory, and bring their family up too.

A lot of the labour lived in, so apart from the family, the wife had to look after the men as well. A lot of them were hired – the farmer used to go to the hiring fairs at Ulverston, and if you wanted a man and you couldn't get anyone local, you'd get on the train to Ulverston and hire one for six months. It would be early Whit week, and they'd come on Saturday, the men who'd been hired. They'd come and live with you and they'd work every day – they never had any time off, and they'd finish at eleven o'clock. They'd finish at noon on a Sunday, and then there was milking time at four o'clock Sunday night. They worked until November, and then there was a break and another hiring fair, and if the farmer was satisfied with the man, they'd come back. If they weren't they wouldn't come back. They were mostly young men, and they weren't encouraged to get married.

Tom Murray

My father was on the radical wing of the Liberal Party, and in fact that was the first introduction I had to political life. He took me to an election meeting in Tornaveen Old School in 1909. There I got my first taste of electioneering. My father was so good at heckling that the Liberal Party hauled him round the constituency to heckle the Conservative candidate, F. E. Smith, who later became Lord Birkenhead. My father was tripping him up quite effectively evidently.

Well, my father had the lease of Easter Tolmauds Farm at Tornaveen from Lady Gordon Cathcart of Cluny Castle. The factor of the estate of Cluny was John Hosie, who had been at school with my father for a short time at Gordon's College in Aberdeen. Under the terms of his lease, Father was entitled to the drainage of certain waterlogged fields. John Hosie said to him, 'Look here, I'll take you into my confidence. If ye carry on with your Liberal activities ye're not goin' to get your fields drained by the landlord.' My father said, 'Well, if that's the case, I'll make it public.' And Hosie said, 'For God's sake, don't do that or I'll lose my job.' So my father didn't do it. I said to him afterwards, 'You know, I think you should have just gone ahead and advertised it.' It was more important to floor this reactionary woman. She had got these vast estates, not only in Aberdeenshire, but up in Rossshire and over in the islands – I don't know where all the Cluny Estates were – but she got them by a simple quirk as it were, in a will. And she married this stupid man, Sir Gordon Cathcart, a baronet. He was an utter nitwit – the way he carried on.

Robert Williamson

The majority of deep-water sailing ships were loaded in the West India Dock. That's where all the sailing ship sailors went and looked for a ship – because there was no unemployment pay. As soon as a ship moored at home, and the voyage ended, the pay stopped. The sailor received what pay was due to him at the shipping office and he had to find another ship or starve.

Opposite the West India Dock was the Surrey Commercial Docks, which were always full of masts and yards, because that is where the Norwegians and the Swedes would bring in timber. There were usually schooners and barquentines – and that was where you saw the bulk of the sailing craft in the Thames, apart from the sailing barges, which ride up and down the river.

The coasting trade was entirely different from the foreign-going trade, and it had its own rules. I didn't know anything about this until I met a chap who explained it all to me. One day I was at a loose end, so I went down to the City Arms. In the bar at one end there was a large, red-faced fellow, and my chum pointed him out to me, and he said, 'That's Barge Billy. All the barge skippers go to him. Any men who want a job in a barge, they go and see Barge Billy, and he brings the two together.' At the other end was a little man sitting there, and my chum said, 'He's Schooner Charlie.' Outside there were all these coasting sailors, pacing up and down waiting for a job – and all registered with either Schooner Charlie or Barge Billy.

I got into conversation with Schooner Charlie. He said, 'What about you – do you want a job?' 'Well, no,' I said. 'I don't want any coasting job. I'm a deep-water man.' 'How would you like to join a nice brigantine? I've got a captain who wants a seaman.' I got interested so I said, 'All right.' He said, 'Come down tomorrow morning and meet Captain Woolley. His brigantine has a reputation among the coasting people, for being slow. But she's a good stout craft, and Captain Woolley is a very fine skipper.'

Next morning I went down, and Schooner Charlie introduced me to Captain Woolley. He said, 'What about joining me?' I said, 'Well, Captain, there are all these men outside – why are you so keen to ship me? I don't know anything about the coast. Where are you going?' He said, 'We're loaded with bagged grain in the Albert Dock, and we're bound for Hull.' So I said, 'What about if I join you and go to Hull with you?' He said, 'That'd suit me. I find it quite hard to get a man here in London, but in Hull I can get men. Come with me to Hull, and then we'll see.'

We were due to sail on that tide late that evening. To me this brigantine was a plaything, really, and I was bustling about doing various jobs. I was interested to find that we had an extra shipmate – a dog named Jack. He was an Irish terrier, and he was chained up to the wheel – he was the extra hand. During the forenoon, the Board of Trade inspector arrived while Captain Woolley was ashore. 'I want to inspect your gear, mate.' So I went down into the cabin with the inspector. 'I want to see your lights.' So the mate handed me one rather battered side-light, I don't know whether it was a port or starboard. The inspector looked at it. 'What's that?' 'Well,' I said, 'I suppose it's a port light, isn't it?' 'Oh, is it? Put it down there.' Then the mate handed me a starboard side-light, which was an even more battered specimen. The Board of Trade inspector glared at it. 'What's that?' 'It's the starboard light.' 'Hmm, put it over there.' Then the old mate handed me what was really an old carriage lantern – and I held this up. Well, the poor fella looked at it and said, 'What the hell's that?' I said, 'Well, I suppose it's the stern light.' 'Good God,' he said, 'that's not a Board of Trade light – it's a damned old stable lamp. Look, all your lights are condemned, and you don't leave this port until you have a brand-new set of lights and I come on board and inspect them'. So away he stumped, and went off ashore.

Captain Woolley came back and the mate had to tell him the bad news. The sailing had to be postponed. Captain Woolley had to go to his agent and raise the money to buy a new set of lights. The new lamps were delivered late that afternoon, but it was too late. We'd missed the tide, so we couldn't leave, but that evening the Board of Trade man came on board and he inspected the lights.

The inspector also had to inspect the life-saving gear. The ship had two circular lifebuoys on the cabin aft, where the mast was, below decks. There was a wooden companionway over the ladder leading down to their accommodation. As was customary in those ships, there was a lifebuoy on brackets on either side of that companionway, which could be grabbed and thrown overboard. The dog was not allowed to go ashore, because there was a regulation that, if the ship had a dog, and the ship had visited a foreign port, the dog was not allowed to be landed in this country for six months. So this poor old dog was in quarantine because the ship had been over to France a couple of months earlier. So every time the ship came into port, he had to be chained up. He'd been chained up rather carelessly somewhere, and he'd amused himself by chewing the lifebuoys. Of course, when the inspector looked at the lifebuoys they had no brackets – they'd been chewed off around the ends – so that had to be repaired.

Eventually he cleared the ship and she was allowed to proceed to sea – but we couldn't sail until early the next morning. Unfortunately, during the night a thick fog settled over London. A real old pea-souper. The fog lasted the whole of the next day and nothing moved on the river at all. It was the most eerie feeling – you couldn't hear a sound – and nothing could move. It was not until the next night that the fog began to disperse, and in the morning we sailed on the tide.

When we got to Hull we had 300 tons of grain in bags to discharge. The rule on the coast was that if a man wanted to leave, he couldn't leave until the cargo was discharged – then he received all the money due to him, which was calculated on the number of days since he'd joined. Well, after the grain was all discharged – it took four or five days unloading sixty tons a day – I went off to see Captain Woolley to draw my money and leave.

I went back to the South West India Dock – looking for a sailing ship again. As I entered the dock, the first thing I saw was the old *Discovery*. She was the last vessel carrying sail which made the voyage from London to Canada. At that time, the railway had not reached Hudson Bay in Canada. It was still some 200 miles short of the bay, so all the stores had to be sent by sea, during the summer, while it was possible to get through the ice and the channels were clear. It wasn't feasible to send steamers through there, because, apart from the risk of damage to the propeller, there was the question of fuel. There was no coal to be had, so it was essential for the vessel going to the posts inside Hudson Bay to have some auxiliary sail power.

I saw she was fitting out, there were riggers was fitting out, and I saw riggers were aloft and cargo was being shipped. It was obvious she was getting ready. I'd sailed with a man who had actually made a voyage in her, so I knew all about her. The wages there were a little higher than they were in deep-water ships, so I hurried on board, and the second mate was talking to the stevedore. I went up, and he guessed I was a seaman. I said, 'Have you engaged your crew yet, sir?' and he said, 'No, not fully engaged.' So I gave him my seaman's discharge book. He glanced at it and he just asked me one or two questions about my experience in sail. He said, 'All right, you're engaged.' The next Monday I was on board, and Captain Ford, who was a short, stocky man with a beard, was there. The chief mate showed him all our certificates and books – and he satisfied himself, because he would take only youngish men – it was tough, a voyage like that. The oldest chap on board was only about thirty. I was actually nineteen.

Then Captain Ford said, 'Well now, you must realise that this is a very unusual voyage, and a certain amount of hazards are attached to it. The bay is not fully surveyed, and there are lots of dangers there – and the ship is always liable to be lost through ice and currents and so on. So you have to agree when you sign the articles that if the ship is stranded and has to be abandoned, that you will observe ship discipline ashore as well as on board. You understand that? You have to continue working.' Then he said, 'Well, then, you sign the articles on Thursday, and the ship will sail on Saturday.'

On the Thursday morning we arrived at the shipping office in Dock Street and there was trouble brewing, something had come to a head between the unions and the shipowners. The seaman's union had been agitating for an extra pound a month for able seamen and an extra pound for the stokers – the firemen – which the shipowners were refusing to pay. The unions had given them notice that unless they agreed, from that morning, the crews would refuse to sign on. The wages for able seamen in those days was £4 10 shillings per month, and for firemen, £5 10 shillings – but unless the wages were increased they would refuse to sail. When the shipping master read the rates of wages for able seamen as £4 10 shillings per month, one of the men from another ship stopped him and said, 'No mister – that's got to be £5 10 shillings per month for the able seamen and £6 10 shillings for the firemen – otherwise we're not going to sign on.' The shipping master said, 'Well, Captain – what am I to do?' He said, 'I'm instructed that these are the rates of pay and I'm not to pay any more.' Whereupon, all the crew walked out.

We had already had a conference between ourselves that we would have to ask for the same – we couldn't do anything else. We'd been threatened by the union people outside in the street, that we had to get signed on for more or there'd be trouble for us. Then the shipping master came to our table, and he recited all the articles and special clauses to which we'd already agreed with Captain Ford. Then he came to the wages for able seamen. Now the wages in those days was £4 10 shillings for steamers, but for a sailing ship it was £3 a month – that was all. It was a wicked wage – but still that was the rate.

The Hudson Bay Company paid a little more because she was part sail and part steam, and he said £3 10 shillings. We picked out the biggest bloke among us to be a spokesman. He very politely said, 'No, I'm afraid, sir, that, as you know, there's a strike on, and we're unable to sign for that. We must have £4 10 shillings a month, instead of £3 10 shillings.' Captain Ford immediately said to the shipping master, 'You've got to understand that this is a special ship on a special voyage, and we can't afford any delay. The ship must sail.' So he said, 'On my own responsibility, I will offer you another ten shillings a month.' We withdrew and had a little conference, and said, 'We got ten bob – let's stick out for a pound, and if they refuse to pay we'll sign for the ten shillings.' We went back and said, 'No sir, I'm afraid we must stand for the pound.' So the captain said to the shipping master, 'Just a moment, I must telephone my agents.' He went off and he wasn't gone very long. Back he came and he nodded to the shipping master. He said, 'All right, boys, you get another pound a month.' This was wonderful. We were signing for £4 10 shillings a month instead of £3.

On board, the crew lived in a deckhouse between the foremast and the mainmast, and this was a long, big house with a wooden table secured to the stanchions down the middle for a mess table. There was a water tank in which you stored your allowance of fresh water – and that was all. We had to provide all our own bedding. The usual thing was a straw mattress, which one bought from the ship chandler very cheaply, and three or four blankets and your gear. Beside the bunks there was a locker for each man in which you could stow all your clothes. In the sailing ships there were no lockers. But every man had his sea chest which was lashed to the lower bunk, and you kept everything in the old sea chest. But the ship provided nothing whatever – you had to provide every mortal thing for yourself.

There was one thing special to sailing ships which were going to be at sea for at least three months – say on the passage out to Australia or New Zealand. On those trips you couldn't run ashore somewhere and buy things – if you hadn't got it, you had to go without. But it was customary for the master to carry what was called a 'slop chest' – a stock of articles which a seaman might require – shirts, underwear and probably a suit of dungarees, and warm sea-boot stockings and odds and ends like that. Every Friday evening at sea, except in tempestuous weather, all these goods were laid out by the steward in the cabin and if you wanted anything you could go aft, make your selection and sign for it. At the end of the voyage, the captain was entitled to stop that amount from your wages.

The food had to be stuff which was not perishable. The main thing was casks of salted beef and salted pork, which had to be passed by the Board of Trade and have the Customs seal on it. The only other meat they had was Australian tinned mutton, which was awful stuff. We didn't like it – whereas the salt beef and salt pork were very good indeed. The tinned Australian mutton was known to the sailors as Harriet Lane – and I'd been at sea some time before

I knew how it got its name. In the last century there was a terrible scandal about a poor old woman in the East End of London who was murdered, and they always said she was rendered down into tins for the sailors. The Navy had the same thing, but they used to call it Fanny Adams. That was another woman who'd come to a sticky end.

You couldn't carry a great amount of flour, but according to the Board of Trade regulations we had to have baked bread four times a week – because on Sunday we were supposed to have a pudding – a plum duff of some sort. We were entitled to a pound of bread. It was about the size of a bun – and it was very acceptable, so acceptable we used to eat it at once, we were so famished.

Another thing we used to enjoy was haricot beans, and they were very good. The cook used to make it up with a bit of molasses in it. We also had dried peas, and we used to get plenty of pea soup. The best things we had were the pea soup and salt pork. Salt beef we didn't care so much about.

Every ship was compelled by law to serve out to the crew a daily measure of lime juice – and every man had to drink it – he could be fined if he didn't. After so many days on salt provisions the ship was compelled to issue lime juice every day. It was fortified with a certain amount of spirit – you weren't allowed to sell it on shore. It was a very refreshing drink. At noon we'd go aft with our mugs – our pannikins – and we would get it filled with lime juice, which we had to drink right away. There was never any need to compel the crew – we could never get enough of it – but it was effective. I never struck a case of scurvy in my days at sea.

Fresh water had to be very strictly rationed. Every afternoon at eight bells, the pump would be rigged into the fresh water tank and then the second officer had to supervise. For ten men we would get two buckets of fresh water, which was put into the water tank in the foc's'le. One bucket of water went into the tank and the other bucket went to the galley, where there was a big water tank for the cook. That went into the food preparation, for tea, soup and so on.

The only games we played were card games – we used to play

quite a lot of cribbage. Otherwise, you were working. When you were on deck during the day you were working hard. There were all kinds of jobs – you'd be working aloft, and there were always repairs to be done. Afterwards you were quite happy to just sit around, smoke your pipe and yarn, or play a game of crib. On a fine moonlit night it was grand to be up aloft. It was beautiful up there, the ship just gently snoring along – looking out over the sea. My gosh, you didn't need any better recreation than that. You'd think that being, say, three months at sea, it would grow monotonous. Well it never did, because you were entirely dependent on the winds and that kept you on your toes the whole time. You'd see the way the ship was surging away through the sea, and you could hear the occasional creak of a yard. After I was back in steam, as an officer, I remember quite distinctly lying in my bunk and I'd long to hear the creak of a yard again and feel the gentle motion of the ship.

I don't think we missed the company of women. We used to talk about them quite a lot, but never really missed them. It was a life apart – and we loved every bit of it. We used to growl, naturally, especially in bad weather, but on the ship you are all friends – you're all in the same boat. In fact, I've heard many an old sailor say, when you've been together all those months, you've been a united family and then when you get paid off – and it all comes to an end. You often wish you could put the ship around and go back again.

George 'Cowheel' Andrew

When I first started to go boating I can remember up to twenty-nine boats working off Brighton beach. There were two or three Motor Torpedo Boats moored, a boat called the *Pendennis Castle*, another called the *Regency Belle*, and of course the Campbell's paddle-steamers that were running from the pier. Most of the fishing families in Brighton had two boats. They used to cut the boats in half and they made a shed, so they could put their gear in. They're not supposed to be sold or leased for private – they're for the fishermen.

Steve Prebble

When I left school in 1907 I went fishing with my father and Jack. The bigger boats as a rule didn't carry a boy, but occasionally one might have had three men and a boy. There were two men and me on my father's boat.

You'd start drifting for mackerel about the first week in May and carry on till the end of July. Then in September, you used to go what we called autumn mackerelling. The summer mackerelling was done in the west bay and the autumn mackerelling in the east bay between Dover and Dungeness. You see, in the summertime mackerel are coming from the west to the east and in the autumn they were going east to west – going back again. Then, the latter part of October, you'd take your mackerel nets out and put your herring nets in. The herring season was done along the shore, mostly from smaller boats than we had for mackerel. Never got further than a mile out pretty often. Sometimes we put our nets out alongside the shore as close as you could get. If there were any herrings you'd carry on with the herring nets perhaps up to Christmas, or sometimes you'd start catching sprats in November – it just depended on where they were. Then we carried on with sprats right up till the end of February. But we had a spell till about May when we didn't do any fishing. We were getting our nets and boats ready then, but we'd got no income unless we got a job for a month or six weeks on the groynes there, or at the Brooks.

Robert Dale

You didn't know how long you were going to be gone. It all depended on how long it took you to get there and how long it took you to get home again. If you had a fair wind and could get out of the bay at daylight, then you could start right away. You couldn't get out of the bay at low tide after a certain ebb, so often we had to go very early, then if the wind happened to be against you you'd have to tack all the way in. In fog the watchboat would ring to help you get there. We often rowed for oysters for six hours in the boat. Three men rowing, and one man with a dredge shooting it over the side.

Sometimes we were gone thirteen hours in total, but we were only paid for six.

Steve Prebble

With fishing, it wasn't just a case of going out there and coming home again. Sometimes you went hours before it was time, because of the tide. Other times it took you hours to get home because of the tide. You used to be fishing from the time the water came over the sand till it went back again and you came ashore just before it left it.

We used to have to put boards under the boats to get them up and down the beach, or else they'd have dug right in the shingle and you couldn't move them then. You couldn't get them across the sand at all. Launching off the beach you'd got to know what you were doing. You'd watch, if you were on the shore, until you'd got four or five big waves come in and then four or five little ones. Well, if you went off sometimes in the big 'uns, they'd fill your boat up full of water. So you waited until you got a smooth, as they call it, and let her down before the next big ones came. If it was a bit rough we'd get the boat down close to the water and then we used to have a rope on anchor out there about fifty yards out, to pull her through the surf. One or two men, depending on how many of you there were, would get in the boat and pull, while another put the last board underneath and the others pushed. Then you'd got to turn the boat round to sea, because we always went out stern first.

Bob Bishop

Whitstable whelkers never used whelk pots. They didn't know what they were. They used to go what they call 'trotting'. They used to get fish offal, fix it in bunches, sink it in the sea and leave it for a time, then they'd go and pull these up and the whelks would be stuck to the bait. A whelk has got a tube that sucks everything up. It'll clean a crab out, suck out the legs as clean as a whistle. So these whelks would actually be sucking the bait. But in other places whelkers used whelk pots. These had iron frames, iron ribs and rope twisted round the iron stays. They curved over at the top, where there was a small hole, and hanging inside that was a small net called a crinny. The crinny was about four meshes deep and it used to hang down inside the pot, so when the whelks tried to climb out, they came up against this crinny.

There was also what we called a strop – a short bit of rope to hold the pot fast to the tows or rope. These whelk pots were then put in lines of about thirty with a buoy at each end. We never had big buoys, they were just two-gallon paint cans. We used to cork them and tar them. Each day you went out and hauled them up, emptied the whelks out and put the bait in. While one man was hauling, the other used to stack them in the boat. After you'd got all the lines up and baited, then you turned them over a different bit of ground, like. We used to shoot them across the tide, and you had to know which pot was next to throw over the side because you'd got a hell of a lot of rope there.

Sometimes, when it was very rough, the pots used to move about on the bottom, and it was surprising how the lines used to get tangled up. We had to get them up the best way we could, sometimes two or three at a time. Then again, sometimes we'd get foul of the dredging boats. They used to cut them when they were dredging. We'd lose perhaps five, six, eight or even ten pots if they cut some out of the middle of the line. What we had to do then was grapple for them. We had a long iron, about a foot long, with all these hooks on it, and we dragged it along the bottom until we got hold of the rope in between two pots, and then we pulled them up, and sorted them out. Sometimes the dredging boats used to pull two or three up and they'd bring them ashore themselves and bring them round to the whelkers, and we had to give them something for bringing them ashore. That was a bit of a racket because the boats that were dredging, like the whelkers, had poor weeks and they used to make a bob or two the best way they could. The whelkers used to have quite a bit of trouble like that to start with, but in the end they got used to one another and eventually the dredgers wouldn't foul the gear if they could help it.

Whelking was often a matter of luck too. One day your whelk pots would be right full, and you'd turn them over thinking, 'Oh, they'll be all right tomorrow,' and perhaps then you hardly had any whelks at all. They would go off in all weathers too, as they were afraid of losing a day's money when things were a bit tight. Sometimes though they wouldn't be able to go to sea for weeks, if it was pretty rough. I've known my father be ashore for six weeks in the winter, but I think that was the longest. In that time a barge came ashore at Tankerton loaded with Quaker Oats, and people were getting that and living on oats. The dredging boats were the same. Things, at times, in Whitstable, used to be pretty dodgy as regards money and feeding.

We had wonderful boats. They were called crab boats because they used to go crabbing with them at Sheringham as well as whelking. They could put up with some weather, they could. They were double-ended, sharp fore and aft. They weren't all that big – about eighteen, nineteen foot – and when you were hauling your gear in it was hard work pulling, especially if there was a bit of a tide running. The early boats never had engines. They were all lug sail, what you call a dipping lug and a pair of oars. You pulled the sail up and when you wanted to come on another tack, you had to lower your sail, unhook it off the mast, put it back and round the other side of the mast and hook it on the stern forward, hie on the sail. You used to have a ring – a crinkle – in the lug sail, and you used to hook it on this and pull it up the mast. You could only sail on one tack with the sail up, otherwise you'd got to keep working really hard to let your sail down, pull it back, and pull it up the other side. We used to make what we called long boards when we were tacking.

As for the oars – well, you never had rowlocks. You just had holes cut in the timber of the boat, and you poked the oar out over the side and pulled it back in through the hole. Actually, that was better than rowlocks because if it was rough and you were rolling, the oars wouldn't come out of the hole like they would out of the rowlocks. And you had leather fixed round the holes so that the oar wouldn't wear the wood. We used to tack these bits of leather round and wet them to quieten them down a bit, so they didn't keep screaming when you were rowing.

As kids we used to go and help paint and tar these boats. They were mostly tarred up to the top planks and then painted blue or white. Blue, mostly.

You never had weather forecasts in those days. Yet it was strange how they used to forecast the weather and very seldom they were wrong. Lots of old fishermen could look up and tell you what the weather was going to be. When I was a school kid and I went with my uncle and my father in the school holidays, the sun would be shining and hardly a ripple on the water. My uncle would say, 'Come on, hurry up – let's get this haul aboard before it blows.' And sure enough, once we got home it was blowing hard. How he knew I just don't know. My father was the same.

Ed Gillett

The weever fish were a damned nuisance amongst the mackerel. As soon as you dabbed your hand down they'd sting you. I've had lots of little ones sting me, but only one time I've ever been stung by a big one. He'd got his prongs sticking right up and as I pulled the net, he dived and he got me right in the calf. When I pulled the net up, there he was, but he was dead. I said to my father, 'I can't go no further.' He brought me home. That made me queer. I had to go to Dr Proctor and he burnt it out for me and I fainted then.

Steve Prebble

Mackerel catching, you never put your nets over till it was getting dusk. It's no good putting them over in daylight because the water's clear and they'd see your nets. At Dengemarsh, about half an hour after low tide, the flood tide goes east along the shore. Then you'd anchor perhaps five or six hours and wait for the evening to come. You'd go and get what we used to call a berth out at sea, half a mile from the next boat. If you got too close to him he'd catch all the fish and they wouldn't come along to you. There used to be the

Hastings boats and the Rye boats out there too. There was a bit of swearing sometimes!

Bob Bishop

A lot of the whelkers used to go to the Salvation Army. Even my father used to go and listen on a Sunday. Although he'd been in the pub and had a drink, he'd always come out and listen.

Steve Prebble

When you pulled your nets in you didn't pull the nets to the boat – you pulled the boat to the net. Except when you got nearly to the end, then you'd pull the net through the water. In the middle of the boat was the net room as we used to call it. You hauled the nets in and put them back in the boat with the fish still in them, unless you got only perhaps a hundred or so, then you picked them out as you went and put them in the box so you hadn't got all the nets to pull out again. Then on the beach, you got all the nets to pull out to shake the fish out of them – count them up and put them in the boxes.

Wintertime, when you were catching sprats, it could be night time when you came ashore, and if there'd been any rain in the evening and the beach was still wet, the beach would freeze like concrete. Then you'd stand there, for a couple of hours perhaps, shaking your sprats out of the nets with the beach all frozen. The sprats would be frozen stiff on the beach before you could pick them up.

Albert Packman

I got down to Folkestone, and my cousin met me there in the van. He'd put on the telegram that he had found me a job – but he hadn't. The next morning I went out with him along the Leas. A big hotel there wanted a pageboy. I went in and, of course, I'd got my best suit on, which wasn't a suit to measure or anything like that. If fitted where it touched.

'Well,' said the supervisor, 'you want to be a pageboy. What have you been doing before?' I said on the farm. She said, 'Oh yes, I see. Well, you know a lot of other boys have been after the job. I'll have to leave it and let you know.' Of course, we didn't hear.

My cousin said, 'You'll never get a job in those clothes. I'll go and get you a suit and some different shoes.' So he bought me a better suit, and a pair of socks – not hand-knitted like we used to have – and a pair of shoes. He made me quite smart. He came in one morning and he said, 'I think I've got the job for you. It's a kitchen porter in a hotel.' I said, 'Well, it'll be something to start on, won't it? I can work up from that.' It was at Sandgate – the Royal Kent Hotel. An old coaching inn right on the front.

I got five shillings a week, all for myself. Nothing to buy, no food, just my clothes. I was fourteen and a half – so five shillings a week, good lord – I was a millionaire before I started.

As a rule they had about thirty people staying there and I had all the crockery to wash up for these people. The saucepans and all the plates and dishes – I had a double sink and big draining board and all the rest of it. The first night I thought, 'I'm not going to wear my best clothes for washing up,' so I put my boots on. Anyway, I got in there and I had to go up three steps from the scullery into the kitchen and collect all this dirty stuff. I came out with all these plates up to my chin – I wanted to show I could do it right – but I forgot all about the three steps to go down. You never heard such a clatter in your life. I went down and the plates shattered the flag-stones in the scullery. I thought, 'This is it. My five bob's gone. I've lost my job and everything.' The missus – it was a woman that owned it – she came running out there. 'Oh, I'm awfully sorry. I really am sorry. I won't do it again. It was these boots. I shall get some lighter shoes to wear. I'll pay for them at so much a week. I won't do it again, honestly.' She said, 'Oh, don't worry about that. But do try and be more careful – that's all.'

Ray Head

An unwelcome task the police had in those days was administering the birch to young offenders. My father who was a policeman, used to say how difficult it was to punish a bloke that he'd never seen before.

Albert 'Smiler' Marshall

One day, whilst trudging along home with an empty basket, Mr Dickens passed in his milk cart. I asked him whether he would give me a lift. He asked what I did, and suggested that I should come and work for him, plucking chickens and looking after his best pony. As I had ridden from such a young age, I was delighted, and for the rest of the summer I went with him on his milk round. When he was ill, which lasted for months, he asked me to drive the milk cart and do his round – a great experience at the age of thirteen. All those houses and having to remember who had what and whether they had paid. Then on Sundays I took great pride in getting the best pony and trap ready to take Mrs Stead and her daughter to the Wesleyan Chapel. My wages were four shillings and sixpence per week. I gave my sister two shillings and sixpence and the rest I kept, gradually collecting enough to have my first bicycle, with solid tyres, which I bought from my brother for three and six.

Henry Allingham

When I left school, my mother couldn't support me and I had to get a job. I went to work at St Barts Hospital as a trainee surgical instrument maker. I used to get twelve shillings and sixpence a week. I'd give my mother ten bob and I had half a crown to pay my fares and lunches. Lunch was always meat pud and potato. I began to look like a meat pud. I got my food there Saturdays and Sundays too, but then I chucked that job. They were very, very nice but it wasn't what I wanted to do.

I worked at Foden and Scammel, the car body builder in East Dulwich Road. That was a very high class of work. The first week I thought I was going to get fired, but the second week, I pulled all the stops out and Albert, the boss, came to me and said, 'You're a good lad. Can you carry on next week? I'll see what I can do for you.' I got twenty-five bob a week – that was a lot of money for a kid really. I finished up with twenty-nine shillings a week. Well, there were gents going to the city for thirty bob, so I was making a lot of money. I used to be at work at six o'clock in the morning, then I took half an hour for breakfast from eight o'clock to half past. You brought your own breakfast and you were ready for it by then. You had a beer can for your tea. The smithy would fill your can with a measure of water, and you had a whistle of tea and you added milk. At lunchtime the boy used to come round, and he'd go to the shop. You could get steak for ten pence, a good steak, and if I was flush I'd have at least twelve ounces of steak. Whoopee! You could braise it on the smithy's fire or you could fry it in a pan. You'd get it white hot – I became a master at doing steak – and you'd have lovely fresh oven-baked bread to eat with it. You would keep it in your toolbox so if there were any vermin around, they couldn't get it.

Bob Rogers

My first job was at a sealing wax factory in Stoke Newington. Seven pence a week, carrying the sealing wax about. While I was there, I broke both my feet. It was the weight that I was carrying. It pushed the bones down. There was no compensation and I was given the sack. I had to go to the workhouse hospital in Hoxton and they put me on sticks, but my feet have never been the same since. The hospital put bandages round my feet and then they put some kind of black tar around them. They said that was all they could do.

Jenny Billis

Suddenly there was a boom with cigarette making, and all the mothers were saying, 'Oh, it's a very good trade. You can earn lots of money.' A lot of English Jewish girls went in for it. Actually, it was slave labour. It was all piece-work, and you had to work like a devil to make two thousand cigarettes by hand. I started work in the factory at the age of fourteen. In the big factories the tobacco leaves were blended in the factory. There were hundreds of girls employed to strip the leaves. The tobacco was brought in, in its raw

A policeman on duty at one of the earliest games of rugby to be
filmed: Hunslet vs Leeds, 1901. Much to the annoyance of the
players the motion photographer was allowed on to the field.
Hunslet won the game by 16 points to nil.

A pint of old and mild at a village alehouse, c.1906.

state, and the girls used to strip the leaves and throw the stalks away. I used to go down there just to have a look. After it had been stripped, the tobacco was blended by putting the leaves through a machine.

I started as a cutter. I would cut the ends off the cigarettes after they'd been made. I made a few mistakes at first and I got told off. When the cigarette maker has a bad cutter, her work is being spoiled, and as it's piece-work she doesn't like it. But you learn by watching and trying, and soon I graduated onto being a maker.

The maker received the tobacco and made it into cigarettes. You used something called a 'clonky'. It was blue paper and linen combined, and it came in sheets. It was stiff and gave a good grip, which helped to roll the cigarette up. You'd cut out a square of it and stick half of it onto the edge of your table with some starch. The other half was free to roll the cigarette. Then you had a pound or two of tobacco in a tin, loose, on the floor with a lid. You would take some tobacco with your hand and put it on the table. As it would all be stuck together, you'd loosen it with your fingers. Then you'd take a fingerful – the amount for each cigarette – and put it along the clonky. After that you would take a piece of parchment paper which was cut into the shape of a steeple and put it into the clonky. Then you'd roll the tobacco up very tightly in the parchment paper. Then you took one of the cigarette papers, called cases, and you pushed the parchment through the case with a pusher, which was like a knitting needle with no point. That's how you made a cigarette.

We worked at a long table with three makers and three cutters on each side. The table had a trough running in front of it, almost in the lap of the maker. When you had about a hundred cigarettes, you'd take the whole hundred in your hand and you'd put them on the cutter's table. The cutter had a narrow strap, also made of linen, to hold these cigarettes. When she had a hundred cigarettes, she'd pick up the strap each side, hold the cigarettes together, and they'd have to be patted down with a block of wood. Then the cigarettes were put in trays and they'd be straightened out by shaking them. When there were about two thousand cigarettes in these trays, the cutter would take them to the forelady. Each room contained about two hundred girls and two foreladies. The forelady would examine the cigarettes, and if she saw one had a little tiny hole, or had a drag of tobacco, she'd take the cigarette out and throw it away. She'd call out the maker's number and she'd say, 'Take these back to the maker, they've got to be thrown out.' So all your cigarettes had to be torn up and you'd have to use the tobacco all over again.

The foreladies were like prison warders. One was a Mrs Murray. She was from Scotland, and she was very, very strict. I think we earned three and six per thousand cigarettes. Now, there were some girls who could put their nose to the grindstone and sit and roll and roll and roll and do nothing else but concentrate on their work. The quickest worker could do three thousand a day – ten and six a day – £3 a week. Well, I earned about £2 a week because I could only do two thousand a day – and sometimes not even that, because I liked to have a chat and a joke with my next-door neighbour. It was very monotonous work. I mean, you could think of nothing while you're rolling these cigarettes, because you did it automatically. You got backache – and the smell of the tobacco got up your nose and gave you terrible catarrh. It was horrible work. It was nerve-racking, I didn't use my brain, it made me feel ill and I hated it.

You had to be in by eight o'clock in the morning, and about ten to eight you'd see a stream of girls running as fast as their legs would carry them down Worship Street to get there in time, because if you didn't get there on the dot of eight, the door would be shut in your face. More than once I got shut out, but only for the morning. In the afternoon you could get back in. Sometimes I was frightened to go home, because my mother would tell me off. Once you were in, you had a ticket that you put on a board. It was a brass ticket with my number – 242 – and a little hole, and you had to put it on a big board where all the numbers were. We worked from eight to one without any tea break and from two to six without any tea break. I'd bring in sweets. We weren't supposed to eat sweets – but as soon as Mrs Murray was out of the room, we'd pass a few round. We wore a pinafore because the tobacco would drop into your lap. And if you wanted to go out in the evening with your friends or to a dance, you'd take everything off – I mean everything would be smelling of tobacco.

About five years after I started, they started introducing machines to make the whole cigarette. They introduced these machines gradually, so they didn't get rid of all the girls, but they became very, very strict with us. It was like school. We weren't allowed to talk to our neighbour. Immediately that Mrs Murray left the room, there'd be a noise – people would start talking. After a while, Mrs Murray would come back in and you'd hear a voice booming out, 'I've been watching you for the last half hour, number 242. Tomorrow your seat will be changed!'

Then they took liberties because they didn't really need us any more. Machines were coming in and they were looking to lay us off. They started picking out all the cigarettes that would normally have been passed. The foreladies started to find fault. We became terrified of them. Once, the forelady took out a lot of my cigarettes, and I had this little learner cutter who was really spoiling my work. The forelady called me out, and said, 'I can't understand your work, maker.' So I said, 'Well, I think it's this learner cutter who's spoiling my work.' She said, 'You are not paid to think, maker! We expect you to do good work. It's nothing to do with it.' So I had to stand there like a lemon, but I couldn't answer back. Eventually, the factory went fully over to machines and everyone was laid off. There were no hand-made cigarettes any more.

Freda Ruben

My mother went out washing. She charged one and six for the whole wash. She used to go and do it in their homes. I remember one day when she'd done a day's washing she came home – and our Morrie was born! She was so heavily pregnant and we'd begged her not to go, but she needed the money, and she had my brother as soon as she'd got back home. She didn't go to hospital – she just had Morrie there and then after a hard day's washing.

Joseph Henry Yarwood

I had a job while I was still at school. I worked for a baker. I used to help him pull the barrow round delivering bread. We started at nine in the morning and we worked till six in the evening, and at the end of the day he gave me ninepence and a loaf.

Mrs G. Edwards

When you went to the bakers to buy your bread, they always weighed it on a scale. The big loaves weighed about two pounds. If it didn't weigh that, they used to make it up with what they called the 'makeweight'. That was a big loaf at the side of the scales and they'd cut a lump off and put it on the scales so that you got what you paid for.

Joseph Henry Yarwood

I got a job with a greengrocer who supplied high-class houses in the Clapham Common area. I started at nine o'clock and delivered baskets of fruit and vegetables to the big houses and he gave me ninepence and a bag of vegetables.

Daniel Davis

There were two different kinds of tailoring work. In the cheaper line of work, in the East End of London, everybody had a job to do. One person made the material ready for the machiner and then he gave part of it to the presser to press out. He only had to get the garment ready for the other people. In the better class of work, you had to make an entire garment. You had to do everything, your own pressing, your own machining. There was a special cutter there who would cut the garment and give it over to the tailor. The tailor used to make the first fitting, and when it came back again he used to do the second fitting, and in many cases there'd be a third fitting. The customer paid so much for each fitting.

Mr F. Davies

My father was a tailor who specialised in waistcoats. After the season was finished in July, all the gentry left London and there was no work for the tailor at all. Things got really bad. There was no money coming in and no dole, so we had to go to the soup kitchen. It was either that or starve. We were also part of a great tradition; my father's suit, or his rings, would be brought out on Friday and my mother would go up the pawn shop first thing on Monday. It wasn't just us. Everybody was the same.

May Pawsey

Before I started sewing, I was put to work sweeping and dusting the sewing rooms. We had to take all the pins out from the dirt in the morning by putting the dirt into a sieve and shaking it. We had much more work during the season. The Derby and Ascot were very important and then it faded out because London became empty in August and they didn't want us, so they sacked the work crew. We knew when the end of the season was coming when we heard the lavender girls on the streets, with their big baskets of lavender, singing:

> 'Won't you buy my sweet blooming lavender?
> Sixteen branches for a penny.
> Buy it once and buy it twice,
> It makes your clothes smell very nice.

Daniel Davis

I was apprenticed from the Board of Guardians, and they said, 'How would you like to go into ladies' tailoring?' 'Well,' I said, 'I wouldn't mind. I'll try.' So I was sent to a place in Shaftesbury Avenue and got on very well there. I was apprenticed for five years and the guv'nor put me under a Jewish Frenchman. For the first twelve months, I was sent doing errands, buying the cloth and silks. I learnt the prices of the stuff better than the guv'nor! And I kept my eyes open, and I used to watch this Frenchman like a cat watches a mouse. After twelve months I went down to the guv'nor, and I said, 'I've been running about for twelve months,' I says. 'Don't you think I ought to be put on a table?' So he thought to himself it was a bright idea and he put me under this Frenchman.

In six months I had made my first suit complete, on my own. It was the best class of work and I had to do everything, including 'felling', which is when the lining is basted down. Felling is very delicate work – the lining has to be felled with small stitches to hold it onto the material. So the guv'nor examined the suit and eventually, he took sixpence from his pocket and gave it to me as an encouragement! After that, I was put on regular.

Half the way into my apprenticeship, I decided that it was time that I received lessons on cutting. So I asked the Frenchman. Now, it might seem funny, but he didn't know how to cut himself. He used to cut material, baste it together and then fit it on the customer. A baste is a large white tacking stitch to hold different parts of the garment together before you make it firm. So he said, 'What d'you want to know cutting for?' What he meant was that he couldn't teach me – because he didn't know himself. He said, 'It's nothing. You just cut the cloth like this, you baste it together, and you fit it on the customer.' I thought to myself, 'That's no good to me.' So I went to the Board of Guardians and I explained the matter and they said that they would send me to the Polytechnic just opposite Selfridges to take lessons. There was a cutting school there. So the guv'nor used to let me go there one day a week to learn. I learnt to do the pattern cutting, and then I practised during the week because the guv'nor gave me a length of material to work on.

Freda Ruben

When I left school at fourteen, I became a dress-machinist. I came home one dinnertime and I told Mother how bad I felt in that workshop. My mother said, 'Don't go back there – too much hard work.' So I left and started at Millers, Greenfield Street. I started right away on the machine and my wages were a shilling a week. A shilling a week! My mother used to sit by the gate on Friday evening, waiting for me to bring the shilling home. There were six of us working there – all machinists. They were very nice to me. One used to sew half a crown in my coat sleeve. I'd take my coat off and find the half a crown sewn into it. They knew I was poor.

One day when I arrived at work and it was pouring with rain, Mrs Miller, who owned the workshop, took me opposite to a shop, threw my shoes in the gutter and bought me a new pair. Now, my mother would never let us wear old things from anybody – we weren't allowed hand-me-downs. If we couldn't buy it, we never had it. So when got home and Mother saw these new shoes, she was annoyed. 'What's this?' she asked me. I started crying. I said, 'My feet were all wet, and Mrs Miller says to me, "You'll get pneumonia – you won't be able to work, and what will your mother do?"' So mother took me across to a little shop and bought me a pair of shoes and threw Mrs Miller's straight in the gutter.

Bessy Ruben

My mother's cousin had a very small workshop in the Cannon Street Road. It was just a room at the very top of the house with a skylight. He didn't employ a lot of people. He did his own work. Things became very busy towards Christmas and Easter, and the work had to be done. I was on school holiday and he came round and said, 'You come over and do some stitching for me, I'll treat you.' So I did. He showed me what to do – the bottom of a coat and the inside of the sleeve. He did such good handwork.

Mamie

I remember Wilson and Carter, the drapery store, which we patronised most. We were always met by a shop walker, and they really were characters in appearance and manner. They wore frock coats and cravats and always addressed you as 'Madam', and led you with an exaggerated walk to the department that you wished to go to. I remember them pulling out a bamboo chair for Mother to sit at the counter to make her purchase.

Miss Earnshaw

We never bought goods on credit – we always paid. We used to go into this shop run by a man called Garfinkle in Dean Street. Garfinkle stood there with a book open in front of him and he'd put a ha'penny here and a ha'penny there, all the way down. And then when people came at the end of the week to pay up, their bit of paper didn't tally with his book – but his book was always right.

Daniel Davis

We used to go on the book – but that was a dangerous business, because many times the shopkeeper used to put extra money on the book. My wife's grandfather used to go to synagogue every morning, and when he came back he used to stand on the balcony to get a bit of fresh air. The grocery shop was just facing him and the grocer kept milk in large churns just outside the door. Well, one morning my grandfather watched as a man came along the road with a jug, opened the lid of one of the urns and helped himself to a jugful of milk. Then, when the shop opened, he watched the grocer come out and empty a jugful of water into each of the milk churns. Later that day, he went down to the shop and started talking to the grocer. He said, in Yiddish, 'You know what I saw this morning?' The grocer said, 'What?' He said, 'I saw a man come up from the lodging house with a jug and he opened your milk and he helped himself.' 'Did he take much?' asked the grocer. 'Not really,' said my grandfather, 'he only took as much as you put water in.'

Jack Brahms

We used to do our little bits of shopping at Mr Garfinkle's shop. I asked him if he wanted any help in the evening. 'Yes,' he said, so I started working there every Monday, Tuesday, Wednesday and Thursday evening. I would leave at half past ten, just before he closed. All I was doing was weighing up sugar, flour, or whatever he wanted weighing up. I was paid with a bag of peanuts at the end of the week, and since I was only twelve, that seemed very fair to me.

When I left school I took a job in a grocery shop in Wentworth

Street. I was there for about six months. In those days, we sold broken biscuits for fourpence a pound, and one Sunday morning I took a little bit of biscuit, and the shopowner said, 'Go home and tell your father I want him.' So I went home – I didn't know what for – and told my dad that 'The guv'nor wants to see you – I don't know why.' It turned out it was because I'd taken a broken biscuit. He said to me, 'Well, if you can take a broken biscuit, you can take something else, can't you?' I shall never forget that as long as I live.

Mrs Crosby

My dad was what they called a journeyman butcher – he went out around the country and bought these animals, and then came back to the abattoir at the bottom of Brook Street, to have them slaughtered. Then he sold the meat on the stall.

There were about six butcher's stalls by the old police station, all competing against one another. In those days you could get a shoulder of lamb for one and six. You could get a leg of lamb for two shillings. Brisket was fourpence a pound, and pieces of beef were just thruppence a pound. One day an old lady came and said she wanted big pieces – so my dad said – because he was a bit humorous – 'If you wait a minute I'll sew them together and make you a roast.'

The stall always had a clean cloth with the meat all laid out nicely, and there were the S hooks with all the legs and shoulders and poultry and sausages hanging – it looked lovely. We started on the stall at six in the morning on Saturday and we didn't finish until one o'clock on the Sunday morning. Then Dad bought a shop in Brook Street. He had it converted into a butcher's shop, but he still had the stall in the market. At Christmas it was beautiful – there were all these pigs with oranges in their mouths, lambs and beef all hanging out. Some people were really hard up, and they had what they called a shilling wrap-up where you got a few potatoes, carrots, onions and a few pieces of beef – ends of beef – and a rabbit. If there were any sausages left they'd put those in too. There was no electricity on the stall, just naphtha lamps for light, and to keep warm in the winter you had a little round stove, although you had to keep it away from the meat. The lamps did smell, though.

There were no cold stores, so my father couldn't store meat, he just had to get rid of it – and some people would wait until late at night when any meat left over had to be sold off at auction. I've seen a leg of lamb go for eleven pence.

My father never sold live poultry – they did at the Public Hall though, and rabbits, and little dogs in crates. The farmers would sell them, and there were men who bred dogs for pets. Then there were eggs – eight pence to a shilling a dozen – but you got thirteen – what they called a baker's dozen. I worked on the market when I was thirteen and I enjoyed it. It was interesting – you met such a lot of people. We knew all the other stall-holders. I've watched them kill the cows and sheep and lambs – and they used to skull the pigs. I wasn't frightened – but the pigs used to scream. They used to put them in boiling water, alive, because if they had been killed first, they wouldn't have turned out white. Uncle Bill was a champion pig killer, and when he used to kill them they were really white. I watched him scrape the hair off. They killed the cows with a poleaxe, but the pigs, they used to slit their throats.

On the other stalls there was jewellery, and you could buy bits of material and perhaps a little girl's dress for one and eleven. There were the women with the Southport shrimp stalls on a Wednesday – just a few of them because most had push-stalls in the Public Halls. Some of them used to walk from Southport, pushing their little trolleys. They used to wear a bonnet with a frill – in fact I used to wear that too, with a flap down the back – but always nice and clean. And we wore dresses with the big puff sleeves and a white apron. Some dresses were really nicely embroidered. Some had a black skirt, and some checked.

Mrs Avery

In the morning we would take the shutters down, take the bar off, the lock off, and three shutters that was the door. If we had any kind of a parcel in our hand, we threw it in first before we went in – we were dead scared, because there were rats in the shop. We always took something to throw in the shop before we went in there. Then, when we went in, we used to go around the back of the counter, to turn the gas on, to light the light at the back. It was black dark. We were dead scared.

We had a cage to catch the rats in. And Billy Brewers, this old barber who had a shop further along, he had a terrier dog. Every morning I used to find him to come and get the cage with the rats in. And where the Swing Bridge comes on to the Sandhill, he used to open the cage and let the rat out, and the dog used to go for the rat and he used to catch them just like that.

Allott Smith

I used to deliver the groceries, and sometimes I got a penny off somebody, or an apple, and if anybody paid the bill, you always got a quarter of sweets. When I first started in Walter Wilson's, the manager said, 'Now, there's some sweet jars there.' There wasn't much to choose from – mint imperials, caramel, black mints. 'Eat as many as you like, but don't steal.' About a week or two after he said, 'I haven't seen you eating any sweets lately, Allott.' I said 'No, I've got sick of them.' He says, 'That's what I told you to get them for, we always do that with errand boys. I tell them to eat them, I don't mind how many you eat. Then after a while, they can't look at them.'

James Oates

When we got to Ireland my father's sister had a little tea shop. This was in Cootehil. On market day she used to set out cups of tea for refreshments for the farmers, and she used to sit at the door with a great big black dress and a big apron on, and they used to throw her coins as they were going out the door.

Ted Harrison

There were two doctors in Hoxton – Dr Sullivan and Dr Llewellyn. Some people favoured one, some favoured the other. Some people didn't like Sullivan because he had no bedside manner. He was very abrupt. For the doctor to come round to your house, it was sixpence, and then you'd go back to the doctor's place and he'd make up the medicine. If you couldn't afford a doctor, you paid thruppence and went down the dispensary on Wilson Street. You'd sit in there, lined up for two or three hours. If you didn't have a cold when you went in, you ruddy well did when you came out. They always used to give you cod liver oil. It was like eating raw fish. I didn't like it. They held your nose and shoved it down. There was no option. If ever there was anything very wrong with you, you went 'down the slope' to the workhouse infirmary. If they thought you were going to die, they took you inside. You didn't need a letter, they'd just take you in. I was taken there in a horse-drawn ambulance. Everyone used to call it the 'fever cart'.

Mrs Brown

When I was twenty I left to be a nurse. I started at the Royal Victoria Infirmary in Newcastle, which was a new hospital in 1907. I was there until my feet let me down, I had terribly blistered feet. I worked sixty-five hours a week and I got no wages for three months. I had nothing except my keep, as I lived in. At night I used to be so tired I used to scream when I put my feet on the bed. It was exceptionally strict. You were never allowed to start a conversation, you were never allowed to speak unless you were spoken to, and you were never allowed to walk in front of a senior. You had to do exactly what you were told – you could never answer back. You had no social life at all. I remember saying to a sister that I had an appointment with my young man, and she said, 'Nurses in training have no business to make appointments.' I wasn't allowed to go.

Mildred Ransom

When Mrs Grundy realised that while training, girls and men sat side by side listening to technical lectures in physiology and anatomy, she said it was 'impossible for women to do this without losing their modesty.'

'And what about men's modesty?' someone asked – and while the old lady was trying to remember what did happen to men's modesty, another objector called out, 'I feel certain that if women were doctors they would sooner or later be called in to doctor men, and how terribly improper that would be.' 'No worse than a man doctoring a woman,' somebody replied cheerfully. 'And what about the impropriety of a nurse putting on her apron and nursing men? Men would indeed be in the soup if left alone to get well.' 'That,' said Mrs Grundy comfortably, 'is different. For a woman to know all a doctor must know would inevitably "unsex" a woman.'

I began by qualifying as a Sanitary Inspector and lecturing on health. The general public had discovered 'hygiene' and liked lectures, and I obtained engagements. The work was well paid and interesting. I was engaged at one time by a Midland County Council to go and stay for three months in the county town and give four lectures a week in the villages nearby. If the village was inaccessible by train or bicycle the local hotel was contracted to drive me, and when we became friendly, the driver used to bring a colossal landau round, horsed with one steady old horse and one almost unbroken. He said he felt sure I should not mind, and it was such a good way to break in a young 'un, and the hotel would not charge extra. The young 'un was so unbroken that a second man used to get down and run alongside to calm his nerves when we met a pig or a traction engine or anything exciting. We used to arrive in magnificent style at the local rectory, with one man running, the young 'un rearing, and me sitting in state in the enormous turnout.

I was in lodgings with a dear old lady who prophesied that 'something black would come down the chimney' to remove me when I worked on Sunday. Being young and enthusiastic I pressed on her the value of the vote, and pointed out her wrongs in being deprived of representation. She put up with these eccentric ideas for some time, considering that youth and common sense never did go together, but when I let out that in my mature opinion there was no reason why women, who I thought formed the more spiritual sex, should be debarred from the priesthood, that got her going and she replied, 'A woman be a parson! Didn't St Paul say she weren't to speak in church?' 'He did. And he said too that she wasn't to plait her hair.' The old lady patted the plaits of what remained of a handsome head of hair. ''E 'adn't no call to trouble about that,' she said firmly.

John William Dorgan

The wheelwright was an important job because there were few motor cars. It was all horses and carts. Mr Tommy Tulley was the wheelwright's name and he took me on because he liked the look of me. I was very happy there, but I'd only worked a few months when I had an accident. I was polishing one of the machines in the workshop and my finger got entangled with the cogs. It mangled my finger up to the knuckle. I went up to see Dr Spence, who said, 'Jack, should I take the finger off or not?' I said no but I wish I had because it's been a bother all my life. That finished me as a wheelwright.

Jenny Billis

My father was a bootmaker and I used to take him his tea. Mother used to send my brother and I to the workshop with his tea in a can. I can remember my father always having a mouthful of nails, and when we went in it would be very dim and somebody would say, 'Sadliemein'. We didn't know what it meant. When we asked our father, he said, 'It means stop swearing.'

HOME

Albert 'Smiler' Marshall

On leaving school there were few openings for girls, who nearly all went into service. The pay was three and sixpence per week. Hours were long, and there was only one half-day off each week.

Mrs G. Edwards

My first job was at Wetherby Gardens in the West End of London. I was fifteen years old and was an under-nurse in the nursery. The Head Nurse was above me. I called her 'Nurse' and she called me by my Christian name. The house had a cook, a kitchen maid, a housemaid, a parlour maid, a coachman and a groom. My job involved attending to the children. I got up at six o'clock to walk the children's dog round the square. Then I went downstairs to fetch anything up for the children. I used to have to take their shoes and boots down to be cleaned in the kitchen. The children lived in the nursery and we had our food sent up to us, but sometimes the two eldest children went down to dine with the family and I would go down with them to serve them. I stood in the dining room with them.

I lived up at the top of the house in a room I shared with two other servants. That Christmas, we all hung our stockings out and I thought we were just hanging them out for fun, but the other girls put things in my stocking. It was ever so nice really. Apart from that, I didn't really have anything to do with the servants. There was no reason for me to be with them. I only went back to my home in

Brixton about once a fortnight, for an afternoon off. I used to get very homesick. I missed my home but my mother said I must stay for a year so I could get a character reference. But I decided I didn't want to be with children again, so after that I became a parlour maid at a house on Streatham Hill.

Mary Keen

I worked for Mrs Johnson in a big Victorian house with long flights of steps. I cleaned the steps with the hearth-stone and I did the brass, dusted the front door, cleaned the area and the bits around it, and then swept the hall. I worked from eight in the morning until eight at night and on Sunday from eight until four, and I was paid two shillings a week.

Working conditions were very bad. Mrs Johnson never so much as offered me a cup of tea. I had my midday dinner and tea, but I didn't get enough to eat because she was a very mean type of woman. I didn't like her. She had four children – Billy, a boy of my age, Douglas, ten, Mabel, six and Maurice, three. I had to mind Maurice because the two elder boys went to school. Mabel went sometimes but she wasn't very strong. She had heart trouble. Between two and five, I took Mabel and Maurice walking in a blessed cart. It was all right in the summer but very cold in the winter. I walked to work and I got very tired because I was only a skinny little thing and my feet and legs were very bad.

I'd been with Mrs Johnson for nearly a year when my mother said to me, 'Tell her you won't be coming any more. You'll be leaving her next week because I'm going to have a baby.' Mrs Johnson didn't like that very much, but I was very glad. I went home on the next Saturday and the baby had already arrived – a little fair-haired, blue-eyed girl. She was a dear little thing. My mother was in bed for just over a week and I took charge of her.

Connie Edgerton

I did all kinds of things for this Mr Huddleston, but I didn't like his ways. One time he went away for the weekend and he brought me back a pair of kid gloves. They were very nice gloves, so I thanked him. But the next time I threw them back at him, because he wanted me to go with him. Well, this old fellow, he didn't want to take no for an answer, and every time from then on he started chasing me round this big oval table in the middle of the room. I used to set off and he would be running after me. I've had him on the floor many times because he used to fall on the slippery floor and as soon as he fell, I ran out. Well, then I got a young man, he was the head baker for the Co-Op, and I'd told him about this old fellow. One night he came up and this old fellow was after me and I heard my boy come into the back door. I made a dive and got away before the old fellow caught me. My boy, he'd have knocked him down, but I didn't want him to be making any bother. This night the old fellow, he'd got his pay packet and was accusing me of stealing a half-sovereign, or something out of it. 'The old bugger,' my boy said, 'you go to bed Connie, and I'll tell you what goes on.' He went and he lay on the rug near the fire all night and then when the ashes had cooled he poked away and found the half-sovereign.

Ronald Chamberlain

In Canonbury, the houses were rather large. Our house was four stories, with a little staircase leading to an attic where the servant had her bedroom. It was usual in these houses to have some kind of help. A woman with a family couldn't really look after a house without any of the modern conveniences. There was no central heating, so fires had to be lit. The whole place had to be swept in old-fashioned ways. The more affluent people, certainly the people in Highbury New Park in North London, would have several maids and a cook and so on. My father, with his very humble income as a Post Office clerk, had the cheapest form of labour – a little girl straight from school, fourteen or fifteen. She had her keep, her board and lodgings and five or six shillings a week. She had to work awfully hard.

My mother never thought she was being oppressive to the little girl. She wasn't being brutal or anything like that – it was the

'Cats' meat man' on a slum street, London, 1905.
His cat can be seen between the wheels of his barrow.

The house party at Stonor Park, Henley on Thames,
gathered for a pheasant shoot.

accepted way of life. The little girl would bring in her alarm clock to be wound by my father, who would wind it and set it for half past six the next morning. At half six, the girl would wake up, make some porridge, light a fire and she would work right through the day with very little breaks. She'd have her meals by herself in the kitchen and go to bed at half past nine. She had two little bits of freedom in the week: one evening off, but she had to be in again sharp at ten and Sunday afternoon off. Other than that, she worked tremendously hard. Indeed, on more than one occasion, when they couldn't stand it any more, one of these poor little girls would run away. I remember going with my mother down to some part of Islington where one of the girls came from to see what had happened to her. Not to fetch her back – she wouldn't want to come back – but to see that she hadn't come to any harm. My mother was really a very kind person.

Ethel Barlow

When I was still at school, I used to have to go and help this old German woman. This old girl used to make me scrub the floor. If I didn't do it properly she used to hit me round the earhole. I'd go home and cry and tell my mum but she'd just say, 'I suppose you didn't do it properly.' One day, the woman said I'd pinched a farthing, but I hadn't. She said she'd have me locked up. She was horrible.

Frank Honey

I was never forced to go out to work. I was expected to, let's put it that way. In those days everybody had to. I was one of a big family and every bit of money was welcome to my mother.

My father would never let me be a newsboy. That was undignified. I couldn't be a newsboy, but if I worked in a house where I wasn't seen, that was all right. My father was the foundry foreman at H. M. Biggleston's and I worked for one of the family whilst still at school. I used to go as a houseboy and I had to be there at six o'clock in the morning and I stayed till eight. Then I walked down to St Peter's to school. I worked there for about two years when the family closed their house down and I got another houseboy's job with a wine merchant's family. They had a house at South Canterbury, but I didn't like that place at all. It was hard work. They had boys going to King's School and they used to have these heavy brogue shoes and I had to clean them with a skin blacking. That was one thing I didn't like there. Anyway, I gave that job up.

When I gave my second houseboy's job up, I went doing other odd jobs around Canterbury, including the veterinary surgeon's job, bottle washing, running his errands and still going out with him in the evenings to the farms. In addition to that, I was with other boys too up at the stations carrying parcels for a ha'penny or a penny, to various parts of Canterbury.

I went with another boy who used to live in Notley Street and his father used to do shoe repairs, and he had to take these shoes back one night to a house in the New Dover Road: I think he was a captain in the army. They had a very big house and a racehorse, and the daughter even had a Shetland pony. We went to this house and the lady invited us in, and she said to this other boy, 'Do you want a job?' He said, 'No.' But I said, 'I do!' So I got a houseboy's job there and that was the best job I've ever had in my life as a boy. Again I had to be there by six o'clock in the morning.

My first job was to groom two big black retrievers they had, and then I had to let them out into the garden. Then I used to have to chop the wood and clean the shoes, the knives and forks. There was no stainless steel cutlery in those days. We used to use brick dust, but the beauty of that job as far as I was concerned was that I had a jolly good breakfast. Prior to that I might have taken a piece of bread and butter to school with me when I went out, but I used to get eggs and bacon there – something I never got at home. I could also work there on Saturday mornings, and if I worked that, I got an extra sixpence on top of the two shillings. Of course, I only got about a penny or two of that, because in those days we only got about a ha'penny a week pocket money.

In addition to all my part-time jobs, we all had our chores at home as well. There was always Dad's boots and shoes to be cleaned and the knives and forks – and we had to scrub the big table and chairs once or twice a week: chop the wood, fetch the coal, and fill the boiler on the kitchener. I was scrubbing floors when I was eight. It wasn't all pleasure, I can tell you, but we didn't regard it as a particular hardship.

Ray Head

My father was a policeman and he was moving from what you might call the upper labouring class to the lower middle class, and the result was that he built his own house in Hounslow. It cost £250 and it had a kitchen, dining room, two lounges, three bedrooms but no inside toilet or bathroom. It had a bay window and Venetian blinds – he was imitating the next grade up – getting above his station, if you like. He named the house 'Longleat' because he came from Wiltshire and Longleat was the prestigious place of his youth. Naming your house made it a little above the cottages, which were all numbered.

Ernest Hugh Haire

We lived in Rock Ferry, a part of Birkenhead that contained large houses with gardens, stables and coachmen. My father had a grocer's shop and our drawing room was above the shop. It was one of those Victorian drawing rooms with an oval table and a stereoscope on it. The visitor would come in, look through the stereoscope and see its three dimensions. If I walked from our house round the corner, it was only houses for a hundred yards and then it was farmland.

Rose Trinder

We all had our districts, and the very fact that you lived at New Cross meant you were someone better than people who lived in Deptford. I mean, the Deptford people would in their way think themselves someone better than those that came from the other side of the river. Anyone the other side of the river were seen as rough people. Now, I've heard of people who lived at Islington who were quite respectable and lived in nice houses. But at the time, the general impression was in our district, that as there were more working-class people there was likely to be more pub crawlers, dancing on the pavements when the public houses shut, and that sort of thing. In New Cross you were that little bit higher and you wouldn't do that sort of thing in the street. And if you went a little bit further along to Lewisham or Bromley, you were really sociably somebody, you know. You never did vulgar things like sing in the street or anything. Oh no! Good Heavens no! You were made to know your districts in London. The very fact, I don't know if it was something in your speech, or what it was, or whether it was just the district you lived in, but the districts kept themselves socially apart.

An aunt of mine that lived at Bromley, her husband happened to sell papers and magazines and printing material, that sort of thing, and she always had a daily maid. We were allowed to visit the day the maid was out – to keep the class, you see. She wouldn't have it known that she knew us people that lived in Deptford or New Cross. Her name was Sarah Ann, but she wouldn't be called Sarah Ann – she was Maud. No one ever called unless you sent the card saying you were going to call and that sort of thing.

Mrs G. Edwards

I grew up in Brixton. My father was a clock-maker and he used to go up to the big houses to attend to their clocks. Our house had three rooms downstairs – a kitchen, a little sitting room and a parlour – and three rooms upstairs. The toilet was outside. There were eight of us living there – Mother and Father and six children. The rooms were small but we had a garden. We were really quite comfortable compared to some people. The only time we were hard up was when people didn't pay their bills, but at Christmas time, people usually paid up and we were quite well off. Brixton was a respectable area, full of nice working-class people. There was a new school and I knew all the children. I liked it there. Over time people started to move out of the area because they wanted something better: they wanted to buy their own houses. A lot of new houses were being built elsewhere and you could get them cheaply.

William George Holbrook

I knew I couldn't spend my whole life working on a farm so I looked around and I saw situations advertised in a local paper. So I wrote to them and I got letters back and my mother saw the letters and opened them. She got on to me: 'You be content with the job you've got!' she said. But I didn't listen. I got a job as a houseboy in a big house with a garden of five or six acres with fruit trees. He was a businessman. I had to clean the boots, take care of the pony, clean the harness and chop the wood. He used to drive his trap to his business in London and I used to drive it back. I remember one Saturday morning, he came down while I was sawing some logs. Well, I wasn't sawing them. All I'd done was go down to the barn with a saw, I sat down and read a paper called *The Union Jack*. He came in and said, 'How many logs have you sawn?' I hadn't sawn any so I pointed at a log and said, 'When I've done this one, sir, and when I have done two more, I'll have done three.' He walked away with a smile.

Alfred West

I had bad bronchitis and the doctor said I should get a job in the open air, so I started work in a gentleman's house at the top of a hill in a pine forest. The family were all in government work abroad. The two boys would work for two years and save up four months holiday and then they'd spend it together at the house. The old gentleman – 'Daddy' as they called him – was wonderful. He was riding horses to the hunt until he was eighty-eight.

I helped with the horses, the garden, and I looked after Daddy when we went shooting. I loaded his guns and looked after him in general. We'd leave Newport at six in the morning, put the dogs and the guns in a great big car and go for a day's shooting in Herefordshire. We'd stop at one of the hotels in Monmouth at eight and then we'd go on to the shoot. The game was wonderful. I used to be treated very well. When I was working in the stables, washing down the horses after a hunt, I was able to go into the servants' quarters in the 'Big House' and I was given the same food the toffs had had, after they'd finished with it. There was pheasant, duck and venison. It built me up no end. My health improved while I was there, but in the end I became too old for the job. They wanted someone younger, but while I was there, I fitted in wonderfully. The young toffs taught me a lot.

Minnie Lane

My brother Manny wanted to be a gentleman's valet, and he went off to a house in Manchester. He was away for three months, and at four o'clock one Sunday morning we heard a noise. Mother got up. 'There's a knock on the window!' she said. 'See who it is!' So I looked through the window. I couldn't see anything, but then we heard, 'It's Munny! From Munchester!' It was my brother and he'd picked up the Northern way of talking. 'Ooh,' said my mother, 'let him in.' And there he was. We asked him why he'd come home and he said that the gentleman he worked for wanted him to cut his toenails, and he wouldn't do it. He'd do a lot of things, but he wouldn't do that.

Lena Burton

We had no gas, so we had to have oil lamps. I remember the first gas-jet we had – we were thrilled to bits. My mother used to have to light the fire in the kitchen to warm the water to wash. We had a boiler next to the fire and the oven on the other side. We had to get the hot water out of there.

On the floor we had lino and home-made peg rugs. My mother had a sideboard, and she loved stuffed birds in those glass containers. We had three, a big owl on one side, and three little ones on the other – the middle one was a hawk that was caught at the open rubbish tip we called the middens. There were no dustbins, and you used to throw stuff at the bottom of the yard in what was a cess pool, I suppose. We used to have to go down there to the toilets – there were three at the bottom of the yard.

We didn't have a parlour – it was a tin tub in front of the fire, always. We had a living room and the kitchen and two pretty big bedrooms. We three girls had to sleep in one with two beds.

Bath time: a wife washes her husband in a slum dwelling c.1901.

A middle-class family having tea in 1910.

Minnie Lane

In our kitchen, there was a little fireplace, a coal bin, your cooker, a sink, and underneath the sink was your dustbin – a pail. The sink was a yellow thing – one tap – and very shallow. You had a bowl for washing up. There was a bit of cork to stop the water going down.

The walls of the kitchen were whitewashed brick. There was a dresser in the kitchen too – you'd keep all your plates on racks. We used to pile them up, and you'd have your plates at the top and then cupboards underneath. The cups were in the front room on the dresser and the glasses in the bottom of the living-room dresser. My mother would cook everything on the range. And when she was doing toast, she had a fork, and would toast it in front of the fire – beautiful. And kippers – she'd put them on top of the coal, without a pan. They'd come up beautifully.

Daniel Davis

We lived above my father's tailor shop in Beak Street. We had the first floor with three rooms. My father had the big room on the top floor as his workshop. The main room was the sitting room cum bedroom where my parents slept. At one time there was a piano in there, but my father didn't keep up the payments. There were a few pictures round the walls. In the kitchen was a dining table cum work top with kitchen chairs. In the other room was a double bed for us children. The rest of the house was taken by a clerk who was a dress maker. We had outside flush toilets and no bathroom. The only water in the house was up on the second floor. There was a sink with a cold water tap. For our baths and our domestic washing, we went to Marshall Street.

May Pawsey

We didn't have baths in our houses so we all ran down on Friday nights to the Chelsea Town Hall to line up for a bath for tuppence. You were in a cubicle and they put the hot and cold water in from outside, so you had to be sure the temperature was right before you let the ladies shut the door. If you didn't, you froze and had to call out for some more hot water, and when it came you had to be careful because it was boiling. We were allowed half an hour. If you took longer, the ladies shouted, 'Hurry up, number so-and-so!'

Mary Maughan

Friday night was bath night, a big tub used to hang in the wall in the back yard. My three sisters all had blonde hair, you got a strip of hair and wrapped it around, tied it at the bottom, and the next morning it all came out in ringlets. That was my job.

And I had to clean at home, help Mother with the washing and all things like that, but you felt it was your duty, it was a big family. Stone-built houses, terraces, with big fires, you were never cold. You wore laced boots and the quality was so good they passed on to the next one, and we wore white embroidery pinafores, velvet dresses if you could afford it on the Sunday, and stockings. Your feet were never wet, not in real leather boots. I don't remember wearing a hat, we all had long hair, the girls. The boys had a rubber collar tied with a bit of ribbon.

Nancy Lambert

Some girls used to go to school in plaits. My mother would never let us have our hair in plaits, no matter how we wanted to, but we all had ringlets, there was only one straight-haired one in the family. My mother used to look at our heads, wash our hair, twist the curls. We had our necks washed and scrubbed, though we didn't have a bathroom, just the tin bath. We all had lovely complexions as children. A woman asked, 'What soap do you use for your family?' Mother said, 'Watson's Matchless Cleansing Carbolic, or the Co-Op White Windsor' – cos that was a bit dearer. 'The first gets the cleanest water.' That was true, cos all the water had to be carried up and down stairs from the back yard.

Minnie Lane

If we didn't go to Goulston Street baths, we'd bath in this big zinc bath one after the other in the same water. By the time we was finished, it was like ink.

Ethel Barlow

The people around us were very poor. Next to our house was an old girl with a wooden leg and her old husband. They used to sell beetroots at the top of the road. A penny for the beetroots and a ha'penny for a big bunch of mint. When you went into their house, it had no furniture, no lino, nothing. All they had was bare boards. Everyone was poor. Most people had to steal. You'd go into a shop and come out with a pocket full of biscuits or something. None of us wore shoes and socks. All I had was a dress, like an old frock. The winters were colder in those days. We seemed to have six months of snow and ice.

James Bowles

A funny thing happened – a lady came to our house and said, 'You must get your children out of the valley, we don't want the children to be interbred.' And my family did get out of the valley and were married out of the valley. But there were a lot of brothers and sisters. There was a lot of intermarriage, but they hadn't much chance to do anything different. You couldn't go anywhere unless you walked – so you couldn't go far.

Gertrude McCracken

Most cottages in those days kept their own backyard pig, feeding it on household scraps and vegetable peelings boiled up in the copper and mixed with meal. The day the pig had to die was all bustle. The copper was filled and lit, and a bonfire was made ready to burn the hairs off the carcass. A little man called Mr Payne cycled from Warminster and, if we were within earshot, we heard the pig squealing like billy-oh, and then utter silence. It was ghastly. Nothing was wasted from the pig – the offal and the fleck, the tummy lining,

Domestic Economy School: 'Housewifery, Cookery & Laundry,
Open for Instruction'. Domestic service. although badly paid,
provided the advantage of living in.

Maids on a Cunard vessel, Liverpool 1902.

made faggots, with brawn from the head and trotters, and black pudding from the warm blood. The sides were cured and hung up in the back kitchen. The fat was rendered down for the lard, and we children ate the scraps that were left after the lard was melted.

Mrs Temperley

Every year we killed two pigs for Christmas, one on Monday and one the next. The kitchen table was occupied, we used to make the sausages on that. No sink, so we had to carry the water. We had to go outside to empty the water, and we had to go out to the toilet, coalhouse and pantry. In the winter everything had to be carried in before dark. The meat and bacon was frozen, the milk was frozen. All the food was in the pantry. Many a time the two dead pigs were on the floor, on straw in the pantry, before they was hung up.

Thomas Henry Edmed

We had no drinking water on our estate, which was owned by the National Provincial Bank. We had to go a quarter of a mile to the nearest well. We had a barrow made and we put a beer barrel on it and we used to bring the water back that way. But it wasn't big enough, so we had to drink a fair amount of pond water, which we boiled first. Well, I got a goitre on my neck. The doctor said it was from the bloody pond water, and I had to go to Guy's Hospital to have it removed.

May Pawsey

Chelsea was awful. We had that power station in Battersea that used to cover everything in yellow smoke. We had two rooms and they were not very large. There were four of us – my mother and father and two little girls. We all slept in the front room with the fireplace. My parents had a large bed with brass on it and we shared a bed at the side.

Ernest Burr

Our house was a poky little place. It was in a block turning – a cul-de-sac. There were no carpets down, no furniture, just broken stuff. The rats were as big as cats. They used to make holes in the skirting boards and come out and look at you. If you blocked the hole up, they made holes somewhere else, so there was no point in it. One day when my father was with us, he trapped one with a broom and chopped its nose off. He said, 'I'll hang it on the door knocker. When the landlord comes, let him knock it off.' So he hung the rat on the knocker.

Minnie Lane

In the front room there was a dresser where you kept your crockery near the window. We used to decorate it with crinkly paper, paste, and make fans all round. It looked so pretty. There was a chest of drawers near the door, where Mother used to keep all the cheap glass she valued. In those drawers she kept all her different odds and ends. It was always in a mess and we were always cleaning it out. In the same room was a wooden table with an oilcloth that you could wash off. It was stuff that you could roll up and put away. It looked very pretty – it was all flowers.

We had a square table and wooden chairs that had to be scrubbed. Everything had to be scrubbed – the table was scrubbed – scrubbed white. There was one real wooden chair with the slats in it, and Mother had rheumatism, so my brother cut the legs short so that she could sit in it. There was a couch that opened up into a bed and you put it up during the day. We had a fire and a fireguard, black polished fire and oven. My mother used to cook on that fire and with the cinders we cleaned our cutlery. We'd save all the cinders and we'd polish our knives and forks with them.

Ellie Jackson

When we were off school there were always things we had to do for the family. We used to go down and pick up the coke that fell off the tip carts from the gas works. As the carts came along the road, the cobblestones on the Marine Parade shook the coke off and we picked it up. If it didn't shake off we hooked it off with a stick and it came in very handy for the fire.

There were six of us and Mother said, 'Dad, I wish you'd come out and get a shore job.' So the next day he did and there was a slump for three months. He went down to the old workhouse and sat round the table and was questioned and cross-questioned about all of us. He was given a cheque for five shillings worth of groceries for us all and we had to go to the workhouse twice a week and get two long loaves. That was all the help you got.

Mother used to go to the mortuary, where they had piles of blankets at the beginning of winter. She paid ninepence for one blanket and we used it all winter. She would take it back clean in the spring and get her ninepence back.

Ethel Barlow

The conditions in our house were bad. We only had paraffin lamps at first, and don't even talk about the toilets, they were terrible! We used to have to walk down the garden and round the corner to get to it. And there was no toilet roll. You used to cut up newspaper, put a bit of string through it and hang it on the tank. Every day, the toilet was blocked up! And the rats! You'd be sitting in the house and all of a sudden rats would come out the fireplace. Everyone had rats. For people living near the water, it was worse still, because the rats were bigger. Those water rats were big as cats.

We never got rid of our rats until the First World War. The Germans dropped a bomb on the donkey stable at the back of us, and when it all cleared away, we found that the rats had made a big tunnel under the earth and into all the houses. We dug some more and found a big drain hole in our front garden, where they all were. When I opened it up, there were thousands of them.

Bob Rogers

Our family had the basement back room and the basement front room and the first-floor front room. The other rooms were let out to other tenants because they helped to supplement our rent. I slept in the basement kitchen on one of those old-type folding beds. When we had another lodger come in for the night, he used to sleep with me.

Gertrude McCracken

There was no electricity in the cottages in those days, but we obtained our light from the lamp and candles. Mam's lamp really was a thing of beauty. It had a heavy pierced stand with a glass reservoir for the oil and a chased glass globe on the chimney glass. After the tea things were cleared away, a chenille cloth was placed on the table and the lamp was lighted. Dad always sat with his back to the lamp to read the paper, or sleep. Mam always sat in the circle of light with her mending and either talked to us or sang. She had a rather nice voice and was also known for whistling. I think those evenings held a kind of magic for us, with the fire glowing and blinds drawn. It gave us, I think, a feeling of security.

Being a large family, Mam always seemed to have a needle in her hands. There was no money to spare, so jumble sales were a great help. Home would come the jumble to be washed, unpicked and remade into garments. She had no patterns and after the garments were tacked together, one of us had to stand still while Mam pinned her in for what she called 'sherriping' – in other words, shearing bits off with the scissors. How I hated those fittings. To stand still for about twenty minutes was to me an utter waste of my precious time. I remember Dad having to do it once. Mam had bought a dark blanket and door curtains for thruppence, and made him a pair of working trousers. He came through the ordeal very well and thought it was a great joke. Those thruppenny pants lasted Dad nearly two years.

Ada Wayter with her eight brothers and sisters whom she rescued from a fire at their home in Battersea Rise. The children, lined up in their identical clothes, are barely a year apart.

Daniel Davis

It was a hard job to work out living accommodation in Rothschild Buildings. The bedroom was so narrow that if you put the bed in width-wise you couldn't go past it. Many times I slept on the floor. It was a terrible living. We had no furniture at all. There were a couple of cupboards in the wall – and a table and chairs. It was a terrible life. There were plenty of others like that.

Minnie Lane

Mother made a bed in the front room – she curtained it off and there was two boys sleeping in there. During the daytime, the bed was left there – never put up. The curtain was hung on two screws put in the wall. My mother slept in the bedroom with a cradle on each side. She lay there with her arms out, rocking the children to sleep. My sister used to sleep on the floor, near the fireplace.

We had a paraffin lamp, and in the front room we had gas with a mantle. We were always breaking that mantle. When you went to light it, you'd put the match too near the mantle, and bang! So Mother would send you down to Petticoat Lane to get another one. We'd go to the shop and say the mantle was faulty – but it wasn't. With luck the shopkeeper would give us another.

We had plenty of pictures in the bedroom – pictures of the family, all the faces. That's if you could keep them on the wall. If you knocked a nail, you'd had it. The wall would either come to pieces or if it didn't, you'd have creepy crawlies round the picture.

Outside on the balcony, in your gateway, there was a chute that you pushed the rubbish down, and it went right down into the dustbins at the bottom. It smelled – specially when it was stopped up. People used to stuff things like pillows down it, and it would block up. Then somebody would think of a nice idea, and they'd put a lighted match there. All of a sudden you'd see a load of smoke come up and that would put an end to the stink! Those that lived at the bottom – they had a lovely smell. They also had to put up with the cats running about in the basement – they bred like I don't know what.

I once remember throwing a cat over the top – God forgive me! I went up – it was eight stories high – and there was a cat up there and I threw it over the top. I had to close my eyes. When I looked over, it was running across the playground. It didn't kill it. There were swarms of them – wild cats – but they kept the rats and mice away.

Freda Ruben

Furniture? We had one orange box, covered over with a nice piece of material. We had no lino on the floor, but you'd have come into our house and found it white. Scrubbed white. We had three chairs. My younger sister – a boy wanted to take her home, so she said, 'I can't bring a boy home – we've only got three legs on one chair – where's he gonna sit?'

Alfred West

We lived over a stables in a mews. It was always very warm. The horses were cleared out every morning and they had a big iron rack outside the stables which was filled with all the horses' manure every morning. People came up from the country to collect this manure and we were glad for them to have it.

John William Dorgan

In 1906, we had electric lights installed in the house. We were allowed five bulbs!

Bill Owen

Our house had a kitchen, and a sink in the corner – but no tap. We had a slop store, a fire with two hobs, and a big kettle on the hob. That was on all day – it was for everything. There was one room upstairs, and there was the garret above that – the attic. A straight up and down house. You were rich if you had two up and two down, and if you had a tap in the house you were really rich! The one tap in the court was for all of us. You had to get under the tap to get washed. When it froze in winter you had to go without – or you'd get bundles of paper lit under it to thaw it out.

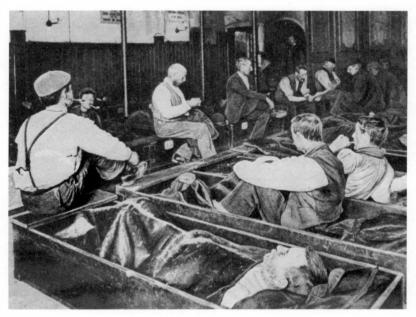

Waiting for lights out in the Salvation Army shelter,
Medland Hall, 1901.

You didn't have midwives, they had a helper – a handy woman with a shawl round her. As a kid if you saw her going into the house, you'd know there was a birth. Births, deaths and marriages – that's what they lived for in them days.

Annie Swain

Me mother the night before used to put the clothes into a big tin bath. We had the water to carry from the middle of the street in pails. Then the next morning me mother used to get up with the first shift of men at three o'clock. She would put a big pan on a great big old-fashioned fireplace, with three pails of water. Now at the side of the fireplace was a big pot which was used both by the men coming in from work and to boil the clothes on a washing day. Then I would get up with the family, get our breakfasts, and then I would start. I would get the tub in from outside, give it a good scrub, because it always went in under the pipe where the rainwater came down. Then get the stick and give it a scrub, and then, I was away to school. I would go knowing that when I came back at dinnertime, that was the day that we didn't get a dinner, we just got what we could from the pantry.

Then I would go back to school and my mother would be washing all afternoon turning the clothes inside out, scrubbing all the seams, then she would rinse them, then put them into clean boiling water, then we would put them through the great big heavy mangle which was almost like a piece of furniture in a miner's home then. We used to use blue mottled soap, and my mother had an old suet grater – we used to grate the soap with that into the water. She also used compo at tuppence a packet and soda powder. I've seen me on a frosty day, going to school and been cut and bleeding with the soda and the cold weather. And of course everything had to be beautiful with starch. Pillowcases, shirt cuffs, collars, petticoats. Everything had to be starched.

Mind, the clothes in those days were white! Sometimes we had to swill six sheets, all the men's shirts, all the chemises with three yards of stuff in every one! Then white knickers, petticoats for the children, which they wore two of every Sunday, and if you had a family of girls you'll understand what it was like, and then the nightdresses all made of calico. We had terrible times in those days, but we were always kept very clean. In those back lanes in those days, it was always to see who had the whitest clothes. It was just like a competition.

Alice Cowen

Of course we used to love coming to Ambleside, as we never cared for Newcastle all that much in the winter, although I dare say it was warmer. Grandmama had constructed three or four large wooden boxes with padlocks, and into these boxes went the kitchen paraphernalia, some of the silver, and I'm not quite sure about the china. We took up a special coach on the train and into this went the boxes, three servants, the carriage, the coachman and two horses. Mother used to get the trunks down from the attics, a round-topped trunk and some flat trunks a week before we were to come and she used to start packing all these trunks. The sewing machine went into one of them – the sewing machine! Everything we could need, the plated cake stand, the silver teaspoons, and all our clothes. Our nurse helping her to pack, then on the great day the cart would come up from the tannery and all the luggage would be piled into it and taken down to the station while we went down by tram.

We travelled by way of Carlisle, where we changed, and Oxenholme, where we changed for Windermere, and there another cart met us to take the luggage the ten miles to the house. We made the last part of the journey in a thing called the wagonette, which was an open carriage with the seat parallel to the road. We took our servants of course, and we all piled into this and were taken round to Balla Wray, where our gardener's wife had prepared delicious homemade bread and boiled egg. We always had the same the first day and in due course our luggage came round in the cart.

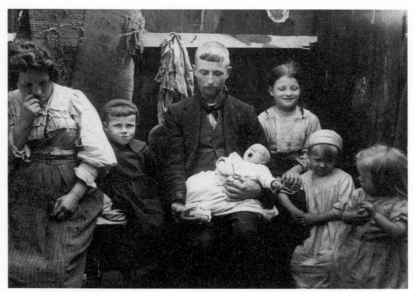

A man with a handful of pawn tickets sits with his family
in London's East End.

Harold Smelton

The bigger houses entertained frequently – it was a big thing, especially shooting parties. These took place from Yorkshire down to Hampshire, but our biggest shoot was at the Duke of Westminster's Eaton Hall, outside Chester. He was the richest man in England: King Edward would be in the party. He had his own little railway to take his guests round. When their friends arrived to stay in the Lake District, although there was not much shooting, they went mostly driving round the different hills, the different countryside, the lakes; that was the main thing.

In the area, an old lady had a carriage and pair with a coachman and a groom, who used to ride on the box with a top hat with a plume on the side. That carriage and pair was kept especially for the old lady, who used to come up for a holiday six weeks in the year. For the rest of the year they did nothing. The groom would take one horse out in the morning for exercise, put it in the light trap and go and call on his farmer friends all round the neighbourhood, and in the afternoon the other one would take the other horse and do the same.

Sonia Keppel

Number 30 Portman Square was narrow and high, each floor of which acquired significance for me as I grew older. The basement spelt breath-taking adventure and, as yet, unknown risk. The ground floor was largely a changing-room (shawls on, to go out; shawls off, to come in). The drawing-room floor was given over to fun. My day-nursery floor was a white-painted fortress, my nurse the garrison-commander; my sister's French governess, a spirited captain of the guard. The attic – my night-nursery smelt of Brasso and perspiration, and soap. And different sounds went with the floors: sepulchral voices and the clatter of mysterious vessels in the basement; muted sounds of perambulator wheels in the hall; enchanted laughter, male and female, in the drawing room; altercations in North-country English and shrill French on the nursery ramparts, accompanied by the rattle as of artillery, from an adjacent pipe; sniffs and the rustle of starchy petticoats came from the attic. The house became my orchestra, and I quickly learned the score it followed.

In the course of the day the position of the floors was reversed. I started at the top and worked my way down. First I had an uncomfortable sojourn in a hip-bath in the night-nursery, with my behind very hot, and my back very cold. Then suffocating layers of merino underclothes were piled on me, topped by a pinafore. Thereafter, I scrambled down the top flight of stairs to breakfast in the day-nursery. For me, 'night' and 'day' nursery had literal interpretations. The attic roof of the night-nursery precluded all human contact and all but a small patch of sky from my sight. The day nursery looked out on to the world, and the light and the people. After breakfast followed an unendingly delightful visit to Mamma in bed, and Papa, breakfasting in his room next door. A brief reversal to the night-nursery before going out. Then a syncopated progress down the main flight of stairs to the hall. And so out. And so in.

John William Dorgan

We moved four miles to the village of Ashington in November 1906. The Ashington colliery owned hundreds of modern houses and we moved into one of them. These houses were in blocks and they were all exactly the same. They had two bedrooms upstairs, and a kitchen and a front room downstairs. My mother and father slept in the front room and we children slept upstairs in the bedrooms.

One night, Father got home from his shift at two o'clock in the morning and he opened the front door and came into the house. He passed through the front room and heard my mother sleeping and walked through to the kitchen. He switched the light on to find that he was in the wrong house. Quietly, he put the light out and crept back through the front room and let himself out. He pulled himself together and realised he was two streets away from where he lived. He got home eventually, and the next day my mother went to apologise to the people in the other house, but they had no idea that my father had ever visited them.

DAILY LIFE

Lady Charlotte Bonham Carter

During the London season, there were many people around. It was very jolly indeed. *The Times* had a list of the balls, starting with the last week of April right to the end of the third week in July, and there were a minimum of four balls every night – six balls possibly. My mother took a house in Eton Square and held a ball for me in 1912. We got a good list of the young men who were available and a list of young ladies who we asked to be accompanied by their mother. The invitation read 'Mrs and Miss So-and-So' and sometimes the father could be dragged along as well. Fathers were often awkward about this but they could be very useful because they could take a lady into supper. Supper had to be taken downstairs unless it was a very grand house like Surrey House. Supper generally began at twelve and might consist of a clear soup, quails with white grapes and potatoes. It was a light but really delicious meal and you could take it whenever you liked. While the ball was in progress, the mothers sat round. There were lovely chairs all round the walls of the dance room. Of course, the really lovely place to have a ball was the Ritz. The really well-to-do people gave a ball at the Ritz – it was perfectly beautiful. I think there was a ball at the Ritz every evening from Monday to Friday during the summer season.

Mary Keen

There were large Victorian houses near where I lived and they used to have grand parties and balls there. We used to go round and watch people going in and coming out. The women were beautifully gowned in evening dress. The ground floor was one large room and they had a red carpet laid down and when the carriages arrived, footmen would jump down, open the door, help the ladies out and hold their trains as they walked up the stairs. You would hear a little band playing and they had the windows wide open. We used to cross over to where we could see them dancing all around. It made me want to dance, seeing them like that.

Sonia Keppel

Sometimes, my contacts with my parents took the form of dress displays. They would go out to special functions – or they would give a dinner party. At all times of day or year their clothes seemed beautiful. And those my father wore were as exciting as my mother's. In a front seat in their dress circle, I had a splendid view.

I can remember a spring dress of Mamma's in a grey and white stripe. Below a boned, high collar, it cascaded in widening folds down her bosom to her slender waist. And from her throat to her knees, it was buttoned with tiny, braid buttons. To set it off, Papa wore a dark blue, skin-tight frock-coat, worn with a top hat. He wore this coat over his shirt and, when paying afternoon calls, he could not take it off. In his lapel he wore a carnation. In those days, if calling on a lady at teatime, implicitly he had to give the impression that he was merely 'looking in'. Into her drawing-room he carried all the paraphernalia of his walk: his top hat, his walking-stick, his gloves. And gentlemen callers on my mother did the same. And I can remember a black velvet, low-cut evening dress of Mamma's, with which she wore a huge, black-feathered hat. With it, as jewellery, she wore a high diamond and pearl dog-collar, pearl ear-rings, and a diamond drop. In those days, the contours of Ceres were more fashionable than those of Venus, and my mother's ripe curves were much admired. To conform to such standards, handkerchiefs padded out some of the bodices of her flatter-chested friends. As a partner in her magnificence, Papa wore a gardenia, and a coat with satin facings and a very tall top hat.

Small wonder that, in my front seat in their dress circle, I sat there, open-mouthed.

Lady Charlotte Bonham Carter

It was very fashionable to go riding in Hyde Park during the day. One generally started at Hyde Park Corner and then one used to ride along the lovely sanded track from there to Exhibition Road. You didn't trot or canter – you walked. One wore suitable clothes – a habit and a rather elegant small top hat that was not too heavy to wear. It was difficult to look smart when you rode side-saddle, but of course one had a really good female saddle with a pummel, so that you could sit on your saddle absolutely facing the two ears of the horse. There were quite a few men about, but the younger men didn't really appear until six p.m. because they were all working away very hard in their offices. In the evenings, lots of carriages went up and down between Hyde Park Corner and Marble Arch. It was the most lovely to-ing and fro-ing. People sat in the carriages and stood all along the side and it was a most delightful sight.

Mr F. Davies

We used to go up to Mayfair. That, of course, was where the money was. Sometimes you'd see the street completely covered with straw about a foot deep. That meant that somebody in the house was extremely ill. Once it was someone on the west side of Grosvenor Square, in the house where the American Embassy is now. We'd gone there because we wanted to look at the kilted footmen who worked for the Sunderland families on the corner of Grosvenor Street and South Audley Square. We loved how the wealthy dressed. You could see your face in the men's shoes. The ladies with their long skirts scraping the ground and their dresses shaped to the waist with the sleeves puffed up. Huge hats with feathers and flowers. Any dress cut lower than the throat line was considered very daring. In the evenings, ladies sometimes wore a plunging neckline but that was to show off their jewels. In the evening, the gentleman wore his evening suit, tails, waistcoat, stiff shirt and gold watch chain right across his tummy.

Lady Charlotte Bonham Carter

Society was an enormous number of persons ranging from the very rich to some people who hardly had any money at all. It was very much de rigueur for every young person to be presented at Court. The courts were in the evening and they were really very glamorous. They were a tremendous occasion and you were there to be presented to the King and Queen. One's parents applied to the Lord Chamberlain's office and the office looked into the application and in due course came a large and splendid invitation – a summons to Buckingham Palace. My mother and I were fetched and you approached Buckingham Palace from the Mall. When you arrived, you took your place in the queue. If you were within the first hundred cards, you would get into the throne room where you waited for the presentation to take place. In due course your name was called and you walked along the row and your name was called again as you approached the Royal Family. We then curtsied and passed on to another room where there was a very delicious supper.

Dorothy Wright

All my brothers went to Eton and did well. The eldest, like a great many people of that age, was sent round the world when he was twenty-one, and he had a whale of a time. He shot tigers with rajahs and all the rest of it. The second brother went into the Church and had Lancaster Gate for several years. The third was an oarsman who stroked for the Oxford eight. I think he overtaxed himself with all that rowing and the doctor told him he must have an outdoor life, so he ran the gardens on our estate for years.

Lady Charlotte Bonham Carter

One day, I had a lunch party. People were due to arrive by four-wheeler and I wanted to make sure that outside the house and all round was really nice and tidy for them. As I opened my front door, a large coal cart drawn by an enormous horse slowly appeared along the street. It stopped exactly outside my front door. I was about to say, 'Would you mind moving on, I'm expecting some people to turn up here,' when the horse started to give vent to the most appalling flow of liquid. It sprayed almost everywhere and one wondered what to do. I looked in despair at the coal man but he didn't mind at all. 'How can I help it if my horse wants to relieve himself?' he said. I stood watching until the horse decided it was ready to move on.

Dorothy Wright

My father was a very keen politician. He was on all the local committees and he was a magistrate and a freemason, like all the big landlords were in those days, until things became more difficult for everyone. In those days, many people had no private investments. They had no firm that they belonged to – no family business. It all came from land and rents which were going down and down and down. So the day came when we were forced to move to a smaller house, to the great grief of my parents. We took the old servants with us, including the old cook, who was absolutely marvellous.

Lady Charlotte Bonham Carter

There were very charming shopping areas for the young – Sloane Street was a very delightful area. When I was young, it really wasn't a good idea to walk up and down Bond Street. One had to have a companion on Bond Street. In those days, all one's clothes had to be made for one. Coats and skirts had to be pinned on and tried on. It was so inconvenient. I was one of the earliest to buy off the peg, and then of course, in no time, the standard of buying off the peg improved as there was such a demand. Hair was always long then, short hair was absolutely non-existent. Everybody had long hair which had to be crimped. There were all sorts of crimping apparatus to use and they were very uncomfortable. We had appointments at hairdressers who came round to one's house and crimped up one's hair. It was such a bore.

Norman Musgrave Dillon

We lived in Jesmond – a suburb of Newcastle upon Tyne. My father was secretary to an iron and shipping works in Jarrow. It was a medium-income background. We had a cook, a housemaid, two other maids and a governess.

Mildred Ransom

London had space and time in those days to appreciate characteristic happenings. There was an old woman in St James's Park, close to the Horse Guards, who kept a cow, and sold milk, cakes and sweets to passers by. She had a tiny hut, but I do not think she lived there. Her right to the land and the stall was so firm that it was an expensive business to buy her out when improvements made it necessary. She was one of the sights of London.

Another sight was Mr Leopold de Rothschild driving his tandem of zebras in the Park. We used to admire, but not touch, the famous Piccadilly goat; we bowed as the old Queen, now deeply beloved, drove slowly by, or the Princess of Wales passed with her three daughters packed into the back seat of a landau. Royalty passed with a stately step then.

Albert 'Smiler' Marshall

I grew up in Elmstead Market in Essex and I remember village life very clearly. There was Mrs Page, who sold sweets, biscuits and cigarettes. A strip of liquorice cost a farthing, a bottle of ginger beer a penny. There was a glass marble at the top of the bottle which was much prized as marbles were at a premium. The Watkinsons sold bacon, dripping and cheese – large round cheeses. Six carriers took the produce to Colchester – a distance of four miles. Mrs Pentney sold haberdashery, women's overalls, children's dresses, stockings – and also tins of bully beef and condensed milk and cake by the half pound. It was here that my future wife was to work. The bakery was run by two spinsters who baked every day, starting at four a.m. Three pony carts delivered bread to outlying farms. Milk from the farms was collected in milk cans –a penny for a pint of skimmed, or for a ha'penny, a pint of new milk. Water was obtained from the village pump, which really belonged to the village pub – The Bowling Green – where you could get beer direct from the barrel for tuppence a pint. The blacksmith played an important part in the village, making metal hoops for the wagon-wheels, shoeing all the horses and repairing anything. Most of the villagers worked on the land – the village policeman went out rabbiting and pigeon-shooting – the pigeons were shared out in the village.

The flower show was an important event in the village. It was organised by the schoolmasters from Elmstead and the adjacent village, Great Bromley. The girls wrote out the Twenty-Third Psalm, the best six being selected for the show. They did flower arrangements and showed pressed flowers and butterflies, while the boys showed the produce of their gardens – vegetables and flowers. And on Boxing Day all the villagers assembled with their pets for an unusual race – pigs, goats, ferrets, donkeys, cats, dogs, tame mice and even a cockerel – all wearing a collar and on a lead. There can never have been a race like it! All through the village went this odd assortment of 'pets', finishing on the village green – the winner having to climb the greasy pole to try and reach the dead duck on the top.

Steve Tremeere

The old man used to do all the cooking and all the washing for us kids after he came from work. He used to go at half past five in the morning. We was ready for school at half past five! We used to get our own breakfast – bit of bread and milk – condensed milk – or perhaps a bit of bread and jam. Then you could go to the shop and you could get a farthing's worth of tea, a farthing's worth of sugar, and a ha'p'orth of milk. As long as you'd got the hot water, you'd got a cup of tea to warm you up before you went.

Marg was fourpence a pound up the Maypole. You had to go to the Maypole because if you didn't go and get half a pound of marg, you didn't get a clapper. That was a bit of cardboard with a bit of paper in it, and as you moved it round, it went 'crack'. We had to watch all these shops where they gave something away, us kids. Where they were giving a little bit of bunce, that's where we used to go. If they hadn't got the clapper, we didn't want the marg. Go down to Pearks's then. What did Pearks used to give away? I don't know if it wasn't a little tin whistle. They all used to give something away.

Father used to make gravy. He'd get a big white metal spoon, fill that up with brown sugar and poke it in the fire until it turned black. Then in the frying pan went the little bit of water and a bit of flour, mixed up, then in with the burnt sugar – and it was lovely bloody gravy, I'm telling you.

Jack Banfield

I wonder how Mum and Dad went on. They must have gone hungry. To get fed as children, we'd go out in the morning with a mug each – in some instances it was a condensed milk tin – and we'd go to a coffee shop in the high street opposite Hermitage Wharf near Wapping, where we'd have a mug of cocoa and a couple of slices of bread and jam. Then we'd be off to school. At midday, we'd go to another coffee shop in Turks Court and we'd have a bowl of soup and a couple of slices of fried bread. When we came out of school at four o'clock, we went to Ben's Chapel in Old River Lane and that was run by social workers and we'd have a mug of tea and bread and jam again.

If there was a young baby, its mother could go to the Board of Guardians to get milk and bread tickets that they had to exchange. But that was charity, and it was looked on as a disgrace to have charity.

Steve Prebble

You could eat all the parts of the blinkin' pig – liver, sweetbread, trotters, even its innards were scraped for sausage skin. All parts of the blinkin' pig. When we killed him we put him in some hot water and then scraped him, then my mother used to have big crocks, great big ones to put the hams in when it was brought indoors. I

The King's favourite, Miss Lillie Langtry, at the races.

remember when she made her brine, she put an egg in it, in the water, then kept putting salt in till the egg floated, then it was right. After it had been in the brine so long, we used to take these hams out, wrap them up in brown paper and hang them round the house. You'd cut a slice off the gammon when you wanted it. Good meat that was. Wasn't everybody that did it that way, but we used to.

John William Dorgan

In 1900 I was going to school and my parents were very, very poor. I knew poverty right to its limit. I was brought up on rice pudding and broth. Those were the cheapest meals anyone in our position could get. I can't remember ever having any meat in my schooldays. My mother made all our clothes. She'd go to a jumble sale or a second-hand shop and buy an old suit and take it apart until it was just cloth, and then she would make me something.

Margaret Jones

Monday was wash-day when everything got washed, including our white cat, Peter. We had a wash-house with a sink and a cold water tap where you were supposed to do the washing. Mother had a table in the kitchen and on Mondays she scrubbed it until it was white. The broom handles were also scrubbed and stood out in the yard to dry. Finally, Peter got a bath in the last of the water, and then he was tied to the kitchen table leg so that he didn't go out in the garden and mess about. We had a safe in the garden in which we kept the meat.

Mr Powton

The family was everything, and my mother used to make all her own jams and chutneys and pickles. There was a garden where we had all our vegetables, potatoes, turnips, carrots, parsnips, celery and leeks. Nearly all Hobson, in County Durham, used to bake on a Thursday. The Minister used to like to come on a Thursday cos there was always a lovely tea, straight out of the oven. There would be brown and white bread and tea-cakes and scones, and always a fruit tart. That would last us a week. Mother always had a fruit basket in the pantry. We never spent money other than pocket money; we used to get a ha'penny a fortnight, but there was always something to go to school with – a piece of chocolate, an apple, an orange or plum or even a biscuit.

Mrs L. Welsh

My father belonged to a savings club, and at Christmas he used to get the money out. He'd take us down the Portobello Road and he'd buy a turkey or duck or goose. In Portobello Road in those days, they had all the livestock. They weren't dead in the window – no, there was a little fence put round the shop and they had pigs, turkeys and geese in the pen and you'd pick one.

Ethel Barlow

In them days we had oranges but we didn't stop to peel them. We ate them with the peel on. We were hungry – always hungry. I remember buying chips and a lovely lump of fried fish and when we got home and started to eat, we found about six big cockroaches all fried up, but we just made a joke out of it, and kept on eating.

George Perryman

My mother cooked on the coal stove. She had big iron pots. Everything was done in these pots. It was mostly stew made from mutton or whatever we could get hold of.

Arthur Harding

We used to get pease pudding and faggots from a German butcher. All the butchers' shops in the East End were German. When we lost those German butchers, we lost a lot of good things, cos you could go there and get lovely food very, very cheap. When the war broke out they were all interned and they never came back.

May Pawsey

We lit a fire once a week. We only had meat on Sundays, so usually it was just soup with a slice of bread. Mother made the soup in a big pot and everything went into that pot.

Minnie Lane

We had a window-box, and if Mother had made a stew and there was something left over, outside on the window-box that stew would go. She'd cover it up and we'd have it the next day. We had no fridge. We had a neighbour who used to sell bagels in Petticoat Lane, and she invited my mother in one day, and she said, 'Would you like a bit of dinner?' and she went over to the toilet and got a bowl of soup out of it. 'No thank you,' said my mother. 'I'm not very hungry.'

Joseph Yarwood

I was the oldest and I would be sent out with thruppence to buy food for a family of six. I would get half a pound of 'thruppenny pieces', which were pieces of fat from the butcher. Then I bought four pounds of potatoes for a penny and a ha'p'orth of pot herbs, which consisted of a turnip, a carrot and an onion. That was a meal for thruppence. Or else I could go to the fish stall in Battersea Market, which had plates of haddock, whiting and herrings for tuppence. Together with the four pounds of potatoes, that made another meal for thruppence.

Arthur Harding

You could get half a sheep's head in those days. There was a stall in Brick Lane. My mother used to buy them. They used to be very nice cold. Every poor person used to buy them, and tripe and all that kind of thing.

Daniel Davis

We got all our food in Petticoat Lane. There used to be a board with a whole mountain of flounders on it. Used to be a shilling a lot. People used to have it with a penn'orth of mustard pickles.

Miss Earnshaw

On Sunday you used to get the muffin-man round. Muffins and crumpets. He had a huge tray on his head, and it was always covered with green baize. He'd ring a bell, about four o'clock in the afternoon. If you wanted crumpets you'd just go out and buy them. And there was a winkle man who used to come round, and a man who came round with fish. He had a barrow with a couple of boxes of fish on it. He put out plaice, perhaps a dozen small dabs, a half dozen small haddocks – threepence a lot!

Florence Hannah Warn

Sometimes a man selling flycatchers would come. He wore a tall black hat with long strips of sticky paper fastened to it, covered with dead flies, and he would walk up one side and down the other side of the street calling loudly, 'Flies, flies, catch 'em alive!' and then sell his strips of sticky stuff. Then there were two men wearing long black coats hanging to the ground, who trundled a small cart with long handles, from which they sold blocks of salt. They called out in very doleful voices, 'Any salt, please, lah-di?'

When the baker came he would gallop his horses to the top of the street and then call at the houses on the way back. At the back of his wagon was a handle at each side, and the boys would hang on and have a good run all the way up, until someone would call out, 'Wheel, wheel, whip behind!' and the baker would slash his whip around and catch the boys' fingers to make them let go.

Often we had a visit from a man with a hurdy-gurdy, which was a portable music machine. He turned a handle to play jolly music. We children thoroughly enjoyed the merriment and also the little monkey, who wore a red pill-box with a tassel on his head and would leap around with a collection box for his master. We also had

Waiting for handouts of food in Cheapside, London, 1901.

The butcher's boy.   The muffin man.

a man selling watercress, which was sold in little bunches standing in a bucket of water. He'd call out, 'Wahder Creese, only a ha'penny a bunch' – whereupon he would lift out a bunch and shower us with water.

Louis Dore

We used to sort through all the half-rotten fruit and vegetables left behind by market traders. It was a common practice – and anything that we regarded as edible was garnered from these piles. I remember an occasion when a friend and I discovered some rhubarb leaves with little bits of stalk left on them. They were devoured avidly and several days of intense pain and sickness followed. We learned that raw rhubarb, especially the part near the leaves, was the opposite of nourishing.

Miss Earnshaw

When I was growing up, we always had chicken and fish, including smoked salmon, because it was cheap. With us, smoked salmon was just an ordinary meal. There was a butcher on the corner of Lolesworth Street and Wentworth Street – a ginger man, a very tall man. My father would never buy anything that wasn't kosher. He wasn't orthodox, but he said that if you buy a piece of meat that's kosher, you know that the beast's all right – there's nothing contaminated about it. He was very strict about that. In those days they used to kill on Saturday nights, so you got the fresh offal on Sunday morning.

Freda Ruben

My mother used to put us to bed at five o'clock. And that was because we had absolutely nothing to eat. She was a very orthodox Jewish woman and one day, Dolly, our Christian lodger, told me to go and get her some bacon. When I came back, my mother said, 'Where've you been?' I told her that Dolly had sent me to Mother Woolf's for bacon. I tell you, she had a mind to break both my legs! 'Don't you go there no more!' she said.

Ernest Burr

I had a drunken mother. She used to go to work in the morning and I didn't use to see her again until twelve o'clock at night. I used to stand by the door waiting for her because we were hungry. I remember going upstairs and looking around to find something to sell. I took the brass bed knobs off the bed and took them round to the rag and bone shop. Then I said to my brother, 'Get half a loaf and a penn'orth of jam in a cup.' They used to sell the jam in a gallon jar with a big wooden spoon in it. When you pulled the spoon out, it was covered in flies. Sometimes, we would go up Rathbone Street, that was the market, and we'd get some orange boxes and bring them home. We'd chop them up in the scullery and I'd send my brothers out selling the wood, to get some grub for us.

Another thing we used to do, we used to get underneath the stalls at Rathbone Street and pick up the potatoes, carrots, turnips, cabbages, anything they used to throw under the stalls. I was the eldest and I had to look after my brothers. I had to do a bit of 'tea-leaving' as well. I had to do it in order to live. Petty 'tea-leaving' like going up the market to see what I could pinch. All the kids were at it. The man in the boot shop – he got so many pairs of boots pinched, he used to put one boot out with a nail through it. Of course, we went around without boots or stockings. My feet were in a terrible condition. I used to knock them on the kerbs and they were covered in tar and so I used to rub in a little bit of margarine to get rid of the tar.

Polly Oldham

When we were babies we had a pram – it was made of wood, like a bowl, with the handle at the foot end. For baby food we used to have gruel made with sago, steeped and boiled with milk. After that, when you got a bit older, you got bread and milk. Then you'd go on to solids – but the sago gruel was horrible. Even when we grew up, if we weren't well she'd make sago gruel and make us drink it. The milkman used to come with a big churn, and he'd measure it out and put it in a jug. You could have blue milk or buttermilk. The blue milk was like skimmed milk.

Teatime we had bread and jam mostly, but Saturday we always had Finnan haddock, done in the oven, and barm cakes. We had a cooked meal at dinnertime – she'd make a potato pie or rabbit pie. She was a good plain cook. We came home for lunch from school, but when the lads started work, they didn't come home to lunch – they used to take sandwiches.

Lena Burton

For breakfast we had mostly porridge and bread and butter. My mother used to do a lot of toast and dripping, because she didn't have a lot to go on with my father having to be off so much. She would bake her own bread – I used to come home from work at dinnertime and knead twelve pounds of dough which she'd put into loaf tins, or she'd make muffins. It was good plain food – a lot of beefsteak puddings in the rag, and broth – sheep's head broth more than anything. We used to make potato pie – meat, potatoes and onions done in the oven with a suet pastry top. If we weren't well, it was nothing but bread and milk – what we called pobs. We ate a lot of oranges, which were fifteen for fourpence ha'penny then. My mother used to have to come across from the Horsforth Road with a huge rag poke – that's what we used to call it – with twelve pounds of flour in it.

My father was very partial to brains. My mother used to beat it up with butter – delicious, really. We used to have a lot of rabbit pies – and hare soup. A man used to come round – a pork butcher – with dripping and sausages. Then the ice cream used to come with a horse and trap, and we used to go out with a cup for a ha'p'orth of ice cream. That was lovely. We got a ha'penny a week for our spending money, and the little shop down Piccadilly used to sell tiny mint balls and 'hundreds and thousands', and because there was a lot for a ha'penny, we used to buy those. Then there were everlasting strips and Spanish ribbons. There were pear drops and aniseed drops and clove drops. We used to love those.

George Hewins

The thing we ate most of was bread and dripping, or on Sundays leaf lard, out of the pig. Pure leaf! There's a big leaf in the pig when he's cut open, about an inch and a half thick, width of his belly. Folks rendered this down and put rosemary in it. We ate it like you would eat butter; it was lovely on toast. When I was in work we had meat and two veg on a Sunday, always stew because we had no oven. Two bullocks' livers were enough for five, more at a stretch. I used to bring them home still steaming. Then the butcher's shop stayed open Sat'day nights, till eleven. We got cheap meat – a leg o' lamb for one and ninepence, a shoulder for ninepence, breast for tuppence and thruppence. There was nowhere for the butcher to store it, you see. 'Buy me leg, buy me leg!' he'd be a-shouting when we came out of the pub. If he had any meat left it went to the Gas House to be burnt. There weren't no cats' meat in those days. Cats and dogs got their own living.

Mr Lockey

I used to supply a doctor in Tyne Dock. The doctor used to go and trap a few seagulls, and bury them in his garden for a couple of days. He told me that when he took them out, they were just as good as partridge. He was the only man I knew shot seagulls for food.

Mark Croucher

Poachers had an old trick for catching pheasants with birdlime – a real sticky glue. They used to make these little three-cornered brown paper bags, same as they used to get with a penn'orth of toffees years ago, and they used to find out where these pheasants were feeding, and then they used to feed them, encouraging them to come to this particular place. Now when they'd got them accustomed to come to this place, and given them a bit of feed, they used to put a little paper bag down with food in it, and get them accustomed to eating out of the paper bag. As soon as they got accustomed to that – which didn't take them very long – they used to smear birdlime around the inside of the paper bag and just fasten them with a little bit of wire. Then Mr Pheasant used to come along and he used to say, 'Oh that good man's been around again and fed us.' They used to feed out of this paper bag, but they weren't aware that there was birdlime inside. So they used to feed and find out that, with the birdlime stuck on their feathers, they couldn't get the paper bag off their head. Then, very early in the morning, the poacher used to collect what pheasants he'd got, pop them in his bag and off home.

There was a lot of pheasants in those days, and a lot of game-keepers, but there was also quite a number of poachers. They always used to say that the best gamekeeper was made out of the best poachers. If anyone advertised for a gamekeeper, if the poacher was fed up of his poaching activities, he could apply for this gamekeeper's job, and nine times out of ten, he got it because he knew all the tricks of the trade.

Florrie Passman

In Black Lion Yard there was a cowshed, and in those days it wasn't pasteurised milk – the cows used to be milked in your jug, because we thought it was pure, you see! We always used to drink out of huge mugs.

George Hewins

The missus would send one of the older kiddies to the Co-Op with a pillowcase. She'd say to our Edie – she were no bigger'n a bee's knee: 'Ere's thruppence. Go to the Co-Op and say, "Could I have this filled, mister? And could I 'ave some change?"' She came back with an old brown loaf, a currant loaf, lots o' tops and bottoms of broken cottage loaves, stale cakes and a bag o' broken biscuits!

William Keate

People supplemented their wages in different ways. One such couple were a man and wife who lived in a cottage near the bottom of our street. They sold fish on days when they could get it – it would be laid out on a table near the open windows, and many a time I have been sent there for a couple of bloaters for tea if we could afford them.

That wasn't all that often, as my father's wages in those days were eleven shillings a week, of which he kept a shilling for pocket money. I was always told to ask for hard roes, and the man or woman would pick the fish up in their hands and squeeze them around the middle. Apparently they could tell which were hard or soft roes. Perhaps they would pick up a dozen before they found the right ones, and throw the others back again. They never concerned themselves if their hands were clean or not, and you accepted that as a way of life.

Friday and Saturday nights they sold faggots and peas and always did a roaring trade. You took your basin and they would put however many you wanted into it with a few spoonfuls of peas and a fair amount of gravy. You then ran home as fast as you could, before they got cold. They were a very special treat.

Mrs Lynch

The men who were doing the road up, they used to make a fire and fry bacon pieces on their shovel and finish that off with a cup of tea for their lunch. Those were real pioneer days, they were, just like when you see the cowboy ranchers.

Ethel Barlow

I can remember a lovely gypsy girl who came round once a year, selling lavender. Sid used to come round too. He was the cat's meat man. I used to watch him cutting a big lump of horsemeat into bits. Then he'd put about four pieces on a skewer and he'd come round every day and chuck the skewer through your letterbox. It was food for the cats. He came round on Saturday for his money.

Bessy Ruben

We used to live in Rothschild Buildings in the East End of London. I remember a Mrs Morris living there. I was friendly with her children. She had seven of them. This Mrs Morris got on to a chair to put a penny in the slot for her gas to go on, and she fell and broke her leg. She was taken to the London Hospital – but what should she do with her seven children? Well, it was no problem. All the neighbours collected around, and said they'd take it in turns each day – one would go in in the mornings to give them their breakfast and see that they got off to school, and in the evening when the husband comes home, he'll take in a pot of whatever it was and they'll all feed together. This went on until Mrs Morris came home. Now, on the day that she came home from hospital, the neighbours all around collected together and washed the children, made them all clean, and sat them up in a row. There was a baby there, tied to a chair with a towel so he couldn't wriggle out. When her husband brought Mrs Morris home from the hospital, she was so overwhelmed by this party – they'd collected some cakes and things, and made it all look very nice – that she burst out crying. It was really wonderful to know that her family were being taken care of by her neighbours.

J. Tickell

I remember Mr and Mrs Lindsay who lived next door to me. When Billy Lindsay came home from work, he would go out and he would be poaching all night long in Shincliffe Wood, sometimes as far as Croxdale. He would go to work the next day with a cricket bag full of all the rabbits and pheasants that he'd poached. He took them to the shops in Durham and he went along with a stick, a bowler hat and his cricket bag.

His wife was a tall, strapping woman – she would be nearly six foot tall. She never used to come out of the house – she was mad. While he was out at night, she did the strangest thing. All night long, she would walk backwards and forwards with a pail, throwing water down the sink. We had some ducks and these ducks would go and sit in her grate, waiting for her to throw water over them. Or you might see her curtains going back and forwards because she was throwing buckets of water over them, trying to clean them.

Sometimes, you'd suddenly hear her singing at the top of her voice. She would sit down at their out-of-tune piano and sing as loudly as she could. She'd been a teacher once. She was very keen on jam tarts and Billy used to have to spend a fortune on them to placate her.

Freda Ruben

My mother was a widow at thirty-seven. She never grumbled. She didn't have a single penny coming in, but she didn't grumble. She'd come from a very comfortable family, and her father used to say a girl mustn't learn a trade, because a girl gets married and she doesn't need a trade. So she had no trade and we didn't have a penny coming in. So she went to the Board of Guardians and they gave her twelve shillings a week. For six children! And the rent was five shillings a week. Oh, the Board of Guardians were terrible – they wanted to take away Becky and Hymie to Norwood, to the Jewish orphanage, but my mother said, 'If four'll starve, six'll starve. If I have a piece of bread for four, I'll have a piece of bread for six. I'm not giving anybody away. We're all happy together.' So the Board of Guardians stopped her money – so I started work.

I worked from eight to eight in the workshop, then when I got home, Mother used to give me work to do at home. When I got home on the Friday, with my wages, Mother would be sitting outside on Thrawl Street with a shopping bag and I would run back to Petticoat Lane to get a few bits and pieces. She had nothing and she was waiting for my money. I was the 'father' in the family. I never got married for that reason. I could have got married as good as anybody else but I'd never have left my mother – never – because without me she'd have been lost.

Richard Common

I always had good shoes, but often I would run out without them just to be the same as the other lads. My father would play war – 'You've got a pair of shoes, you're not wearing them.' I was quite happy running around in my bare feet, as we just had the fields to run on.

As for the farmers, they used to get their potatoes up and they would just open the field for anybody to go in and we would pick the potatoes that were left. We used to clear the field for him.

Bessy Ruben

We may have been poor, but life in Rothschild Buildings was very companionable and very colourful. In the summer, nobody went far afield – there were no cars in those years, and very little transport that people could afford, and consequently you lived in the street. Your off-hours were spent amongst your people – your neighbours. The children were very, very friendly, and you were in and out of each other's houses.

Arthur Harding

I used to know chaps who worked at Spitalfields Market coming home with bags of potatoes, and they would share them out amongst the people in the block. The poor were the salt of the earth. There were no class distinctions – no racial distinctions. I can remember the Jewish people coming along Commercial Road from the docks, with big sheepskin coats and a pipe and that patient look in their eyes. They were just arriving in this country, and they used to go down to work in Columbia Road. They used to walk down the middle of the road, so they wouldn't disturb people on the pavement. They would always give something, even if it was only a farthing.

John Tickell

I remember a man who used to get up a tree and he would stand and shout 'Cuckoo' at eleven o'clock every night as people were walking past. This chap was always pinching cabbages out of people's gardens, so we used to shout up at him, 'Who stole the cabbages, cuckoo?' He used to do that at eleven o'clock every night.

Ethel Barlow

I remember when the man opposite shot himself. We saw him do it. His wife had left him, they were lovely people and I think it broke his heart. I don't know where he got the revolver from but he stood at his front door, outside, and he put the revolver to his head and BANG. The top of his head all blew up and it went all over the wall and window. We watched him do it.

William Keate

I remember seeing a skimmington ride – as such an exhibition was called at the time. I was coming home to dinner when I heard an almighty din and I wondered what was happening, but it seemed that a woman, whose husband was in the Army, had found some consolation with another woman's husband. When this was discovered, all hell broke loose. The family of the wronged wife – and they were pretty numerous – collected all the buckets, tin cans, saucepans, in fact anything that made a noise, then paraded in front of the sinful woman's house, banging their instruments and shouting filthy abuse at her.

She daren't go out, or they followed her – it was really vicious, and she quickly moved to another village. She eventually became reconciled to her husband. The man, however, went from lodgings to anywhere he could find shelter and died some years later in an institution.

Edith Turner

We moved to Stoke Newington, but my mother, being a country girl, was rather bent towards religion and we went backwards and forwards to West Hackney Church. My father became very friendly with the vicar and his wife, who had two daughters and they used to give us all their cast-off clothes.

Richard Common

Nearly everyone in Stanley Street had chickens out the back. You'd just open the back door and the chickens were running round in the field. They'd come back to their own place at night. One time, my mother bred some ducks. As the chickens went broody, she started putting duck's eggs under the hens, but as they were hatching out, the mother hen had a look at them, decided they weren't hers and started shaking them and killing them. So my mother picked them all up and put them into the old-fashioned oven, like a pit man's oven with a square front. That kept them warm and they hatched out in there. When they came out, she kept them in a box. When they were old enough, I had the daft idea to get an old mat and I stuffed it down the sink in the back yard and turned the tap on, filling the yard with about two or three inches of water, to let the ducks swim about.

John Agar

In the colliery village we used to call it overweight. I think why it got that name was, if you bought a pound they gave you a pound. My mother used to say to us, go up to the dairy and get a pound of overweight, a pound of margarine. That would differentiate it from butter.

There was a lot of chewing tobacco, especially among the miners. I don't know why, but a lot of old miners chewed tobacco. They gave out coupons with it, and with so many coupons you could get a watch. I think that most of the people who had a watch down the mines were watches that they got through the coupons of tobacco.

Arthur Harding

Women used to suckle their children. They used to open their blouse and feed the child. There was nothing indecent in that – it was a natural thing. People weren't ashamed of it at all. I might tell you, men used to strip themselves in the kitchen to take a bath – remember these people didn't have a dozen rooms, they had sometimes the one room where the fire was and it was nice and warm. Women often got a hernia carrying that bath of water out to empty it after doing a day's washing.

Bessy Ruben

Petticoat Lane was a very colourful part of the East End. The Lane was a lovely place to shop – everything was very fresh. On Sabbath, everything closed down, nobody would dare to open their shop. Sabbath, Pesach or Yom Kippur – those were the days everything was closed. You could tell it was a Jewish area. Cable Street and round there, there was Jewish people, but intermingled with a lot of Christian people.

Ruben Landsman

My mother had come over here from the open villages of Russia, and she never really got used to the confined spaces. So she had these window-boxes outside our tiny flat in London and she used to grow all sorts. She'd show me a potato growing, she had peas and beans. Blimey, I still remember that cockerel standing on the edge of the bed screeching its head off. She had a few hens in the flat too. When she thought it was time, she used to get hold of one of the hens and put it in a tin bath. She covered it with a washing board and kept it there until it started clucking. Then she'd take a look under the board and call out, 'It's laid!'

Mary Keen

Somehow, we were never behind with the rent. Rooms were quite cheap in those days. You could have two rooms for about five shillings a week. You could have a whole house with a nice garden for a pound a week. People often used to do 'moonlight flits' if they couldn't pay the rent. It was quite a usual thing for people to do. They'd leave their rooms in the middle of the night and you'd see them in the streets with all their belongings on a donkey cart or a barrow.

Minnie Lane

There was many an eviction because people couldn't pay their rent. Bailiffs would come in and throw their things out of the window. I remember my grandmother living in Artillery Lane, and she came round to Mother one day and she said she owed rent, and my father, God rest his soul, was a great big man. He looked like a policeman, really. Mother sent him round and said, 'See what you can do for her. See if you can frighten them a bit, you know. You might be in the police force.' Which he did. And they didn't touch her, because of that – otherwise she'd have been thrown out into the street.

William Keate

An event I remember vividly was a bailiff evicting a family from their cottage. Every article they possessed was thrown out into the road. The father was a navvy, and there was his wife and seven children. It was really pitiful to see, as we went to school with these children, and played with them very often. They were left in the road for hours, but as night came, they were given shelter in a stable just outside the village – perhaps the Lord remembered.

Florrie Passman

I lived in a block of flats directly opposite Rothschild Buildings in Commercial Street. I used to worry about the steps looking dirty. Our lights used to go off at eleven o'clock at night on the stairs, and every Thursday it was my job to clean the stairs, so I used to have a candle stuck in a candlestick. I used to get my water ready in my pail, and I used to scrub the stairs. In those days we used to use what they called a 'hearth-stone'. It came in a lump and you had to wet it. It made the stairs all lovely and white. Everyone who came up used to say what lovely clean steps they were. Everybody was so proud of living where they were.

Bessy Ruben

Living downstairs in the basement there was a family called Binstock. They had eleven children, including two sets of twins. They shared two rooms and a kitchen. When it was hot in the summer, the husband and wife used to spend the night on chairs out in the playground, because they couldn't sleep with all that crowd of children.

251

Mr Forrester

There used to be coopers coming round, they used to put rings on the washing tubs. The fishwives used to come round with cradles on their heads selling fish. On a Friday the gypsies used to come round selling buttons and thread, they would sit on the roadsides and smoke little clay pipes. They also used to sell pictures and oilcloths, because there was no carpets then.

John Wynn

I remember Johnny-come-Fortnight. He used to sell a lot of cast-off clothes or second-hand things. He generally had a large crowd around, and we boys having spent our Friday penny or ha'penny, most likely, we used to fill empty packets with water from the trough, then climb up and throw them on his crowd. They'd chase us, so we'd run off down to the market square, where there was only some small gaslights, so we were very soon in the dark. That was our great fun on a Friday night – until occasionally we got caught and got our ears clipped.

Harrison Robinson

At one time my father was off poorly for months, and the Co-Op shop let us have stuff on tick, without paying for it. We used to go down every week for years after paying it off.

Minnie Lane

We used to have the chimney swept every now and again. There was many a fire in Rothschild Buildings because people wouldn't have the chimney swept. The firemen were round about three or four times a week. If that happened, you were fined. One day, Mother was very ill and she had to go into the hospital. At eleven years old, I was the eldest daughter, so I was left in charge of the housekeeping. She said, 'Minnie, I've got a little bit of money. I've put it up the chimney – and if you put your hand up, you'll find it.' 'Oh my goodness,' I thought. 'I'm gonna have a find here.' So I put my hand up and I got a whole handful of soot – but there was a bag up there.

A greengrocer displays his wares . . .

. . . and the butcher his.

There was five shillings in it. She went off to Vallance Road Infirmary and they saved her life. She was about fifty something and she was going through the change of life.

People used to throw any food that was over out of the window – and God forbid if you walked by – you got a lot of fish hanging down your face. You might be walking past when an old mattress would come out of the window. That happened to my brother once – an old mattress came flying out of a top-floor window and just missed him.

Ernest Burr

My mother used to have a real fight against the bugs. My sister had a baby before she got married and that was a terrible thing. One night all the bugs went on my sister's bed and ate her alive and my mother said, 'That's God's judgment on you.'

Freda Ruben

Bugs? We didn't have one – we had the whole army. My mother used to smoke the rooms out with a sulphur candle twice a year and sit outside all day long, eating our food. When we went back in, there were huge piles of them, everywhere. God love us – we had thousands of them. You couldn't keep them away. They were under the window sills, the cracks in the walls. I always remember I had a friend to stay and the bugs were crawling up the walls. I didn't know where to put my face. We weren't dirty – we just couldn't stop them. When we finally moved, my mother left everything there – except the table and chairs. She wouldn't take nothing with her, cos she said, 'If I take anything it will start the bugs again in our new place.' We just left it all and walked out.

George Hewins

There were two years when the winters were terrible hard, terrible. The men had no work, and no dole. The women couldn't go mangling, cos they couldn't pull the mangles up, they was froze in the ground. They got chilblains on their hands; those as went washing or charring like Widow Bayliss, they'd come home crying where the soda had got in the cracks. Old folks died of the cold. The young 'uns like us with families growing had to scratch their heads to know how they was going to live.

Bessy Ruben

My mother-in-law and father-in-law used to come and visit us. 'How could you live in Rothschild Buildings?' they used to ask. But my father used to say, 'But what's wrong with Rothschild Buildings? The walls are straight – you don't have crooked walls, and you don't get crumbling stairs' – which was true. I'd grown up there and a child doesn't know it's poor. What comparison could I make?

Bill Owen

We used to go to Milner's Safe Works, and when all the men used to come out, we'd be there asking, 'Any bread left, Mister?' Then we would be down at the landing stage where there were all the emigrants going out, and you'd get a penny for carrying their bags. I once found half a sovereign in St John's Market, we used to go down there looking for 'fades' – faded oranges, faded apples. I didn't know the difference between half a sovereign and a sovereign then. I didn't say nothing. I picked it up and I ran from the market all the way home to my mother. Oh, they were made up! I got thruppence out of it. For us that was half a week's wages.

In those days they always put the coffin in the house – if it was a youngster all kinds of schoolchildren would come in. If they were Catholics they used to have wakes – they were all right, they were. For us young men, our best do before we got married was a wake, because the day before the funeral they'd have all sorts of eats in the house and all kinds of bevy, and there'd be singing. They used to dress the corpse up in their best suits, and the body was there in the room. Some of them slept in the same room with the body laid out.

We never had wakes in our house, but we had a death in our family every year. You see, there were thirteen children, and about eight died between me and my eldest sister. There were six or seven births and about eight deaths. They died mostly of convulsions – but they were all underfed, too.

Jane Long

Many a time in the night there'd be a knock on the door for my mum, 'Please Mrs Wilkinson can you come now, somebody has died.' But no trouble to her. She'd be out with her stretcher. Then they were laid out, either on the bed or on the stretcher – or on a big clotheshorse. The way the bed was draped, that was beautiful – a big bow of either mauve or white ribbon.

Joe Garroway

My dad used to be what they call a bearer at funerals. When I was twelve, some local people had a little child die – he was about a year and a half – and they came to see if I would be a bearer, but I didn't want the job. My mother said, 'Now look, you go to funerals, you don't know when you'll stand in need.' So I had to go. We carried that child, the four of us. We were all lads, all mates, and we carried that coffin down, all the way from the common, right up into the cemetery. That was my first introduction, and after that I never refused being a bearer at a funeral, never. You never knew when you'd stand in need yourself.

Mr Jordan

My father was much in demand. He was a big, strong chap, and he must have carried hundreds of bodies to the grave. He did that for years and years and years – and all he would get was a glass of whisky.

Polly Lee

They used to have black for people who died in the workhouse, and hardly anybody went to the funeral, just the bearers to carry them. Funerals then were horrible for children – you had the feeling you should die when someone else did. The horses had plumes on, six lots with plumes on. It was a fearful thing, a funeral.

When Father died we got little black bonnets. My sister was younger than me, she got a bonnet with ribbons on and I got elastic. How I envied that bonnet with ribbons on! I had to have the elastic because I was the oldest. I remember seeing my mother sat beside my father in a little low chair. I remember the funeral, and my aunt lifted me and said, 'Look hinny, there's thee da, ganning away.' I can see the coffin on a light birchwood chair, and singing outside. When they came back from the funeral there was the long pipes and tobacco. When they died, the first thing the family did was stop the clock. The pictures all got white cloths draped over and everything was covered up. There was such a funny sensation, when there was a death in the house. There wasn't very many rooms, you were living with it all the time.

It was all black clothes in those days, men would go and borrow suits. They would say, 'I can't come, because I haven't a black suit.' 'Well I'll see if I can get so and so's for you, I think he's about thy size.' And they'd put on somebody's suit. You used to have crepe on the whips, and the hats. They used to seek me out to carry the babies and little ones. I used to hate it.

James Bowles

When somebody died there were Lakeland customs that had to be followed. The clocks were stopped, and the windows were all shut. The blinds were drawn. Then, as soon as the body went out, somebody would be left and they would open all up and restart the clocks.

They didn't have to sit up with the bodies – though my sister did when her husband was killed. I remember her sitting by the coffin all the while before they closed it. The children all went to see the body when people died. I remember going to see a boy who had died of consumption – he was out in a hut in the garden in his coffin. You all went to see the dead people. I think that was why I was never really frightened of death. It never bothered me.

Everybody had to touch the corpse. You just put your hand on the brow. The old legend was that if anyone had been murdered –

if a murderer touched the corpse the body would bleed. So everyone who touched the corpse was proving that they hadn't murdered them.

George Hewins

If anybody died, if a kiddie died or a husband, all up that street they'd go collecting, so's they didn't have a pauper's funeral. But in winter folks hadn't enough for themselves. They'd got no money – nothing. Then the child was put in a home-made box, a crate from the Co-Op, anything.

Jim Davies

People used to pawn everything, and for a while I was a warehouse-man for a pawn shop in Ladbroke Grove in West London. I slept over the top of the warehouse. Everything that had been pawned was kept in the warehouse. I worked twelve hours a day and fifteen hours on Saturday, and had half a day off a week. For five shillings a week.

Things up to ten shillings were called 'lows'. You'd get a suit for a couple of bob, with shoes, boots, shirts. Over ten shillings, it was known as a 'pound'. A new suit would get a pound on it in pawn. That was about the limit. Jewellery, wedding rings used to come in regularly. We used to take five hundred pledges on Monday alone. You would come in there with a suit, say, and ask for ten shillings. They'd look at it and see it was a bit worn and offer five and you'd agree on six. So then, you'd get a 'low ticket' for which you'd pay a ha'penny and you'd get your six shillings. The interest was a ha'penny on every two shillings per month. So if you redeemed it on Saturday, that would be three ha'pence interest and you'd pay back five shillings and three ha'pence and you'd take your pledge. If it was over a pound, generally jewellery, you paid a penny for a ticket instead of a ha'penny. After a year and seven days, if it hadn't been redeemed, it became the property of the pawn-broker. But it was kept for another month after that and it was still redeemable. After that, if it was over a pound, it used to go to a sale. If it was a 'low', the pawnbroker could do what he liked with it.

Every pledge was done up in a duster, never in brown paper. The ticket was in three parts; the top part went to the person who had pledged it; the second piece went on to the pledge – it was pinned; the third piece went into a little box to be entered into the book. The pledge was then brought up in a basket and it was put away in racks. I had to stack the racks, keeping the warehouse up to date. There was an awful smell of mothballs all the time, and there were fleas everywhere, but I got quite used to them.

Arthur Harding

Attenborough's was the biggest pawnshop. There used to be a long queue outside on Monday morning and the peculiar part about it was that in most cases Mrs Attenborough didn't even open the parcel if the person that brought it in was a regular. She was a rough one with her tongue and she wouldn't stand any nonsense. The parcel used to be done up in part of an old sheet and inside there might be an old blanket or perhaps a lady's best coat – anything to make up a parcel. Mrs Attenborough would give a shilling or a couple of bob – something like that. Sometimes she'd take the pins out and have a look and see that she wasn't being swindled.

Bill Owen

I often went to school without eating. The pawn shop was my job every Saturday. You used to wear a coat and vest and corduroys, and I used to have to put the coat and vest on the Monday morning before I went to school, and wear an old jumper, then on a Saturday I had to take the ticket to Willie Spencer and get them back. We used to wash clothes, iron them and wrap them up, and pawn them to get about sixpence or threepence. They'd pawn anything. They'd have pawned me, if they'd got a chance! We lived on the pawn shop – without that we'd have had nowt to eat.

George Hewins

I was doing a job at the workhouse, slating the roof. It was a bitter cold morning when we started, frost was in the air. The door opened and the slummocky woman they'd got for a nurse brings the babies out, one by one. They'd messed themselves. She peels their clothes back and swills them under the pump. November and ice-cold water! How they screamed! Those screams echoed round that square yard, then later the older kiddies started to congregate. Who should I see but Hilda Rowe and Violet. They'd had their hair chopped off, they were wearing long Holland pinnies with big red letters: STRATFORD-ON-AVON WORKHOUSE. They did some sort of drill and then they was marched in a straight line to the National School across the road. The babies' screams and those red letters haunted me all day. If I weren't hearing the one, I was seeing the other.

Freda Ruben

My mother pawned everything! She didn't even have a wedding ring on her finger. When she came to this country, she had plenty with her. But before she knew where she was, it was all gone. After my father died, Mother kept his suit – that suit went in and out. In on Friday and out on Monday. We always laughed about that suit – Father was dead but his suit still went in and out! Everything went in, including the candlesticks – but we always had them back for Friday night. She never got her wedding ring back, though. In fact, when my sister first brought a young man in, we said to Mother, 'He'll think you're not married. He'll think you've got six kids and you're not married.' So we went out and bought her another ring.

Nina Halliday

The roads were covered with gravel and so very dusty, especially in windy weather when the dust blew up in clouds. It was very noisy with the horse-drawn traffic. The butcher boys always had very smart horses, and the milkman too, with his rattling cans. He had one big one which stood on the floor of the van with a tap to draw off the amount the customer wanted in her jug. Alongside were cans of pints and quarts hanging around the rail at the sides of the van, which was rather like the shape of a Roman chariot. It had two steps for the driver to get in by, and the big churn stood in front of him.

People who were very ill found the noise of carts trying, and peat was laid down on the road to deaden the sound. We had it down twice – once when my mother was very ill, and again when my father was the same. I liked to walk on it and I liked the strange smell, and having it down made me feel important.

John Wilkinson

The only operation I had was when I had a squint. We tried all different types of glasses, but they didn't work, so they had to operate. I didn't go to any hospital – it was done on my kitchen table in South Shore. I climbed on the table with my head to the window, lying on my back, with my pyjamas on. I soon went out – and I knew nothing more until I woke up later on and found that I had an eye bandage. I enjoyed many meals off that table later.

James Bowles

My mother's first husband was killed in the quarries. He left her with seven little children, one just a week old. There was no pension, no money, nothing coming in. All she could do was to sit and make shirts at a shilling a go. She did try to do a bit of spinning, but she was never quick enough. The farmers that she knew would give her bits and pieces, but eventually she got married again. She married my father, and then there was four of us, so she'd eleven altogether.

When there was illness, she sat up with people, she nursed them, and at their end she laid them out. She brought children into the world, and if she was there the doctors never bothered to come. There was no going to hospital, because there was no hospital. She was relied on for everything. You just suffered.

The doctor used to call with three bottles. If it was a cough it was a brown bottle, if it was stomach it was a white bottle, and if you had pains it was a pink bottle. She'd administer one of these, and she'd stay sitting up with them.

Shoppers and horse-drawn traffic in
London's Oxford Street in 1909.

The locals always said if they saw her going out in her blue coat she was either bringing 'em in or taking 'em out. She was really the midwife for the valley. She was the only one and she never lost a child, and she never lost a mother. She would stay quite a while, and see to the baby and bath it; see there was something to eat, and then she went back again next day. She didn't get anything in return. She didn't want anything – she didn't charge anything. She just did it because it was friendship. If it was a farmer, they might give her a pound of butter or a dozen eggs.

There were bad colds and things like that, but there were few cancers. She sat up with those who had cancer, and it was very bad when they did die. She used to take a lot of strong mints and big white handkerchiefs when she went to lay them out, because she knew that they wouldn't be in a very nice state. People who were sick died at home. There was nothing else for them.

There were working injuries in the quarries. One chap was killed by a rock-fall off the wire rope used for carrying the rocks. If there was an accident they were nearly always killed – it never was an accident like a broken leg. One lad fell down the quarry – and he survived, but later was killed. He was blown off the wagon going to Coniston and he dropped on to the points on the wire fence. Another lad, Joe Dixon, was killed and this other lad had his leg blown off but the doctor didn't get there in time. It was very raw was life in the valleys.

Harrison Robinson

You had to pay for the doctor. He would give you your medicine too – there were no prescriptions. The doctor would come and do little operations on the kitchen table, and they'd set broken arms and legs there too – you didn't go to hospital. You had to be recommended if you went to hospital. If you had been in an accident or were very ill, they would use a stretcher on wheels and cart you all across the cobbles to the hospital.

Emma Mitchell

We only had one chemist, and that was Mr Kelsey. Many a time I have run there when my mother was ill, for a sixpenny leech. Me granny would get the neck prepared for me coming home with it. It would be put in a box by the chemist. I would run helter-skelter home with it, so she could get it on her neck. Once it got on the sick place it wouldn't leave until it was full and rolled off. Granny would be there with a saucer to catch it. She'd put it back in the chip box and I'd run back to the chemist – the druggist as they called it – and he'd give me fourpence.

James Bowles

The vicar from Chapel Stile conducted the funerals. Even for regular Sunday services he had to walk from Chapel Stile to Little Langdale – but there was no burial ground there, so everybody had to walk to Great Langdale. Bodies were taken in a dog cart or perhaps a hearse with horses. There was often a meal afterwards, back at the house – cold ham or beef with pickles and bread and butter – it would depend if they had the money. If they couldn't afford it, you just went home.

Mrs Avery

One time I had a spot on my face, it was a canny big sore, the size of a threepenny piece. This tall black man used to come in the shop and said, 'One day I'll take that off your face for you, it's a long time in getting better.' I said, 'My mother won't let me touch it.' He says, 'I'll take it off for you.' The next day he came in with a stick of chloride of zinc, and he just ran it over my face. The day after I found a great big sore, three times the size it was before! I thought, 'I'll kill you!' But then it just went away and left no mark at all.

Joe Armstrong

Just before Christmas, when I was about nine, I was sitting in class in the workhouse, not paying much attention. I was chewing on my pencil and I actually swallowed it. A chap named Clark who must have been about fourteen put me over his shoulder and carried me to the Lancaster Infirmary. I must have been one of the first to have an X-ray taken. They put me in a ward with a nice Christmas tree and I thought to myself, 'This is all right!' Anyway, they gave me some medicine and the pencil must have been just the right size and it passed through me and they sent me out on Christmas Eve. I remember wishing I could stay in the hospital for ever. But we weren't prisoners in the workhouse – we were allowed to leave – so one day, when I was thirteen, my mother brought us out. She had got a job in a cotton factory and earned eleven shillings a week. The rent was three and sixpence and we didn't have a stick of furniture – but at least I wasn't in the workhouse.

Mrs Calver

I remember going to the dentist's. I had an abscess when I was three and a half, I had to go to Mr Brumble of North Shields. I had to have a pain-killing injection. He was very kind, he held my hand. Afterwards I had a swollen face, and in those days the cure for this was poppy heads and camomile flowers. You took the poppy heads in a basin with hot water and made a sort of liquid with it, and bathed the place with it, and as you did this you sprinkled in the camomile flowers. It was a very pleasing sort of smell. I suppose the poppy heads might have had something to do with opium!

Jack Edgell

It was Epsom salts, sienna pods and castor oil – that's what you used to get. No one had constipation in our family.

Gertrude McCracken

I noticed Mrs Sewell's very young baby had a dirty piece of rag around its little finger. On being asked what was wrong, she replied, 'Oh, the baby was lying on the floor kicking, and I stepped on her little finger. I squashed the top of her finger off, so I popped it in a basin of home-made lard and stuck it on.' I think this was true, because when Aunty rebandaged the baby's hand with cleaner linen, the little finger had a bluish-red ridge around the top joint and she, Aunty, could move the top of the finger.

At that time whooping cough was rife at school, with three weeks' isolation for the victim. The popular remedy was to take the child into a flock of sheep in an enclosed space. This certainly seemed to help. But this one child's mother went one better. After fourteen days she returned to school, so we children promptly told her that it could not have been whooping cough. 'Oh yes it was,' she said. 'My mum caught a mouse and baked it and gave it to me in bread and butter.'

Mildred Ransom

The fogs possessed a special acridity which inflamed eyes and throats temporarily, and were so dirty that eyelashes and eyebrows became coal-black. They were so dense that traffic was often stopped. They were also very cold. Many is the day when in a thick fog I have stopped before a hot potato stall and bought two large, beautifully hot jacketed potatoes and put one in each pocket to warm my hands.

One evening I was due in Buckingham Gate. When I went out I discovered that if I wanted to get anywhere I should have to walk, as all traffic was stopped. Snow and ice were on the ground, so it was not so dark as it might have been. It seemed possible. The only difficulty would be to cross Hyde Park Corner. Except that a bus got on to the pavement near Grosvenor Gate and scattered the pedestrians, all went well. I even piloted a distinguished old General across Piccadilly, who no doubt was very brave in war, but who was very nervous in fogs. I found the Palace wall and marched beside it looking out for the break in the wall which marks the entrance to the Royal Mews. Suddenly I found myself in a wide silent icy space blanketed with yellow fog. No wall, no Mews, not even any pavement. I could not account for it and the worst of a really thick fog is that the deadly clammy silence which is apt to produce panic. In some extraordinary inexplicable manner I had walked out of a familiar world with nice thick walls and plenty of people, into yellow space, silent as the grave. It seemed to me that I wandered in this empty space for hours, and just as I began to be really nervous a soldier loomed up and placidly told me I had gone through the Park Gates and was near Wellington Barracks. We sociably marched to Buckingham Gate together.

John Agar

Of course, Christmas was a great time, and as children we used to go around singing, with what we called a chuck – it was a soap box. The shop used to get soap in a box, about eighteen inches by two feet by eighteen inches deep, and we used to get one of these, put two wooden handles on either end, and then get hoops from apple barrels and put them across the top of this box. Then we'd decorate it with different-coloured tissue paper and fasten glass toys on, and stand the candle in the bottom. Then we used to go from door to door, one at each end, knocking, then we would sing. One short verse went:

> Spread out your table and cover it with the cloth,
> A piece of mouldy cheese and piece of Christmas loaf.
> Joy and peace be with you, we'll all whistle too,
> And God send you a Happy New Year.

There were lots of verses like that one. The majority of people would give you a copper or two. When you had been around a bit, you got to know where the best houses were. At the end we would share out what we had. It was a great time, that.

Mr Powton

About six weeks before Christmas we used to make our spice cake, and about a week before, everybody used to get a Christmas tree. More often than not your door was left open, so anybody could come in, and we used to go round and see who had the biggest and best tree. At Christmas there was always a social evening at the chapel – a supper, and for the younger ones there would be Postman's Knock and games. We would go home between eight and nine because Santa Claus was going to come and he wouldn't be there until after the singers had been. At long last our mother would say, 'Yes, he's been,' and we'd hurry downstairs. On the table there would be a doll for me, and there would be building bricks for the boys, and boxes of sweets. We had a stocking full of nuts with an apple and an orange and all sorts of odds and ends. I used to love to empty my stocking, because after that you could see all your other toys.

Mrs Anderson

Christmas time was really nice at home. I can picture my mother making the Christmas puddings. We all had to have a stir and then it used to be boiled and boiled and boiled. She used to make her own ginger wine, even though we were all teetotallers. I don't know why – but it used to be really nice.

Ethel Murray

I went to work in the shirt factory, in the afternoons. On Saturday all the girls went in the fields with our rackets and we played tennis, and instead of going home we went to Chingford Hotel two stations along. There we would have a wash, go to the dance, and come home on the last train. On Sunday morning we'd all meet outside a shop and cycle to Southend and all over, and Epping Forest. I could play the piano, so we went into this old country pub and I'd play the piano. Sometimes we didn't leave till four in the morning.

James Bowles

The quarry apprentices would live at home and take the money back. But in those days there was a lot of drinking done. On payday, the wives of the quarrymen would try generally to be at the pub, before they started to drink!

John Smith

There were so many thrills for us children. The Coliseum in Park Row where they had a 'Menagerie of Wild, Untamed Beasts', and once Professor Stevens, the Demon Barber, shaved a man in the lion's cage in the Coliseum menagerie. There were peep shows in Castle Street – the tattooed lady, the strongest man on earth, the bearded lady, the fat boy, the human beast from the jungle. All sights for a penny! A children's roundabout on a horse-drawn trolley toured the streets, charging a penny a ride. In winter there was ice-skating in the flooded fields at St John's Lane, Bedminster. One could earn money by bringing a chair for the skaters to sit on and screw on their skates. The whole scene was lit up by paraffin flares.

My mother was left with nine children and the pub to look after. The pub had three entrances. There was one long bar and a small one called The Ladies' Bar. The women weren't allowed to drink with the men. It was one bar for the ladies and if a man wanted to give his wife a drink, he had to call across and ask her what she'd have and then my mother would serve her. Most of the ladies had just an ordinary glass of beer. Some women would come along with a little jug and take the beer home.

One of my jobs was to clean the handles of the doors and put the sawdust down and empty the spittoons. When we opened at six o'clock, the coal porters would come in. Sometimes they never went to work. Some stopped there all day until eleven o'clock at night.

Albert Packman

I went to the Bricks Music Hall and nearly fell over the front right up in the gallery trying to look over, because it's very high. There were acrobats on the stage, and impossible things going on that I'd never thought of in all my life – all for twopence!

The next day I went to Sandgate, just outside Folkstone. High up on the hills there was a soldiers' camp, and all the soldiers used to come from there to the fish and chip shop. I followed them, got my turn, and there were little windows there where you ordered your fish. They were all saying 'two and one' – so when it came to my turn I said 'two and one' and then I said, 'How much is it?' She didn't half swear at me, this girl. I suppose she thought I was stupid

269

or having her on. I didn't know a two and one meant a tuppenny bit of fish and penn'orth of chips.

I gave her threepence and went and sat down with all the others. God, that was a day of days in my life if ever there was. That was absolutely smashing. It was the end of a perfect day. I went back and told the porter and he laughed when I told him about the fish.

George Evans

At that time we had got a cinema which came visiting about twice a week to the Coniston Institute. They were silent pictures, and someone from the village used to play the piano to the films. The projector always broke down at least once during the evening. When the local squire, Jimmy Marshall, was in residence he would bring lots of friends from London – he lived quite a gay life there. The seating was turned round, so that the stage had the best seats and all we wee things were down at the bottom in the cheap seats. The screen was on the other end of the hall, and when it broke down, as it invariably did, Jimmy Marshall used to bang his stick on the floor and all his friends used to whoop and make awful noises. They thought it was terribly amusing of course, coming from London.

Edgar Johnson

Our main entertainment really was going to the Hunt Ball, which used to last till three in the morning. We used to have a real session with a knife-and-fork supper. Sometimes I've come down after being at work in Colwith Brow, and I've heard music carried by the wind – and we went on listening to it all night. Once I sat up all night with a cow that was calving, and the next night was at the Hunt Ball, so I had been up for two nights. I sat down to milk a cow next morning, put me head up nice and quietly against it, and just dropped off to sleep – dropped the bucket and the cow knocked me down into muck. That woke me up again!

Grace Fellows

Ambleside used to be a grand place for dancing and balls – we made our own entertainment. We had a good opera company formed by local ladies, and there were all the various balls – the Conservative and the Liberal, then there was the Fire Brigade and two others. We used to take gallons of cream down to Mrs Banks at the paper shop and to Mrs Watson down Lake Road, and they made all the trifles to serve up at the dances in the Assembly Rooms. The stairs there were all beautifully decorated and great long trestle tables all laid out with flowers. There were three classes of people at these dances – there was the Redmaynes, at the very top close to the orchestra, then there were my friends, and farmers and suchlike. Then down at the very bottom was what they called the laundry clique – a lot of girls that worked in the local laundry. They always had the bottom of the floor.

Ted Harrison

I'd just come out of hospital with double pneumonia and my mother took me to Holley's, the photographers. This was about 1908. My picture was taken in a long room about twenty foot long and five foot wide with a lot of windows, and they used to rely on a lot of sunlight. They didn't use gaslight to take photographs – they used a mirror to reflect the sun. All the pictures had backdrops like a garden gate, a fence, an aspidistra stand, the corner of a cottage roof – but you didn't get to choose your background. You took what you were given. Pictures were only taken on special occasions – when Dad joined the Army or Uncle Fred got married. Things like that. You'd pay sixpence to have the picture taken, then the next week you picked up the proof. The proof would be on paper that went dark red after two or three days, so it was no good to you. You had to decide if you liked the picture or not and whether you wanted postcard-sized prints or what. If you wanted them, you went back and ordered them for a shilling.

George Perryman

We used to have pigeons in the yard, but my dad didn't go in for racing. He wasn't interested in training them but we used to watch these other chaps who used to train them in Canal Road and all around. They used to put them in baskets and take them in a pony and trap out to Stamford Hill, where they used to let them out and they'd fly back to Hoxton. Sometimes they'd have races where they put the birds on a train even further out, to places like Theydon Bois. A chap would pick them up from there and he'd put rings on them and he'd let them go. The crowds would be lining the streets round our way, waiting for the birds to come back. As they came in, they used to dive on to a platform where someone would get hold of them and put them into a little bag. There used to be prizes for the bird that came first – and there was betting as well.

Ted Harrison

The police used to run down the canal to catch the blokes gambling on the towpath on Sunday afternoons. They'd be playing 'Up the Stick'. A circle was marked out on the towpath. The men would have a little piece of wood made up like a cricket bat. It was very prized by the owner – it was like a man with his darts. You had two ha'pennies on the stick and you spun them up in the air. They landed in the circle and if you got two heads you won and if you got two tails you lost. They caught one bloke cheating. I was amazed. He had taken two ha'pennies and he'd ground the coins down and soldered them together so he was left with one coin with two heads. Everyone was gambling for shillings and half-crowns. If you did well, you won a week's wages.

George Perryman

There was whippet racing on Millfield Road opposite the Clapton football ground. Six or eight whippets used to race each other. Two people were in charge of each dog. One would stand at one end of the course with the dog between his legs and the other stood at the other end with a handkerchief which he used to shake and shout at the dog. The course was about four or five hundred yards. The betting was organised by different bookmakers such as Billy Chandler – but it was illegal. If the police came along, the bookies used to shoot off quickly.

Harrison Robinson

The Bigg Market in Newcastle on a Saturday night was full of turns – strong men snapping chains on their chest, a blind concertina player, who used to play on request, and a chap who would get a cricket ball and light it with paraffin. He'd throw it high in air and catch it in a leather cup strapped on his head. We kids used to watch him, wondering if he would miss, but it used to bang down into his cup and he never missed it. You could easily have a full night's entertainment in the Bigg Market.

Arthur Harding

You used to have Italian organ grinders with a monkey. Weekends were the days when people had money. People would dance to the organ grinders, especially on a Sunday afternoon after the boozers closed. They all danced together in the streets, the young, the old, the men, the women – all together in a crowd. The more drunk they were, the more they danced. A chap with the grinder went round with the hat.

Kitty Marion

People used to send these amusing little postcards, but reactions to them used to be so different. For example, I sent out a postcard of a puppy, sadly contemplating the puddle from a dripping umbrella, wondering, 'Will they blame me for that?' My friends Ethel, Kittie and Jack, whose family was never complete without a dog and cat, were mirthfully sympathetic, whereas Bee Buckell was shocked and offended at my sending her such a coarse, vulgar postcard openly through the post.

George Hewins

On dark nights, soon as the missus came home, we went to bed. That way, you might think, we saved more trouble – but that's how folks like us got so many babbies. There was nowhere to go, Sat'day night, only the pub. You could drink eight pints o' mixed beer for a shilling, three ha'pence a pint, or a pint o' the Oddfellows' rhubarb wine for thruppence. Two penn'orth o' stout the ladies had – or gin. The Oddfellows in Mansell Street, that's where me and my pals went, it was a home-brewed house. Milly and Teddy Eborall kept it, their father and mother afore them.

Jim Fox

At thirteen, I took up boxing. A professional boxer called 'Seaman' Nelson came to live near us. His backyard faced ours and he had a boxing ring in there, where his two sons and me and a few others used to box in the evenings. We wore gloves and he controlled the bouts. He wasn't a great boxer – he was one of those who went round the towns like Newcastle, Sunderland and Middlesbrough. I remember going to see bouts in the covered market place in Durham. There were thousands of people there. There was a referee and a timekeeper – it was properly controlled.

Ted Rayns

I remember going with my dad to watch Newton Heath play football. They became Manchester United in 1902, but I saw them when they were still called Newton Heath. I remember how vast the stand was, with all its steps. There was no tea at half-time, but we did have pies.

Joe Fitzpatrick

I was football mad as a youngster. I played football for my school, and when I was sixteen, I played for a team called Cheetham Lads. We had a real good team and we played every Saturday on Number Three pitch. I could kick with either foot and run like a hare. My favourite position was left halfback. I once played on Manchester

United's ground. It was during a snow storm and we played against the men from the cinema. I also played at Hyde Road, where Manchester City used to play. That was a bit of a mud-tip. They moved to Maine Road after the dressing rooms burnt down. I remember when Manchester United won the Cup in 1909 and I can remember that team; Moger, Stacey, Hayes, Duckworth, Roberts, Bell, Meredith, Halse, Sandy and Jimmy Turnbull and Wall. They beat Bristol City one-nil. On the Bristol team was Charlie Wedlock. He wasn't a very big feller, but he was a good centre-half, and he stopped Charlie Roberts of United getting many international caps.

Maud Gascoyne

It was in 1904, when I was five years old, that my father took me to watch Nottingham Forest, and it was such a big responsibility for him because he couldn't watch the match – I was running about all the while because I was bored. We went home and he never said anything all the way home and then he said, 'I'm not taking you any more until you get a big girl.' But we tucked into our sausages and things and enjoyed those.

Sydney Woodhouse

We went in as 'boys' around 1906 or 1907 and my recollection is that they were a pretty rough crowd at St Andrews, Birmingham – but they were an orderly crowd. They weren't a boozing, shouting crowd. They were mostly cloth-cap and on the poorer side, I would say. Large crowds of working men. Of course they seemed old to us but I suppose they were mostly between the ages of about twenty and forty then. And they went in their thousands to Aston Villa, West Brom and St Andrews. When they got a local match they filled the ground.

George Ovington

Thomas Lipton used to come to West Auckland, that's how West Auckland got to play Juventus, because West Auckland was just a local football team then. They went first in 1909 and then they come

The Cup Final, 1905. Aston Villa beat Newcastle United two
goals to nil.

Enthusiastic crowd at Hull FC's ground, 1902.

back home again, and then they had to go back and play in 1911 and they beat them again, because my brother scored the winning goal.

Thomas Lipton paid a lot of money for some of them to go. That's how they came to call it the Thomas Lipton Cup. He was a tea merchant, but that's as much as they knew about him. When they went there they were called WA. It was up in big print wherever they went – WA. And when they were WA the Italians thought they were Woolwich Arsenal instead of West Auckland. They were all miners. They had never been no farther than Scarborough. We used to get one day, one trip away, a year. That was the chapel trip, we called it, because I was a big chapel lad. They beat Juventus twice. That goal my brother scored. I heard about that goal till I was tired. When they come back they hadn't a cup, see. Nobody had the money to bring the cup back. So this lady, she was rich, she belonged just out of West Auckland. Well, she paid for it. So this lady bought it and it were years and years before they racked the money up to buy the cup off this lady. The club got their raffles and fun-fairs and all sorts, and men gave money till they bought the cup, and then they brought it back and put it in Sid Outhwaite's pub.

Alfred Finnigan

Deep down I wanted to live in St John's Wood so I could watch the cricket at Lord's or get the tube to the Oval. My father took me to see the fifth Test match at Lords in 1909 – England and Australia. One of the Australians was Ponsford – and it was a draw.

Reece Elliott

'Booling' was done over a mile. The last one I saw was down Blakeley Lane in Chester, down the posh houses, and Frankie Doodle booled against Jack Robeson, for money. It was a proper bool. Grandfather used to make them, a bool was about 25 ounce, but you could please yourself what weight you booled. Joe Ferguson used to bool a 50! You could please yourself, sideways, or through your legs, Joe Ferguson was a champion through his legs, what they called haughing. He haughed across the town moor. It was from leaving your hand to the first bounce it was measured, then the lowest number of throws won.

Jack Brahms

The very first girl I ever took out, it was rather a strange thing. I was at a party at Alf Bernstein's and there was about six fellas there, and we were one girl short. So Alf says to me, 'Well, next door there's about three or four girls.' And this one girl came round and her name was Mary. So we invited her in – and to cut a long story short, we ended up getting engaged. Mary never danced, so we'd go to Hyde Park or walk around the West End, looking at the shops and so forth. Or we'd go to the pictures in the Paragon in the Mile End Road. We used to go there very often. We never went to pubs.

I took her back to her house one Sunday after we'd been out, and evidently my father had been round to her parents and demanded a hundred pound dowry money! I never knew anything about this! She said, 'You can have your ring back!' I says, 'Why, why? What's the trouble?' She says, 'Your father wants a hundred pounds.' And that was that. That ended that. I didn't argue with my father about it. I mean, in those days it was usual to demand a dowry – but £100 was a lot of money. I was very upset and very disappointed, because I liked her very much, but that's how it ended. I didn't even try and talk my father round – that was that.

Bella Hindmarsh

Long skirts – oh, they were all long, and the latest styles that came in when the hobble went out. When you went to go over a stile you had to hike them straight up. Once I had a lad and we were coming from Crookhall into Iveston and we had to get over this stile and it was a hobble and he just got a hold of my leg to pull it up. I waited till I got home and when I got to the door and he was saying goodnight and I just spit in his face and said, 'Don't you come back any more.'

Kitty Marion

I had been taught that a man never kissed a woman outside of his own family unless he became engaged to her, and no self-respecting woman would permit any man except her fiancé to kiss her. Like every normal girl I had my dreams of a wonderful, ideal, hero lover in whom all the finest qualities of the Knights of Chivalry were concentrated. Sex, except as a distinction between boys and girls, was a closed book to me. It was taken for granted as a mixture of something very private, personal, mysterious, sacred and nasty, not to be openly discussed.

Arthur Harding

When I was eighteen and I'd come out of Borstal, I'd heard the boys talking about girls and women. I really hadn't any idea about that sort of thing, though. I was just learning – you learn a lot in prison. I used to knock about in Brick Lane, and just round the corner in Slater Street there was a block of buildings for Jewish people. Up at the top flat was a chap we called Fiddler who had a furnished room he used to let to a prostitute. She was a nice English girl, tall and slim. That was the first time I'd ever been in a house where they had a bed-covering such as an eiderdown. We were talking about her one day when out she came. Not quite as glorious or glamorous as she looked when she was out on her business, but she came down, and somebody said, 'I'd like to have a go at her' and I said, 'I could have her any time.' You know how you boast about these things. So we had a little bet, about a shilling, and I said, 'I'll bet I go home with her tonight.'

I had no more idea of going home with her than a fly in the ear, but I wanted to be somebody. So, next night, she must have done well, because it was about twelve-thirty when she got out of a hansom cab. I was waiting. I came over and said, 'Hello, do you want to take me upstairs?' She said, 'Do you really want to come upstairs?' I said 'Yes.' So we went up these stone stairs. I said, 'Will Fiddler know?' She said, 'No, he won't know, he's no trouble.' It was the first time I'd ever been in bed with a woman. She really had to instruct me in a way. Afterwards we lay there talking, and I was trying now to convert her, you know? I was saying, 'What a lovely girl you are, why do you do it? I wish I had a lot of money and I'd take you away.' I left very early the next morning – about five o'clock, and my stomach felt empty, I seemed so weak and I said to myself, 'I'll never go with another one.' I said to her later, 'You've made me feel ill.' She said, 'No, it's your first experience, it's not that, I haven't done anything to you.' I said, 'It's funny, I feel terrible bad.' She said, 'You'll be alright. I'll see you tomorrow night.' I said, 'I don't think so.' Not long after that, she disappeared from the scene. I asked a friend of hers, 'Where did she go?' He said, 'She didn't come home one night.'

Perhaps she got time. Most got a period inside. It was a shame, I liked her very much.

Kitty Marion

Connie Angus and I visited each other on alternate Sundays, and I told Mrs Hillier if I was not home by ten o'clock I would be staying with Connie. Sunday trains were inconvenient and the trip had to be made by bus and tram. Returning on Sunday, I got off a tram to walk across Westminster Bridge when a lady, to all appearance, asked me to direct her to Waterloo Station. Thinking it easier to show her the way than explain it in words, I said I was going that way and if she did not object to my company I would be pleased to conduct her. She was quite agreeable and we talked and exchanged confidences as to names, occupation and so forth. She said she had an appointment with a friend at nine o'clock, but when we reached the station a few minutes later, she looked around saying, 'He is not here, I won't wait.' So we walked across Waterloo Bridge together, I with intentions of taking my bus to West Kensington. However, my companion told me of the cosy flat she had in Gray's Inn Road, and feeling lonely, which apparently I was too, she invited me to stay the night with her. She liked me and we could be very good friends.

Feeling appreciative, I gladly accepted her invitation. Near Temple Bar and Chancery Lane, she slightly collided with one of two men coming in the opposite direction. Mutual apologies opened conversation, the older man talking to her. The younger, who might have been his son, started talking to me. In making some casual, complimentary remarks on meeting me, he edged between the others and me, advancing as I retreated, until we were out of earshot, when he said very abruptly, 'Is that woman a friend of yours?' I was surprised and told him how I had met her, and that she had invited me home, whereupon he became most concerned, and said, 'Little girl, she's no fit companion for you, come along, here's your bus,' and he hailed one. He helped me up the steps and said, 'Good night, dear,' as if he had known me all my life. It all happened so quickly, I seemed in a trance. Years later, when relating the incident to two then very dear women friends, they said, 'You must have been a greenhorn to go off with a strange woman like that, you might have known what she wanted you for.' Well, I had not known and I was a greenhorn. I had no idea that women had 'evil designs' on others. This one was so 'ladylike' too.

The young man, I never saw again, though if ever there was a case of 'love at first sight' it was so with me. His good looks, charming manner, the courtly, protective 'Little girl' and 'Good night dear', impressed and thrilled me beyond words, like a meteor of love flashing across the firmament of my life, leaving just a beautiful, heavenly memory.

Reuben Landsman

Parents never taught us about sex. We didn't learn it from parents – parents never told us anything. But we grew up with it. Flower and Dean Street in the East End had its lodging houses. On the right was a men's lodging house, on the left was the women's lodging house. The street was only wide enough for one cart to go through. Well, prostitutes were walking down all day and all night along there, but we never interfered with them and they never interfered with us. We knew who they were and we had to pass them to get to Hebrew Classes in Brick Lane – but we were two worlds and we never overlapped.

Bill Elder

In Yarrow I remember Mary Whillans, who was to be married to one of the two Wilson brothers. The brothers were very close – too close – and she had a hard time keeping them in order. At one stage, the single brother asked her, 'What do you think *we* married you for?'

Mary Keen

When my mother and father weren't able to work, my father went to see the Board of Guardians. If you were in great need, they helped you. They never gave you money, but they gave us cards for the butcher, the baker, the grocer and the coalman. They had a list of names of shops we could go to and we took the card and they gave us the goods. Times were hard for a lot of people. I can remember a hundred or more labourers and builders marching together round our way. Every now and again, they'd stop and shout, 'We want work! We want work! We don't want charity! We want work!' But they couldn't get it. I used to think how cruel life was.

Freda Ruben

You've never seen such a queue in your life as at Butler Street soup kitchen. We used to get a can of soup and a brick loaf. The loaf was all right but the soup was lousy. There were people standing outside the soup kitchen who'd stop us as we came out and ask us if we had anything to spare from our soup. Very often I didn't like the soup, so I used to pour half of it out for them. For Passover, we used to get a packet of matzos and a packet of tea, cos they closed up for the week. A woman who lived in our flats saw me coming out of the soup kitchen and she called me a 'schnorrer!' That means 'beggar' in Yiddish. I cried. 'I'm not going no more, they're calling me a schnorrer.' I hated her for that. I really hated her.

Bob Rogers

When you were out of work, you could go to the Relief Office and they'd give you a day's work. As a single man, that's all you'd get.

You'd get two bob for some manual work – chopping wood, scrubbing floors. You'd get a ticket for about two bob.

Edith Turner

My father was a kosher butcher, working for Nathan in Middlesex Street. When he came out of that, he tried to get back into English butchering, but no one in the English trade would take him. He never worked as a butcher again. After that, he was in and out of work. I remember when the bailiffs came. They took all our home away. They left us with a bed in one room for us children and a double bed in the front room for my father, my mother and the baby. Apart from that, they just left us a couple of cups and saucers.

Freda Ruben

I remember when my mother owed the shop all this money, and the woman who ran it wouldn't give her any more credit. In those days shops were open till twelve or one in the morning, and then one night my mother was watching outside the shop until the woman had gone to bed and her husband was alone – then she sent me in to get a loaf. The husband didn't know that we'd been refused credit. After that, my mother did some washing for the woman, and instead of paying my mother she said that she'd take it off the book. My mother said all right. Well, when I next went down to the shop, she said to me, 'Your mother owes me the money,' so I went back and told my mother. And my mother said, 'I done all her washing, and she said she'd take it off the book.' Well, I went back down and I gave the woman what for. I was only a kid, but I had the jaw. I said, 'You're a wicked woman.' I'll always remember, she was pulling a cabbage leaf off, and telling me how my mother owes her money. I went back up to my mother and said, 'You'd better pay up her money. She showed me up terrible.' My mother said, 'I done her washing. What more does she want?' She went to another shop after that.

Ernest Burr

Every Friday night, we used to go down to Silvertown. We used to stand on this little bridge, waiting for the men to walk home from work, and we used to follow them, calling, 'Got any lunches, mister?' and sometimes they used to give us some pennies. Sometimes we got three or four pence and we all thought how lucky we were.

Minnie Lane

When my brothers came out of the West Norwood orphanage, they were like hooligans. They had been so caged in – it was very strict – that when they got out, Mother made a fuss of them, but they were bad. They used to smoke in bed – many a time Mother used to go up and there was a smell of smoke. Oh, my mother had a handful with them, but in the end, they were still frightened of her.

Arthur Harding

When I think back on it, it was a terrible bloody existence. We didn't know it at the time because we didn't know any better. There was no door on our house at all, because the workmen had to carry their work right through from the yard to the back. We did have a door to our room – we could lock that – and I'll tell you why. We lived in a period when Jack the Ripper was a thing of the day and people talked about it as if it happened yesterday. There were plenty of child murders and people were afraid to trust their children with other people. I remember the notorious Amelia Dyer – she killed six children and she was hanged at Reading. She strangled them with white tape. People remembered this and they'd be afraid for their children.

On top of that, we were living in the midst of criminals and thieves. It wasn't that they wanted to be thieves, but necessity drove them to theft. These things were a part of everyday life, like the sun shining and the rain coming. I can remember we would always put something against the door – fix the Windsor chair under the lock. That would stop anyone opening the door at night.

Joe Armstrong

I was born in Morecombe on the twelfth of April 1895 and my father was a tailor. I was the eldest and I had two sisters and a brother. I had a good mother but I can't say my childhood was happy. When I was about six or seven, I remember eating one of my father's tomatoes from his window box and he got hold of me under his arm and held me under the cold water tap. Not long after that, he did a bunk. We understood he joined the Black Watch Regiment but we were never sure. After he left, I helped my mother sell his sewing machine, his scissors and his tape measures to other tailors.

Of course, there was no social security then and we were soon absolutely broke, so my mother put us all on the tram to Lancaster and we all went into the workhouse. We didn't live as a family. The boys and the girls were segregated. Thirty of us young lads slept in a big dormitory. The food was very rough and we never got enough. I remember getting a bowl of skimmed milk and porridge in the morning, then every Saturday they used to give us a cupful of Epsom Salts. You can guess where we spent the Sunday.

Ted Harrison

I remember looking into the Hoxton workhouse and seeing men breaking stones in the yard. There was a long hut nearby with steam coming out of it, and that was where the women used to work in their grey shawls and their rough grey suits. I remember going up there one day, and this man pulled a bit of rag out of his pocket. It was to wipe his nose and it was all he had in his pocket so I gave him a ha'penny. He didn't want to take it but I made him because I felt so sorry for him. It was hard to get out of the workhouse unless someone got you a job. If you went in, they separated your family and you only saw them once a week. I used to go in there to collect my grandmother's relief. Everyone was lined up, coughing, and one of the old inmates used to come along and shout out your name. He was a bit pompous. He was like Dickens' Mr Bumble but he was only a workhouse inmate himself. He'd say, 'Follow me!' so

I went after him and he'd say, 'Hold your arms out!' and he gave me four loaves, which was Granny's ration for the week. She got no butter, or anything else, just four loaves of bread.

There were certain streets in Hoxton that you didn't want to go down. One of them was notorious. Even policemen didn't go down there unless there was two or three of them, because people used to get on the roofs and throw flower pots at them. It was full of tenements like in Dickens' books. I remember old Screwneck. He was a terror. You used to steer clear of him if you saw him – you'd cross to the other side of the road. He used to have a big belt made of horse irons. It had a ruddy great buckle and he'd think nothing of taking it and wrapping it round his hand. That was his knuckle-duster.

Then there was Dickie Reagan. He was an Irish bloke. He was all right, but when he got drunk he was bad. They called him 'the Warhorse'. He used to fight the policemen quite regularly. It was a matter of honour for him not to be arrested. The crowd loved him and they used to try to get him away from the police. I saw four policemen frogmarch him down the street with a mounted police-man behind on a white horse. When they got to Essex Street, a lot of boys ran at the police with truncheons. They used to make these truncheons out of the rubber from the tyres of the 'Growlers', the four-wheeled cabs. They were thick truncheons, really nasty. So these boys ran out and attacked the policemen and helmets went flying, the policeman fell off his horse and Reagan got away.

Policemen were known as cossacks, peelers, bluebottles, coppers, flatties. It was 'Flatties' because they were supposed to have flat feet. They had all sorts of names. They always used to wear capes – no overcoats. They had oil lamps and a big square patch on their belt for the lamp. When they used to march out of Old Street Station, they all marched down one behind the other and they'd drop one copper off to take over and they'd pick up the one coming off duty, then they'd march back again to the police station.

Kitty Marion

I spent time walking through the slums, which exercised a weird fascination and repulsion over me. The filthy hovels, broken windows stuck together with paper, or the holes filled with rags, the walls of passages I saw through open doors in passing were thick with grime as if they had not been cleaned since they were built. The women lounging about in doorways and on steps, gossiping, were ragged, unwashed, unkempt. Children of all ages, some tiny tots just able to walk, playing and rolling in the gutter, yelling to each other in much the same foul language used by their elders. 'Come 'ere you, Johnny, you 'ear me, come 'ere or I'll break yer bloody neck!' 'I'll kill ye, if ye don't come out o' that gutter, gettin' yerself all dirty.' As if he possibly could have got himself more dirty than he already was. Babies in play chortling, 'Come 'ere you bloody sod!' Some of them quite pretty in spite of their dirty faces, bodies and rags. What could you expect from children bred, born and brought up in such environment? How could landlords tolerate such tenants, turning their property into slums?

For the well-being of the country I felt these slums should be abolished, and the people, particularly the children, rescued from them. But how? I often broached the subject among friends, only to be advised not to worry about it, landlords didn't as long as they received their rent regularly, and the people were perfectly happy living like that, not being accustomed to anything better. I used to say that if I were a millionaire, I would take these children and place them with good homes, with families where it would be convenient to look after an extra child or two. Expenses would be defrayed by the government or philanthropists who had the well-being of humanity in general and children in particular at heart. I was laughed at for wanting to waste good money on a lot of ne'er-do-wells, or else I was called unnatural, wanting to take children away from the parents who 'loved them'. Love them! How could anyone who loved children bring them into such hellish slums?

287

Steve Tremeere

There was always a prostitute in the street. There was two in our street. Good as gold – never interfered with anybody. In fact, us kids used to like running errands for them because you were sure there was a bloody ha'penny from them. Usually you only got a farthing. Prostitutes always had more money than anybody else. Some of them, if they'd had a good time, they'd go and get things out of pawn for people and chuck it at them.

Arthur Harding

The prostitutes used to wait at Aldgate, and the late buses would come up from the West End and sometimes a cab would pull up. This was around three in the morning. Or perhaps the girl would go up to the West End. In Old Compton Street in Soho, the girls were allowed to parade up and down after eight o'clock at night. The men who were looking for a girl had money. Ten bob was a good price. There were two classes of girl. There was the prostitute, pure and simple. With her you take your coat off, you hang it up and she'd get ready to go to bed – that's if you're going to spend the night. Otherwise you might just spend an hour or so with her. She might talk to the man and weigh him up. If he was a wise fella, she wouldn't go too far, but if he was a chump, if he wasn't quite all there, she might say, 'Two quid, for you. I'll do it for two quid', and he might say, 'Alright, where are you going to take me?' She'd say, 'Only a couple of turnings round there, wait there and I'll get the key.' She'd come back and say, 'She wants the two quid up front.' So he'd give it to her and she wouldn't come back no more. That's the profession.

Then there was the other type of prostitute. These were the girls in Spitalfields who'd give you a 'fourpenny touch' – a 'knee-trembler'. Jack-the-Ripper's 'touches' were all the 'fourpenny touches'. If you stayed at it all night with her, you might pay a couple of shillings.

Steve Tremeere

We kids always respected a policeman, too. Mind you, we used to get a clip round the ear off them. If a bloke was drunk, if they could get him to go home or get one of his pals to take him home, they'd say, 'Go on, push off!' But if he got obstreperous, they'd throw him on a barrow, that stretcher they had, strap him down and away he went. And all the prostitutes had their photos taken and put up in the pub. They was barred from all the pubs – they had to do their business other places.

Louis Dore

Whoever it was that conceived the idea of the jolly, fat, laughing policeman, it was certainly not a working-class person. I don't doubt that in the middle-class areas where the odd half-crown was dropped into his fat old hand, he was regarded as the jovial chap described in the old song, but in areas such as ours he was an alien – an enemy. Though it's true that policemen seldom walked through that area singly – two or three at a time was customary – nevertheless, if we strayed outside our usual haunts, the heavy hands or rolled-up waterproof capes would often be applied to the sides of our heads with considerable force, for what seemed like no apparent reason.

The burglar or thief who, according to the literature of the day, spoke those immortal words, 'It's a fair cop, guv'nor,' did not exist. Caught red-handed or not, he would vehemently protest his innocence, and would call loudly to his mate for rescue. If his mate arrived, there'd be a fine free-for-all, at which point, out would come the truncheon and the whistle, whereupon more 'flatties' would emerge from the woodwork or brickwork. They were adepts at concealment. Shop doorways and entrances to dark alleys were commonplace hiding places. The 'flatties' always won and instead of one arrest, several might ensue.

They were past masters at the art of inflicting pain and degradation on their victims. The half-Nelson was the commonest form of restraint. This was painful in any case, but if you struggled, your arm would be twisted higher and higher, and the pain was excruciating. Frog-marching came next. You made a very amusing spectacle being carried along, face downwards, with a 'flattie' attached to each of your four limbs – but if you proved really obstreperous, a two-wheel stretcher-like vehicle was produced, and on this you were strapped down from head to foot, and wheeled through the streets.

John Tickell

The trucks used to come into Shincliffe Station in Durham, bringing in crates of pots. I used to go up to the station in my cart and pick up the crates and bring them back to the churchyard, where we emptied the pots. The pots were all wrapped in nice clean straw. After a while, Albert realised that pots were starting to go missing, so he said, 'I'm going to see who is getting them. Come across with me and we will go in and have a look come night time.' So we took an oil lamp and we sat there in the churchyard, talking in whispers to each other. Suddenly, we heard a noise. I was trembling. Then we heard some pots starting to rattle and we knew this was our thief. Albert quickly lifted the cloth off the lamp and he ran across the yard and grabbed hold of this fella. The man started pulling away and we looked at him – and do you know, it was the village policeman! He was a fool, this policeman, he'd gone and pinched some straw from Nicholson's farm right at the bottom of the village. He'd pinched it to pack up the pots. Well, if you carry a bail of straw, there is going to be a line of straw after you. He pinched a few bails and of course there was a line of straw leading right back to the farm. He got shifted for that.

Arthur Harding

A policeman who was new to the Division came along under Brick Lane Arch where a lot of blokes were gambling. They were playing Crown and Anchor – the cheaters' game. And like a bleeding idiot he considered it his duty to try and arrest them. When he tried, they battered him about terrible and broke his nose. Afterwards, when I heard about it, I set about a couple of the fellows who did it, I said, 'You caused a lot of trouble for nothing. He was new to the Division, he doesn't know – doesn't understand what it's all about.' I gave them a belting. The policeman got to know about this and he came and thanked me.

Afterwards, he wasn't what you call a crooked policeman, but he used to tell me things for my own benefit. I can remember one occasion when he helped me. I had sold Harry Symons a load of cloth. He was in the tailoring business so it was handy to him. He bought it off of me for a few pound. The fella who stole it gave me something for selling it. It wasn't a lot. So I went up to the police courts to listen to a case and I bumped into this policeman. We got talking and he said, 'D'you know anybody over Jamaica Road? Anybody named Symons? Get over there as quickly as you can.' That's all he said to me. So I got over there quick. 'Harry,' I said, 'What did you do with the stuff I sold you?' 'It's in the back there.' So I told him, 'Get rid of it. Go up to Tower Bridge Police Station at once and say a fella left it in your shop yesterday and said he'd call today, and he ain't called. Ask the police to come and take it away. Say you don't want it in your shop.' So that's what he did – and it saved him.

After that I told Harry I wouldn't tell him the policeman's name, but I told him he'd have to give him something. So he said, 'How much? Half a sovereign?' 'Cor blimey!' I said, 'You can't give him that!' Harry looked at me and said, 'You dropped me in it. I lost money and now you want me to pay the police!' So I had to get a pound off Harry, but the policeman wouldn't take it. 'No,' he said, 'It's alright.' He didn't have to say it twice, I can tell you. I put that pound straight in my pocket.

Louis Dore

Counterfeit half-crowns were in common circulation. These were made of lead or lead-tin alloy, and it was probably these coins which initiated the practice of testing by biting. A strong set of front teeth would leave marks in the soft metal, and a little leverage when gripped by the teeth would bend them. Shopkeepers, always on the lookout for them, would test them – test all half-crowns by rubbing them on their aprons and on pieces of white cloth, kept handy for this very purpose. A lead coin would leave a black line like a pencil mark on an apron or cloth – and a dud one would be bent over and thrown back at the customer. Rather less scrupulous shop-keepers would throw them into a box, no doubt with the intention of profiting by them later. If the customer demanded their return, the shopkeeper would threaten to call the police, and that was a threat to be well heeded.

Arthur Harding

I remember coming in front of the magistrate Mr Clewer at Old Street. I was just back from Borstal. I had found out that my mother had been knocked about by some people while I was away and I went potty. I sorted them all out, even the terrors that had done seven years. But I was young and I could fight like a bloody lion, and it was the first time I had used my strength to protect my mother. So I was arrested and came up in front of Clewer. He was really unusual. He was on my side from beginning to end. He said to me, 'You did what you should have done and I'm dismissing this case. You've admitted quite candidly that you did assault these people and justly punished them for what they did to your poor mother. I remember quite well the case when your mother wouldn't prosecute them. The case is dismissed.'

Louis Dore

For minor offences you got seven to fourteen days in the local nick. This may seem a trivial sentence, but in fact most men would have preferred a lagging. A lagging meant a month to six months upwards in recognised prison – Pentonville, for instance. Here you were overseen by warders – you received enough food to keep you alive, and when you came out you were temporarily free of vermin. You were bathed, your hair cropped to the skull – you wore broad-arrow suits, and your own clothes were baked – sterilised. You could always tell a lag when he came home by his lack of hair, yellow complexion, scarred fingers – scarred from picking oakum, or sewing mailbags. In the local nick your custodians were those very same flatties you may have roughed up on your arrest, and you were made to pay dearly for this.

For example, my father, in company with one of my uncles, was coming home one night, three sheets to the wind and singing 'Nellie Dean' or some such song. This constituted a disturbance of the peace, and they were approached by a constable and a sergeant, and told to stop singing. Whereupon my father aimed a kick at the sergeant's rear. Uncle got away, but Father was dragged off, receiving in due course a sentence of fourteen days. Fair enough – assaulting a policeman could have meant a lagging, but the kindly magistrate considered that having no past record, the lighter sentence would suffice. When my father came home, his whole body was black and blue with bruises. A lighter sentence? A month on skilly would have been preferable. Skilly was the watery porridge served for breakfast in prisons.

Mildred Ransom

I was asked to give a lecture to a girls' club in the New Cut near Waterloo Station, and I was warned that the neighbourhood was 'a bit rough'. It was all that and more. I took a bus as directed to a corner near the station and turned down a long dark street on which the club was supposed to be situated. The street was under one of the old arches, and I was told the club was near the arch. The first thing that told me that things were not as they should be was the complete silence and emptiness of the street. Dead cats, cabbage stalks and other refuse lay in the gutters. There was hardly any light from the houses – the only living thing I could see was a miserable cat picking her way across the street. I marched along the middle of the road consoling my nerves with the fact that no one but a fool would attack me, and I had only to go smartly and not look as if I were nosing round, and I should reach the club safely. In the whole length of that street I only saw one person, a woman who stood motionless outside her door. She had a petticoat and a shawl and nothing else whatever. Such streets were not uncommon in London, but one did not as a rule walk down them.

At the end of the street near the railway arch was a closely shuttered shop which looked somehow as if it might be the club. The difficulty was to find out. The place was so tightly shuttered that it might have been a fort. Two girls came up and to my great relief came to the door. I explained who I was and they banged and kicked on the door. This was the ordinary mode of attracting attention. The door opened a crack. 'Oo's there?' 'Gert 'n' Imy.' 'Oo's the other?' 'Lady. Says she's 'ere to talk to us.' 'Oh, come in – and 'urry up.' We squeezed in through the crack and the door was banged behind us, but not quickly enough to exclude some cabbage stalks which whirled in with us.

'The boys is a rough lot round 'ere,' said the doorkeeper disapprovingly, and cleared away the greens.

During the evening things got a bit rough. Bricks and refuse were hurled against the shutters and once the full strength of the club was required to keep the door shut, but unless a member wanted to come in, the lecture went on and no one took any notice except to apologise for the noise.

We had cocoa and a chat after the lecture, and when the club heard I had come down the street instead of approaching it from the other end, they regarded me as an innocent who ought not to be allowed out alone. The police, they informed me in picturesque language, would only go there in pairs – they said it proudly – it was one of the worst streets in London. I ought to have come by a bus which would have put me down near the arch. They insisted on convoying me to my bus by the proper route, and they waited – all of them – till I got in, and then they told the conductor where I was to get off.

Rebecca Bowman

Uncle lived in Stanley: he'd had a daughter murdered in 1910 by a lodger. All the pit houses had lodgers. My Aunt Polly had two lodgers. One was a great big Irish fellow, Johnny O'Connor they called him. He took Auntie's little girl out to buy some sweets at the corner shop. It was Christmas and they found him on the Saturday and they found the bairn on the Sunday, buried in a shallow grave. On the Monday she would have been ten year old. He was hanged.

Ben Hardcastle

Tommy on the Bridge used to stand on the bridge, you know, shaking back and forwards, and he used to have a tin pot. The ropery was just near the bottom of the High Street. The lasses out of the ropery, they were rough – they didn't care if it snowed. They used to torment him – they'd have their money on a string or something and they used to drop it in his tin pot then tug it out again, so he used to think he was getting money – he was blind.

Arthur Harding

I remember this woman called Dolly Marx. She had a brother. I think they were half and half. She herself wasn't bad looking. When I first met her she was in her thirties. She was living with Arthur Howard, the old-time boxer. She was a right bird – a right hawk – and could be very violent. She'd think nothing of having a row in a pub, picking up a glass and smashing it in someone's face. Sometime about 1907 her and her brother got mixed up in a riot in Westminster. They went up after another gang – something to do with Covent Garden Market. There was a lot of damage done, to property and inflicted on people. There were some very heavy sentences dished out and she got seven years. She was sent to Holloway first and then from there to Aylesbury, where she did her penal servitude. That's where they did the long sentences. When they came to take her out of Holloway, she stripped herself stark naked. It was a terrible business to get in there and put some clothes on her.

Mr Jackson

The public houses were nearly always full at weekends in Dipton, a few miles from Newcastle. They were crowded because the beer was that cheap, and when you've got strong beer there's a lot of fighting

295

going on. Saturday nights and Sunday nights in the Hilltop there were open-air boxing bouts, and they used to fight like tigers. It was just the beer making them fight – they could be back at work with each other next morning. There was only one policeman, and he used to keep out the way, because he knew he might get pulled into it. In one case one man was getting badly used and his wife was screaming and ran up to Dipton and called PC Clarke – a young chap, tall and thin. He came down and tried separating one of these brothers, who said, 'You keep out of this.' PC Clarke says, 'Now come on, stop it. Calm down.' One brother stopped fighting, got a hold of him, and chucked him over a wall nearly a yard high. He says, 'You stop there, cos if you don't I'll chuck you over again.'

These fights entertained the people in the village, and every Saturday and Sunday night you would see people of all ages waiting to see which public house opened the door. One would open and some men would come out and fight. They wouldn't even allow them time to get their glasses off or take their teeth out – they would just fight, and teeth and broken spectacles would be lying about. It was an exciting life, I tell you.

Kenneth Crompton

One man was an engineer at Armstrong's, came to the pub every night at half past six. He had a big red handkerchief, which he'd take out of his waistcoat pocket, and put round his neck and get a hold of each end, and go to the counter, pick the pint of beer up with his teeth and pull it up to his mouth, and drink it down in one gulp. I was telling the lads about this at school, and they wouldn't believe me. I said, 'Come at half past six any night at I'll show you.' So they did, and it was the talk of the school for weeks!

Mrs Mills

For my sister, my brothers and I, Saturday night was the night to go to the Walthamstow Palace. We paid fourpence to sit up in the gallery.

While we were waiting, buskers used to come along and you'd get the smell of the artists. Then there'd be the scramble up the stairs. We were youngest so we were quite quick. There were no backs to the seats – they were just platforms, so you often got someone's feet in your back or orange peel down your neck – but for fourpence it was marvellous value. Some nights you got fourteen turns. There was a big indicator next to the box that showed you which turn was on. I can remember Harry Tate, Will Fife and Fred Karno. It was marvellous.

Dolly Shepherd

I went to Alexandra Palace as a waitress in 1903 because I wanted to see John Philip Sousa, the popular conductor and composer of military marches. He came and sat at my table with John Henderson, the theatrical manager. The showman Samuel Cody then joined us. He had an interest in aviation and was at the time touring and performing rifle and pistol sharp-shooting. As the conversation flowed, Cody said that he was stuck for an assistant. He had grazed his wife's head while firing at an egg balanced on it – and he needed a replacement. So I said, 'Oh, all right. I'll come along.'

I remember I was standing on the stage – and he took aim. What I hadn't reckoned with was his son blindfolding him, and at this point my friend, who had come to watch, fainted – but he shot the egg off my head all right. It was made of rosin – it wouldn't have done for an ordinary egg, after all.

George Perryman

There used to be so many music halls near me. There was the London Music Hall. That was a nice place. We used to pay thruppence ha'penny up in the gods. There was another in Hoxton Street, the London Empire on High Street Shoreditch, the Olympia, the Cambridge in Commercial Street, Collins' on Islington Green, and the Islington Empire. Then there was the Blue Hall, which was a silent picture house in Upper Street next to Lyons' Corner House. We went there once a week.

Entertainment at Hull Fair, 1902.

Devon and Somerset Staghounds taking lunch among the coaches.

Ruben Landsman

At the end of Commercial Street in Shoreditch was the Olympia Music Hall. It was a big one. There were four floors and four galleries. A bit further along in Shoreditch, near Kingsland Road, was the London Music Hall. I can remember seeing George Eliot, the Chocolate-Coloured Coon, there – and Ella Shields, Burlington Bertie, Nora Baines, and the redoubtable Marie Lloyd. Once my friend's father took us to a pantomime. It was the first time I'd ever seen Marie Lloyd. 'Come on,' he said, 'I'm going to treat all the kids.' When we came out, he treated us all to fish and chips and we walked home from Hoxton. What a treat that was!

Bessy Ruben

Our amusements didn't cost a lot – we couldn't afford to pay much. At the corner of Artillery Lane there used to be a family called Benjamin. They used to rent all the wigs and clothes to the music hall actors and the actresses. I knew Danny Benjamin and he would give us passes for the first house at the Tivoli – the Oxford, the Alhambra, the Standard, the London – all these places. We always had to go to the first house, but I saw all the famous people – Marie Lloyd, Little Titch, Dan Leno.

Ted Harrison

My dad used to take us all to the music hall on a Friday night. I remember a cowboy play, *Montana Dick*, with rope-spinning and the cowboy firing his pistols in the air. It was marvellous. I remember my dad telling me that Crippen's wife used to sing there, but I can't remember her myself. The band had a violin, a double bass, a cornet and a piano. There was no pub in the music hall so my dad used to leave at half-time to get a drink or else he'd have gone mad. He used to get blind drunk and Mum and I used to come home on our own – then he swore blind that she was with a fancy man and it always ended up in a fight.

Ernest Hugh Haire

We used to go to theatre matinees at Leicester Square on Wednesday afternoons. I saw *The Merry Widow*, *The Maid of the Mountains* – all these musical comedies with Lily Elsie and others. We walked everywhere. On Sundays, we went to the Albert Hall to celebrity concerts where you saw the finest musicians in the world. If you queued, you could stand in the gallery free. It was wonderful. One night, we went to a vaudeville theatre in Chelsea. If we didn't like the turn, we all shouted, 'Get off the stage!'

Dolly Shepherd

When Cody first came over from America he went in for kites – Cody's Kites were well known, and that was what he was exhibiting at Alexandra Palace, apart from his pistol shooting. Captain Goudron was performing with his balloons and parachutes in the same hall. After I had the egg shot off my head, Goudron said, 'Would you like to make a parachute descent?' I said, 'I would – I'd love it.'

He showed me all the works and how to do it – the works were all hung up in the ceiling. I practised first without jumping, and he showed me how to fold the parachute down when you're on the ground. You had to be very careful not to get the ropes tangled. People used to say to me, 'What would happen if the parachute didn't open?' 'Why,' I would reply, 'you'd be killed.'

Joseph Yarwood

I'd been stage struck since was a child. I used to act out Shakespeare scenes for the other kids and I wanted to be an actor, but my father was always dead against it. He used to say, 'No! If you want to go in for that, you do it as an amateur!' One day, I saw an ad in the *Daily Chronicle* saying, 'Twenty-four boys wanted for West End production.' I kidded myself I had a bit of a voice, so I walked three or four miles to the agent's office in Berners Street. They listened to me sing and I got the job. But then I had to get permission from my father. I walked all the way from Berners Street to Barkers, where he was working. I was trembling as I went in to see him but he gave me a cup of tea and said, 'See what your mother says.' So I walked home on air to tell my mum, who thought it was a good idea.

The play was called *The Captain of the School* at the Gaiety Theatre. We played for six weeks and I took the part of a college boy, singing a Latin song in the last scene. I used to arrive at the theatre at half past one for Thursday and Saturday matinee and at seven o'clock on Monday, Tuesday, Wednesday and Friday for the evening performance. While the play lasted, I was paid fifteen bob a week and I was the happiest boy in London. After it finished, I waited for another acting job. A letter came from the agents offering me another job and my people hid it. They never told me about it until after the chance had gone. It would have been for a show at the Olympia in London for a well-known producer – and with it went my chance of becoming an actor.

Claire Ruane

I picked up the newspaper and saw an advertisement that said, 'Young ladies for the stage wanted. Experience not necessary.' That was me. So I went along to Duke Street, Piccadilly, and I saw a man and told him my story. I didn't tell him I was a skivvy – I was working as a domestic servant at the time. You had to pay so much down before he would interest himself. He said that if I paid him, he would put me in a show. I went back a few days later to find a strange, severe man sitting at the table. I nearly bolted down the stairs again. I told him that I'd come to see the man about music hall work. He asked, 'Which man?' I said that I didn't know his name. The severe man looked at me and asked, 'Did you give him any money?' 'No,' I said. 'I haven't got any.' I think the other man ended up going to prison for taking money from people like myself.

Minna Deacon

I became a performer in a very strange way. We lived in a dear old house in Shepherd's Bush and I used to go down to the end of the garden by the railway line and sing as the trains went by. One day, somebody heard me singing and came and asked Mother who had been singing. That's how I was discovered.

Kitty Marion

My aunt had made the acquaintance of a song writer and his family who had come to live nearby. He had a daughter on the Variety Stage and suggested that I should try my luck there. He would coach me in a couple of his songs – all I needed to start with – and give me an introduction to an agent. I had never been to a Music Hall, so I was taken to the old Cambridge, where the great Charles Godfrey and Jenny Hill were appearing. I was disappointed in some respects. It was not nearly so 'grand' as the theatre, and some of the artists in some of their songs were distinctly coarse and vulgar. I had no wish to associate with them.

However, when I felt proficient enough in my songs to face the British public, I sallied forth with a letter of introduction to a firm of agents in York Road near the corner of Waterloo Road, which in those days was called 'Poverty Corner' on account of the 'out-of-collar pros' hanging around, looking for work. I felt nervously anxious, but on the high road to success. There were other 'artistes' waiting in the outer office when I arrived, so I took a chair and waited too. I recognised the junior partner, when he came out. He dismissed some, asking others to wait. On presenting my letter and answering his questions, Mr Dreck told me of a benefit performance to be given the week after next at the 'Star', Bermondsey. He asked if I would volunteer my services. The Star was the roughest of the rough, hard-drinking, hard-swearing environments. I was first turn, the house was full in more ways than one, with drink and noise, and the overture was drowned out. The curtain rose, the chairman announced 'the first appearance of Mlle Kitty', the 'nom de theatre' suggested by the song writer. The stage manager said, 'Go on, throw it at em!'

My future, fortune, fame, life, everything depended on this moment. Dressed in pale pink, with my hair down, I tripped on to the centre of the stage and ignorant as I was, I felt the shouts and applause that greeted me were more ironic than genuine. With all the fight and defiance in me I 'threw' it at them, 'A Glorious Life on the Ocean!' They gradually quieted down and I finished and 'took a call' to genuine applause. 'Very good,' said the stage manager as I rushed past him to the dressing room and burst into tears. I thought I could never bear to go out there again. An old comedian encouraged me and asked me to 'have a drink, just for luck', so I had a small port, which helped to revive life and hope in me. Two neighbours who had come with me and were in the audience were encouraging. 'A bit amateurish,' they said, 'but your voice sounded fine and you stood your ground.' Other turns told me not to mind an audience like that. To take a rise out of newcomers and beginners was great sport to them. They didn't mean any harm.

Annie Hartley

My act was acrobatic barrel-jumping. To tell the truth, we copied the act from two Americans, but my brother and I always did athletic trick-jumping right from the age of eight. Years ago, young men out of work used to stand at street corners, saying things like 'I bet I can jump further than you!' and they used to try. It was such a rage that they used to make bets and then the police got on them. That's how we got started.

Pauline Chater

My mother loved my being an actress because she was so fond of the stage, but my father didn't like it a bit. He was a solicitor in an office opposite the Law Courts in the Strand. He didn't disapprove of the theatre but he wanted me to have something more 'definite'. It was a very precarious life. He stopped my first engagement. I was going to play a child's part and he wouldn't let me take it. My grandmother was terribly upset when I became an actress. She thought I would go to the dogs by going on the stage. But later, my uncle took her to see me in *Charley's Aunt* and after that she thought it was probably all right.

Minna Deacon

I was the black sheep of the family. No one else was in the business. My father and mother said, 'You're not going on the stage. We're not having our daughter on the stage.' In those days the stage had rather a sticky name. They didn't like it at all, but then our financial situation became a bit stretched and I said, 'I must go and earn some money.' And that's what I did.

Claire Ruane

When you were fresh in the music halls, the artists were so helpful and marvellous. You weren't left to ferret for yourself. They would come and talk to you. They'd say, 'Now, dear, I don't think you ought to do that. That don't seem right to me. I'll go out in front and watch you tonight.' And they'd help you that way, you see. They had the knowledge and they wanted to help you.

Pauline Chater

Laurence Irving was Sir Henry Irving's son and he gave me a lot of tuition. He taught me my first costume parts – Juliet for example. Mrs Irving played the lead alongside him as a rule, but she played many masculine parts – she played Figaro in *The Barber of Seville*, so I played Rosina and had my own song written for me. In *The King of the Vagabonds*, she played the Vagabond, Mr Irving played The King and I played the girl the Vagabond falls in love with. So whenever she played a masculine part, I had the ingénue parts. They were so fond of me. I lost my great friends when I lost them. Mr Irving produced a play over here called *Typhoon* and he wanted me to go to Canada with him to take a part in it, but I was very happy playing *Charley's Aunt* at the time, so I stayed where I was.

Kitty Marion

I played 'Dick Whittington' with Vesta Tilley as Dick at the Prince of Wales Theatre, Liverpool. I had quite a nice little speaking part, too, one of the FitzWarrens' impudent apprentices. It ran for three months, a phenomenal success in every way. Our producer and stage manager, Teddie Steyne, was the all-round best I have met. He rehearsed each section separately, so thoroughly that when they all met for general rehearsal, none had to wait, wasting time and energy, while others were trying to learn their business. Sometimes he lost his temper and yelled, 'For God's sake go home and pray to the Almighty to give you some intelligence!'

Jim Davies

I was working in a 'fit-up' company, which was almost the lowest form of acting. It played anywhere – institutes, halls and the lower-class theatres. The scenery we travelled with was only twelve feet, instead of eighteen feet, which was normal theatre size. We used to play 'stock'. That meant that we had a stock of plays that we performed. It wasn't called repertory in those days. We spent all our time rehearsing for the next play. I did props, played parts when necessary. I was the general help. We had about ten members. A juvenile lead, lady juvenile, heavy man, heavy woman, two comedy actors, a manager. People would always play similar roles. These people taught me quite a lot. I used to study them. We performed all the old standard melodramas. We never played anything high-class because we had to pay licences to Samuel French. At that time, I was only playing walk-on parts. I was getting £1 a week but I could get full board and lodgings for ten shillings. We dried up in Dorchester when the manager disappeared. He couldn't meet his obligations so we had no money. So we paid a guinea for a hall and we did a concert to raise money. I got three and sixpence for my share – having been out selling tickets all day.

Pauline Chater

I worked in an act called 'The Crisps'. They were two sisters and a brother and myself. I got on beautifully with them. I was like another sister. Except that I fell in love with the brother. We became engaged, but then he was killed in the First World War. He was my first love – and my only love really. I did marry after that, but it was nothing like the first love. It was really marvellous. I thought of going into a convent when he died.

Kitty Marion

When playing in Hull, I had my first chance to shine. Mrs Beryl had a cold, and on Tuesday night I had to deputise for her. Now I had never felt any sympathy for people who were nervous. I thought it was just affectation on their part. What need was there to be nervous when you know your part? A feeling of exhilarating, exciting expectancy of doing and enjoying your work, I could understand, but nervous – not I! But when the stage manager broke the news to me! I don't know what happened and I am unable to describe the sensation, but my heart seemed to jump up into my throat and stay there. If the stage had opened and swallowed me while waiting for my entrance it would have been a happy release. However, I flounced on, and certainly spoke the dialogue, or rather yelled it, while the stage manager at the side shouted, 'Speak louder! They can't hear you!' It was terrible, like being strangled, shouting for help, and being urged to shout louder.

Jim Davies

I talked myself into a musical comedy because I could do a few tap-dancing steps. I was the second juvenile in *The Dairy Maids* and we played town halls and places like that. I was learning all I could. Then I got a job as an understudy in a play called *The White Man* at the London Palladium. I talked my way up the ranks and after a while, they gave me the part. The chap playing 'Black Eagle' got pissed and I took over. By then I was living in Chelsea and earning £3 a week. There were eight or nine of us in the dressing room. The social life for a two-bit actor like myself was non-existent. Actors kept apart in those days. You didn't read in *The Mirror* about who they were living with or how many illegitimate children they had.

A music hall gallery, c.1902.

The Whip, 1909, one of many grand scale melodramas
produced at Drury Lane.

Kitty Marion

One day, while the overture was on and I was getting ready for my small bit in the opening, the wardrobe mistress came to tell me that Miss Soldene had not arrived and would not have time to dress and make up if she did, so I had better change into her dress and be ready to go on. Asking my understudy to speak my lines, I hurried off with the wardrobe mistress, who helped me into Miss Soldene's dress, and I just had time to light a cigarette and dash on to the stage. I was playing the Maracona, who, with much excitement and singing at the finale of the first half, faints. The audience was surprised at my coming-to to take the call. People thought I had really fainted. What a thrilling, exciting time when the curtain was down, and everybody was congratulating me.

The producer thanked me for 'saving his show'. He had been surprised when I made my entrance instead of Miss Soldene. Her letter saying she was not well enough to play that night came by the last post, about nine o'clock. I had met her the previous night, when, waiting for an entrance, the wardrobe mistress introduced me to her. I bowed with due deference to an old lady and a great star while she tossed her head and snapped her fingers in my face. The following week, when we went to the Theatre Royal, Sheffield, I was surprised, and some were shocked, to see my name 'starred' in place of Emily Soldene, with Georgina Delmar, Alec Marsh and Charles Collette.

Tommy Keele

I found a job in a show at the Drury Lane Theatre, called *The Whip*. Everyone knew that the Drury Lane Theatre was putting on these big racing shows using mechanical horses. Ex-jockeys used to ride the mechanical horses on revolving tracks and I thought that I'd like to do that. *The Whip* was the story of a famous horse that was sabotaged as it was travelling across the country. In the play there was a most frightening train crash that could only have been done at Drury Lane. The stage was equipped for that sort of business. It had hydraulic lifts so that part of the stage could go up and part could go down and it could also revolve. The racetrack scene was wonderful. They set up six tracks on stage. Each horse had its own individual track that was eight foot long and two foot six wide. There were three hundred-odd wheels inside each horse and they were all harnessed on to the track by little wire traces and a steel bar on the offside. It was often a job to get the horses started. One day, something went wrong with the horse at the back and the stable lads couldn't get it going. The curtain stayed down while they struggled with it and I was on the horse at the front so I turned round in the saddle to watch them. I was an agile little geezer. Suddenly, they got the horse going and the curtain went up and the audience saw me riding my horse backwards. They must have been a bit confused. I was always in trouble at Drury Lane.

I used to get twenty-five shillings a week, which was quite good for those days. I was living at home in King's Cross, but if we were touring, which a lot of the shows did, we could get into professional digs, which meant bed and full board for twelve shillings a week. If you paid thirteen shillings, you expected them to do a little bit of washing as well. So twenty-five shillings a week was quite good.

Claire Ruane

My best job was in Drury Lane. The show was *Ben Hur*. It was a very lavish show – very complicated. They could only have done it at Drury Lane. They had a very big man over from America to play the charioteer – Reginald Owen was his name. Kate Rourke was in it, so was Ethel Warwick, and a huge fleet of girls. I was one of them. I used to sing everything in the show at the same time as the principals and they couldn't work out where this other voice was coming from. I was doing the wrong thing. I was singing everything in the entire show. One night, the old man came round and I heard him say, 'I've got it!' and he knew. He'd worked out it was me. I was an Antioch with an enormous fan in that scene, and even though he couldn't see my mouth behind the fan, he could tell it was me singing.

I used to have understudy rehearsals, and when the principals came along to these, I would live the part. I would sob pints. Then, when the show moved to America, I was asked to go with it to play the part of the mother of Ben Hur, and I couldn't go because I was pregnant with my daughter. What a shame ... what a disappointment.

Kitty Marion

I was fortunate in seeing Madame Sarah Bernhardt playing special matinees at our theatre in several towns. It was like a goddess from another heaven visiting us, though we ordinary mortals could not use the 'green room' while it was being converted into a gorgeous boudoir-dressing room for the divine Sarah, until she had departed.

Claire Ruane

While I was on the MacNaughton tour, I was at the theatre one morning when Robb Wilton came up to me. He was a very quiet man – very polite. He said, 'Good morning.' 'Good morning,' I replied. He looked at me and said, 'You know you shouldn't be on the Music Halls.' 'Why?' I asked. 'You should be in the theatres, not the Music Halls. You're not right for them.' He was right, you know. I was too 'Aunt Maud' – too superior-looking. Music Halls were about walking three steps and shouting.

Tommy Keele

After I came back to England, I went back to Drury Lane to ride the mechanical horses. *The Hope* was a similar sort of racing show to *The Whip*. The big thing in this play was an earthquake. It was terrifying. All these houses tumbled down and people were shouting for help from windows and falling to the ground. They were acrobats, of course, but it was a ghastly sight. The race scene was at the end, but there again, silly little Tommy Keele got into trouble. I was supposed to come second in the race but something went wrong on the first night. All of us jockeys had been issued with riding whips over a foot long. On the first night, my whip got caught and it bent and flew out of my hand. The way the tracks were laid out meant that my horse had to come second. But after the play, there was a big knot of people around my track and I elbowed my way through. The producer was standing there looking black as thunder with my riding whip in his hand. I wasn't listening to what he was saying and eventually, I said, 'Excuse me, sir, may I have my whip back, please?' He looked at me. '*Your* whip? 'Yes, sir.' '*Your* whip?' 'Well,' I said, 'if it comes to that, it's *your* whip, isn't it?' He stared at me. 'You little bugger!' he said, 'I'll kick your arse out this theatre!' What had happened was – my whip had flown up in the air, came down through an inch-wide slot and landed across the track of the horse that was supposed to win the race. It acted as a chock and stopped the 'winning' horse from moving forward. So by accident my horse won the race. It was a million to one chance and it changed the whole play. I didn't even know it had happened.

Pauline Chater

I played theatres and music hall. I played in nearly all the theatres and music halls in every town in England. It wasn't difficult to do both. The theatre world wasn't separate from the music hall world in those days. One minute I was singing and dancing and the next I was playing a theatre part. That's one reason why I was never unemployed. I took anything that came along. But I preferred working in the theatre because I could lose myself into the part I was playing. I was much better as somebody else. As a child, I had been nervous, but on the stage I was a different person altogether. I lost my personality and I was the part, whatever it was.

Kitty Marion

One day, I met Mr Sam Bury, the producer of the Thomas Berrasford tour, who offered me Monday next at the Pavilion Glasgow, and the Monday after that at the Pavilion Newcastle at £4 per week. Mr Bury asked me to call at his office to sign the contract. When I arrived, he wanted to kiss me. I told him not to be silly and tried to 'chaff him off'. I had been advised by other artists that this was a better way of handling the situation than simply becoming indignant. So

I said I'd kiss him when I returned from the North. I walked towards the door and he followed me, threw his arms around me and refused to let go until I kissed him. 'All right,' I said and gave him what he called a peck on the cheek and dashed out. I felt sick – nauseated. How dared men take such brutal advantage of their economic power over women! Though I did well in Glasgow and Newcastle, Mr Bury only gave me one more date, in Salford, instead of the whole tour of fifteen weeks. Some time later, while sitting in the dressing room, discussing him and others of his ilk, one of a pair of sisters told me that when she had once tried to resist Mr Bury's advances, he had laughed at her and said, 'I've had your sister. Why shouldn't I have you?'

Claire Ruane

I worked for Fred Karno, along with a girlfriend of mine. He paid us thirty bob a week and we had rent to pay and food out of that. My girlfriend was such a dear – and she gave him 'what he wanted' and we ended up getting five bob a week extra. We tried to keep it secret but somehow the comic's wife found out and we left the Manchester Palace straight away. We left because the other girls would have given us merry hell if they'd found out.

Kitty Marion

Whilst on tour in Huddersfield, Mabel Hensey, with whom I was sharing rooms, and I came out of the theatre, each laden with a brown paper parcel, our laundry. Immediately, two 'stage door Johnnies' in evening dress – in Huddersfield of all places – rushed up with 'Oh I say, I beg your pardon, permit me!' each trying to take a parcel. We held on, saying, 'No thank you. I am quite able to carry it.' 'Oh Lady Disdain, don't be so independent!' said my would-be porter, 'I have been admiring you every night last week at The Grand. You look lovely in that black evening gown!' Eventually, I relinquished my parcel rather than risk its contents being scattered. We hadn't far to go and the situation did not warrant a 'How dare you!' kind of scene.

I had become quite tolerant towards that sort of approach from men. These two were genuinely delighted with the show and had occupied the same box every night during the previous week at Leeds. They left us at our door with an invitation to supper on the following night. Our landlady knew them both, two of the richest men in Huddersfield. In fact, my escort, John, owned the property on which her house stood. So we went to supper at the Wool Pack Inn. Oysters, pheasant, champagne and liqueur were all a pleasant change from our own economic table. On the way home, John P. C. started raving about my neck and arms and suddenly blurted out, 'I'd give you a thousand pounds to sleep with you for one night!' 'I wouldn't for a million!' I laughed back, 'and don't be so reckless with your money.' 'Good Lord!' he exclaimed, 'do you mean that?' 'I do!' I said emphatically. He couldn't understand a woman not having her price. He had never met one like me before and he apologised.

The dressing-room verdict on my refusal was as varied as the moral outlooks of the occupants. There were the conventional, irreproachable, straitlaces, with whom I was generally classed, who applauded my 'resistance to temptation', and then there were others who made no bones about 'augmenting their salary' who called me everything from a prude to a bloody idiot. They thought I damn well deserved to starve. But I was in love with my own idea of love, and despite my two pound a week salary, a thousand pounds had no part in it.

Claire Ruane

I was working in a show called *The Six Sisters Luck*. One night at the Lewisham Hippodrome, all the girls went out after the show with all these men to have a party, but I didn't go with them. My friend Rosie came back and said that I'd missed a treat. She said there was a man there who had wanted me very badly. The man was Austin Reed.

Kitty Marion

In Blackburn, six of us were sharing a sitting room and three bedrooms. One afternoon two of the girls went out shopping and invited one of our chorus boys, whom they met and who carried their parcels for them, to join us at tea, which was just ready. I, being sort of 'head of the family', called out to the landlady to please bring another cup and saucer. When she saw that our guest was a man she fairly exploded. 'I don't allow men in my house. Mine is a respectable house and he's got to go at once or I'll call a policeman.' We were flabbergasted. Here was one of our own boys whom we looked upon as a brother, innocently causing such a commotion. We insisted he should stay, and she went in search of a policeman. 'Girls, this isn't good enough, I'm off,' said the boy – and went. The landlady returned almost immediately with a bobby who lived only a few doors away and had just come off duty. After listening to the evidence and deciding no crime had been committed, I suggested that he should remain to tea, thinking it would be as well to give him some idea what kind of girls we were. The landlady was more furious than ever and threatened to report him if he stayed, to which he replied, 'Well, Missus, I'm off duty and free to do as I like.' He stayed – and evidently that was quite respectable with her.

Pauline Chater

In Herbert Lloyd's burlesque company, there were five of us. There were Mr and Mrs Lloyd – both Americans – another man, a girl and myself. I worked so hard in that show. I started in the front of the theatre, singing to the man on the stage whilst he sang and pointed to people in the audience. Then I rushed round and changed into a page boy's uniform and did a little step dance and took his hat and cigar, still dressed as his page boy. Then I changed into a Scots uniform and did a Scots reel and we finished up doing ballet dancing in spangled dresses. It lasted over half an hour. Herbert Lloyd was a big success, but being American, he didn't work so much over here. I worked with him in Vienna, Hamburg,

Dresden, the Casino Municipal in Nice, everywhere. When I was in Germany, I sang in German, when I was in France, I sang in French.

We were always travelling to get to the next place. We used to travel all night. So on the last performance in a place, every change I had, I had to quickly wrap the costume into a sheet and then when the curtain came down, we were off to the railway station. We used to have a bit of supper on our way. We'd grab a cup of coffee, sandwiches. We often used to have caviar sandwiches. I never used to think anything of caviar in those days.

Jenny Jackson

We went to Australia, and when we got to Sydney we were told to go in the box on a Saturday night to get to know what the audience liked. Well. We nearly died. We sat there and watched two men on stage having a spitting competition. 'We can't do that!' we said. 'We're English! We wouldn't be allowed to do that back home!' 'Well,' said the manager, 'that's the stuff they like over here.' So we had to put in filth like that.

Pauline Chater

When I was sixteen, I toured the United States with Laurence Irving. I spent my seventeenth birthday in New York. While I was there, we were rehearsing at the Hackett Theatre one morning and a silver-haired gentleman came up to me and said, 'I was in the front row last night and I want to shake your hand. I think you're a very clever little actress.' Mrs Irving came up to me and said, 'That's something you'll remember all your life.' When I asked her why, she said, 'That was Mark Twain.'

Later, I was eight months singing and dancing at the Folies Bergère with Maurice Chevalier. He used to call me his 'little pomme frites girl'. He would sing and dance while four of us sang and danced behind him. We wore the most beautiful clothes I've ever seen in my life – all chiffon and spangles. In one number we had pink brocade dresses with the old-fashioned bodice and white wigs and

315

rows of pearls, and when we came on, we were miniatures within a large golden frame.

Jim Davies

I walked to London and I met a clown called Bonzo and he took me on at five shillings a week. That's how I joined Lord John's Circus. I used to march round the town in the parade and I was an 'Auguste' – a white-faced clown. I did a lot of little routines with the team – I used to be slapped up the backside with the slapstick. Circus life was a bit rough but I managed to get myself another five shillings a week by helping with the seating and loading up.

Pauline Chater

Whenever the Irvings played, their dog was their mascot. The dog had to come on stage with them. When we went to America, we couldn't take the dog because of the quarantine restrictions so we had to get a local dog to take its place.

Annie Hartley

At fifteen, I got to London. We played at the Royal Aquarium – that's where the Victoria Palace is now. Then we played Gilbert's Circus. That was before it became the London Palladium. We played the Hippodrome – where The Talk of the Town was. We played the Coliseum, four shows a day. We had a beautiful act. Acrobatic barrel-jumping. I had all the tricks. The act was about seven minutes long. Everything in the act was quick. Had to be quick.

Claire Ruane

I was only in bed for three days when my child was born. I was back on the stage on the fourth day. With *The Six Sisters Luck*.

Pauline Chater

In 1906, there was a strike on in the music halls, and we were playing at the Oxford Music Hall and people called out, 'Blacklegs!

Blacklegs!' and I asked, 'What do they mean?' The little boy in the show said, 'I don't know. I had a bath this morning.'

George Hewins

My wife became a dresser at the Shakespeare Memorial Theatre. It suited her down to the ground. She loved it. I was relieved, I can tell you. She had Violet Farebrother, Ethel McDowall, Mrs Forster – and all their old hats. Soon she had a hat for every day of the week, and we couldn't see the tea caddy nor the clock for signed photographs! And there was perks for me. After matinees, if it was raining, I fetched the tea for the actresses from a cottage in Waterside. 'Keep the change!' they said, and gave me half a sovereign. I prayed for rain.

After the play the actresses got undressed. The missus helped them, packed the costumes in the wardrobe baskets. If they'd been sweating badly she sponged them down and perfumed them. She got extra for that. If she was going to be late, I went and sat on the baskets to wait for her. I was sat on a wardrobe basket one night and the barber, who made up the actors and actresses, gave me a funny look and said 'You got anything to do tonight?' I said, 'No.' 'Well,' he said, ''es a bloke short. 'ow would you like to come along?' I said, 'Ah! Do me a good turn.' I didn't know what I was letting myself in for! 'You do an hour's performance,' he said, 'and if you don't suit 'im, the gaffer 'as somebody else – quick.'

Well, he must've liked me! By two o'clock next morning the rehearsal was over, and I was a super – a super with Frank Benson's Company! We had three bob a show, and if we stopped after the play at eleven, stopped till two sometimes or three, and rehearsed for the next night's play, to see what he thought of it, that was <u>another</u> three bob! Frank Benson would say at night, 'Now, we've got some special guests a-comin', m'boys. I'll pay you extra if you'll stop and go through this play.' I was in my element.

There was considerable public interest in ballooning.
And parachuting from the balloon.

Pauline Chater

Film work was just starting but I didn't like it. I preferred the stage. Film work was so artificial and I'm not good at posing. All my notices were for being natural. In filming you were restricted as to space. I wanted to be here, there and everywhere.

Bert Clark

On Saturday afternoons we'd go to the Palace Cinema – a penny to go in and it was all silent movies with someone playing the piano – oh yes, they were good. They'd be playing while us kids were creating hell. Then we'd buy a bag of sweets when we came out.

Jack Brahms

I remember the very first picture house that opened near us was in Hanbury Street, and they had forms there and they charged you a ha'penny. Round the back they were spraying the screen – with water, and that was the very, very first one that opened.

Mr C. Tomlinson

Every Saturday morning, before the war, the cine operator at the old Hippodrome used to go out and take film of people parading up and down. Saturday morning in Southport was always a very special morning – all the people that mattered always turned out, with their beautiful daughters all dressed up in their best finery – it was quite a sight. Sunday mornings, if it was fine in the summertime, the Promenade was the place to go. But on the Saturday, all the boys had to go and have a look and see what was happening. This chappie used to take pictures, and that was a great attraction at the time, and people would go along the following week to see if they were on screen, and see how they looked. He must have had dozens of reels of film.

They really did dress in those days – beautiful frocks and hats with fruit salad on, or birds – huge hats. I had three sisters and they used to dress up – they used to have papers and roll their hair round it to make it look huge – and then they put a huge hat on. I suppose it's giving the game away really, but it was a great parade, people walking up and down – the mothers and their daughters, and the boys all hanging around.

Ted Harrison

The first time I went to the pictures, I went to the Varieties, which was a gaslit theatre. I saw a film of John Bunny and Flora Finch. They were husband and wife comedians. He was a big fat old boy with a bulbous nose, and she was a skinny, acid-looking woman. After that, I used to go to Charlie Wright's. He was a local philanthropist who would hire the Pickfield Baths and turn them into a cinema. It was all free and we would all sit on the floor. I saw *Quo Vadis* and *Les Misérables*. It must have been at the time of the Balkans War, because we were shown all these terrible pictures of dead Turks. These pictures were 'the news'. As we watched them, they played a barrel organ in the background.

Tom Norman

You could indeed exhibit anything in those days – yes, anything from a needle to an anchor, a flea to an elephant, a bloater you could exhibit as a whale. It was not the show, it was the tale that you told.

Dolly Shepherd

When you do a balloon descent, you hang under the balloon then you pull the rip cord. In those days you had to twist your hand round and guide the parachute this way and that. You had to go where the wind took you. I've been on a chimney on top of a house – over trees ... nearly on an express train. The driver had the presence of mind to blow the steam, which just drifted me off into the canal at Grantham.

One day I went up in a thunder and lightning storm. The people took a vote – they were Scots, and they wanted their money's worth. So I went – and it was one of the weirdest experiences. You felt the lightning and thunder all around you – you felt you were part of it

– oh, and it was raining. All I know was I was glad to be down. I landed in a churchyard and bump, there I was sitting quietly on a gravestone.

I used to wear high-legged boots and a navy-blue knickerbocker suit, and a tight-fitting tunic – and I had a gold balloon and parachute. I used to wear a cap or a woolly hat, according to the weather. I used to take a little Union Jack up with me and I waved it – people loved that. Every town and village seemed to have a flower show or fête each year – and it usually ended up with fireworks – but a balloon ascent was a major attraction. I was billed as the Parachute Queen.

There was one time when I went up at Alexandra Palace when the balloon was not full enough – the hot air was getting out. The man hadn't turned up to do the parachute drop, but people recognised me in the crowd and said, 'Oh, Miss Shepherd's here!' So I had to do it. But I was just wearing normal clothes, so I tucked my skirt between my legs and fixed it with a big safety pin, and went up – otherwise the whole event would have been a flop.

When you went up you'd wait until you got through the clouds, then you'd come back through. They used to love that. I'd disappear, so they were looking out for me, then I'd just reappear – and that was the thrill they wanted. You always looked down at the crowds – but once you'd lost sight of the crowd, you looked where you were going. I used to say to myself, 'Oh, isn't it lovely here? Isn't it lovely – and silent? Beautiful.' No one knows that calm sereneness unless they've been there.

I had one very bad accident, and I became more famous after that, particularly because I carried on. On one occasion, I went up, I went up very high – about twelve thousand feet. It sounds stupid, but I'm sure I heard a voice saying, 'Don't come up again.' And when I came down, I gave all my things away – my hat and my Union Jack. I never went up again.

Ron Taylor

My great granddad was a mountain fighter, and fought when it was illegal in the days of bareknuckle fighting. My dad used to tell me all about this, and this is what his dad told him. They used to stick four sticks in the ground, put a rope around, and then they had backers or challengers and nobility would back them and most of their payments would be the nobbings. The nobbings are when they used to go round with the hat, because they used to fight mostly on grass so they couldn't chuck money in the ring. So if they'd put up a good fight, they used to get the nobbings.

When they brought out the Marquess of Queensberry rules, where they wore gloves, and they legalised it, my great-grandfather could see that there was potential in it, so he opened a booth on the fairgrounds. So my great-grandfather and some of his friends, they challenged anyone out of the crowd to fight, and the public paid to go in and see them. Before this they didn't pay to see the fight and the boxers relied on nobbings and the showman got nothing because all the money was made on the betting. So that's how my family graduated then to the fairgrounds.

Esther McKeowen

I've always been involved in boxing. My dad had a booth and my brother was a good fighter. My grandfather was a fighter and they used to take him in hansom cabs to his fights, and for three years he was travelling in the Midlands.

I was nearly twenty when I got the booth – my father had it before then, and my brothers used to box in it. My brother was known as 'One-Round Gratton', because he would knock them out straight away. We bought the booth from my dad and travelled it by truck. When I was a child my father had horses, I walked more miles than I rode. I know we went to Portland Fair and I always know how far it is from Weymouth to Portland – eight miles. My brother Johnny used to walk most of the way between Barnstaple to Bridgewater, to try and find the watering holes for the engine.

These electrograph shows had music and dancing girls outside.

Mrs Brewer's show was a small show and Anderton and Rowland had a big show, and they had three Scottish girls who came down and paraded on the outside. Well, although Mrs Brewer had two sons who were very good drummers, they were too close to Anderton's big show to take any money. These girls were dancing on the front, so they'd got to put a pole across to keep the people back. Mrs Brewer asked my mother if I could go on the front because one of her girls had broken a leg, so she only had one daughter to go on. I was only about nine and it didn't take Mrs Brewer long to make me a Scottish outfit.

The crowd had never seen a child dancing like that before, and I was there doing the Scottish dance, and we end up pinching their pitch and their punters, because they turned from one show to the other and we were packed out. It was about threepence to go in and I've never seen anything like that in my life – for a little show to go up against a big show and get all those people in.

Sidney Race

At Nottingham Goose Fair there was a Fine Art Gallery and what was apparently a fat woman show. The last was of a very dubious character if the signs that it displayed were any index of what was shown within: 'The Egyptian Dancers', 'That naughty little girl', 'All sorts of positions', 'The Oriental Dancers from the Harem', 'The Girl with Two', 'The Man with Three' and, as a significant warning, 'NO ladies admitted unless accompanied by a gentleman'.

Esther McKeowen

One time we were at Dawlish and everybody could only have one show up. This particular showman had got a fat girl and I'd got a fat girl – mine was a nice clean-looking fat girl called Nellie, but his was fatter than mine. So we worked it out that I opened my show and he'd put his strip show up. So we are at this place and before we're open, this showman is letting his fat girl walk up and down outside my show. So I get the megaphone and I call out, 'Ladies and gentlemen, that's her little sister we are showing you for nothing, can you imagine what it's like on the inside.'

John Wynn

I remember in the market square where they used to have wild beast shows, and the first running picture show, run by a person called Payne, and on the stage in front, Payne's daughters used to come and give a little sing-song before the show started. I remember one song I used to sigh for – 'The Silvery Moon' – and right up in the top corner they had a silvery moon hanging up, and then after they gave this little performance the show would start. Now and again the fair used to come in, with Crow's hobby horses and other such things, and that made the place quite lively for us lads.

Polly Lee

There would be a show at the top of the market place – Cooper's show with rides and all sorts. There were swings, and there used to be something called the 'ships on dry land', big ships that went round and round. There used to be matinees there, with dancing on the front way. We used to get underneath and pick up all the sequins which came off their dance frocks. Mrs Cooper would stand in her black satin frock with a pocket on each side, taking your pennies in for to look at the peep show – it was just a picture behind a magnifying glass! That's all it was, a big bull's-eye you looked through, and you saw a magnified picture of the Battle of Waterloo.

Tommy Keele

Racing was still in my blood. I'd heard of somebody in Germany who was buying blood horses to ride show jumping, and I thought this was just what I wanted to do. So I lived in a village in the middle of Germany. I rather liked the Germans. The German police used to come round to this village wearing the old picklehob hats with the spike on the top. I used to ride round the village with them. One day, I said 'Ich bin halb Deutsch' – 'I'm half German.'

That was only because my name sounds a bit German. Keele sounds like the Kiel Canal. Well, they took me seriously and one of the police officers interrogated me. He asked why I wasn't in the Army if I was half German. I never felt any feeling that there might be a war coming. It wasn't thought of – no smell of it at all. No one thought of the Germans as an enemy in those days. In fact they were most friendly.

Steve Tremeere

All the beggars used to come round singing – they all got a farthing. Even the poorest always used to take them out a ha'penny or penny. They used to sing

> Throw out the lifeline, throw out the lifeline,
> Someone is drifting away;
> Throw out the Lifeline! Throw out the lifeline!
> Someone is sinking today.

They kept on at it till they got some money. Then the Italians started coming over – they'd play music and you could pay and pick out an envelope with your fortune on. Then there was the Russian bear men. All sorts. You could go in and you'd see them round the big fire, with the big stove – all cooking up. They had what they called a padding kens stew. They didn't call them lodging houses – they called them padding kens. There was always some monkeys up the lodging house at the back of us.

When I was a kid I sometimes saw the most pathetic thing. I was up Union Row, where the workhouse was. Us boys would be up there Saturday morning, getting the coke on the barrow. I saw an old bloke come up with an old girl, his wife. He had a little handkerchief tied round the little things what they had got left, the old girl on his arm was crying her bloody eyes out. We'd watch them till they got up to the Union. She was hanging back as they got up near the big doors – didn't want to go in there, but at last they had to go in. The matron got hold of her and took her away, and the master took the poor old bloke the other way. That's the last they saw of each other. Wicked that was, parting them at that old age, when they'd been together all their lives.

Harold Lawton

When I was about ten, I met and fell in love with a little girl of seven called Bessie. On the day that she and I met, my mother and her mother were talking, and they told us to go and have a walk along an interesting little bit of canal. It was all quite proper, and while our two mothers were doing what they wanted to do, my little girl and I would go walking. It was marvellous, she was lovely – and a very long time later, we were married and were happy together for fifty-eight years.

TRAVELS AND EXCURSIONS

Ethel Barlow
The traffic in the streets used to be terrible. There were so many horses and carts and horse buses and horse trams. It was chaos. I remember watching a fire engine drawn by six horses. The one in the middle slipped and fell down and they dragged the poor thing along until the engine stopped, and then they released him from the harness and just left him on the side of the road. He was there until the council came and picked him up.

Mary Keen
Everything was dirty. The transport, the streets, everything. They hardly ever cleaned the trains, so you had to be very careful with your clothes. You generally took a bit of rag or something to rub the seat where you were going to sit.

Lady Charlotte Bonham Carter
With all the horse-drawn vehicles, the roads were terribly cluttered. Sometimes when there was a sudden shower, the streets got terribly muddy, but there were always delightful 'crossing sweepers'. They were elderly men, very often with beards, and if one waved to them as one was crossing the street, they would come over and sweep in front of one. On one occasion, I was having lunch at St James's Palace. Just as I was approaching, the most appalling storm came, absolutely frightful, and the roads became a sort of duck pond, and there was no crossing sweeper about. I had on my very best pair of

white suede shoes and I arrived in an appalling state and there was nothing I could do.

Ethel Barlow
In the East End, we never had any crossing sweepers. That was only in the West End. We did have a water cart. It was like a big tank on a cart and there was a sprinkler on the back of it with a water can. We used to sit on the back of it and wash our feet.

Ray Head
The streets of the City of London were very, very dirty. The horse manure was all over the place. Boys used to collect it up in little pans and brushes and put it in special containers. At night time, the cleaners used to come along with hoses and hose the whole City down.

Alfred West
It was all horses in the streets. There was no other transport. It was a job to get across because the cabbies used to pull their cabs up against the kerb and put their horse's head in a nosebag. So to get across the road, we had to crawl under the horse's belly or under their neck.

Mrs L. Welsh
Bayswater Road up to Notting Hill Gate was a country road, and girls used to walk along there with big milk pails, selling the milk as they went. At Notting Hill there was a farm – my father knew the owners – they had sheep, pigs and cows there.

Ruben Landsman
I remember the sheep coming through Brick Lane from pavement to pavement – droves of sheep, which they'd bring through.

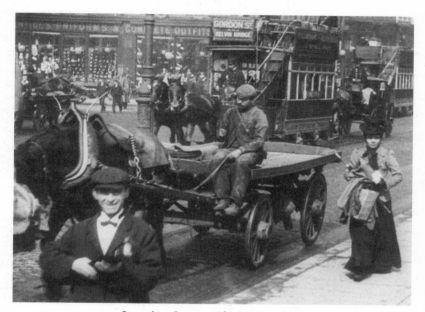

Jamaica Street, Glasgow, 1901.

Lady Charlotte Bonham Carter

In order to get from one place to another in the evening, one had to take either a four-wheeler or a hansom cab. One's parlour maid whistled for them. If you wanted the four-wheeler, she whistled once, but if you wanted the hansom cab, she gave a double whistle. The hansom cabs were very delightful.

Mrs L. Welsh

My mother's cousin had a hansom cab and I kept asking my mother when he was going to visit. 'One day,' she said. When he turned up, we couldn't run to him quick enough. He was a real old-fashioned man with whiskers, a tall hat and a big old cape. I got up by the side of him and he said, 'You've never been in my hansom cab, have you?' 'No,' I replied. 'Would you like to?' he asked. 'Yes,' I said. So we got in. You had to climb up a big step to get in. He was sitting upstairs and he looked through a little window and he said, 'Where do you want to go?' 'Westbourne Grove,' we said. He took us there and we called out of the window to all our friends as we went.

Ronald Chamberlain

Some high officials wouldn't travel in trams or buses. They had a horse and carriage. There were the old hansom cabs with two wheels and a man sitting up the top and driving the horse. People who wanted to travel to the station and had luggage would either travel in that or they'd go in a 'growler' – a four-wheel thing with a horse. But the horse bus was the way of getting about for ordinary folk like us. Of course we boys always wanted to sit on top, where it was open. If it was raining heavily, they had great big tarpaulins which you could put across the seat and button up around your neck.

One nice thing about the horse bus was that you could sit beside the driver, who had a little sort of enclave just by the front seats. There were big notices inside and outside, saying, 'Do not spit. Penalty thirty shillings.' In those days, spitting was rather a common practice amongst working men. That's why they had sawdust on the floor in public houses. The drivers of these buses were great talkers.

Ready at a moment's notice, in the meantime enjoying
being filmed. Wigan Fire Brigade, 1902.

They'd tell long stories and comment on people and vehicles going by in a very humorous way.

John Smith

What a sight for us younger ones to see the fire engines come charging out of Bedminster Fire Station! The engine was drawn by horses. The harness hung over the central draught pole and could be lowered quickly on to the horses' backs when they were placed underneath. The glass sliding doors enabled a quick take-off, and away they went – galloping hooves, clanging bells, smoke from the water-pumps and the tenders with water and ladders. Horses and carts pulled in to the side of the road. Tram cars halted, children ran after the engine, and then came the clang of the bell of the horse-drawn ambulance.

Ethel Barlow

I used to be scared of the horse bus. When it pulled into the kerb you thought you were going to fall out. It was all open at the top and you had a mackintosh apron to cover your knees. The horse tram was better. I often took it from Stratford Broadway to Aldgate East – a return ticket was a penny.

George Perryman

When I was fifteen, I started work as a horse van driver. It was very common for someone of that age to be driving a van. I used to start at seven in the morning. First I'd give the horses their hay and oats, then I'd groom them and rub them down. After that, I'd put the bridle on and the bit in their mouths, and put the saddle and girth on. Finally I'd chain the leads on to hooks on the van. Then, off we'd go with me sitting in my four-wheeled van.

One day, I pulled up with the van after I'd come back from the docks, and somebody had pinched my lights. It was getting dark and I had to get back to the stables, so I drove without lights and this policeman came along and summonsed me. I had to go down to Old Street and I was fined but I never had the money to pay the fine. So I ended up in Pentonville Prison. I was only in there twenty-four hours and my Aunt Daisy came along, paid the fine and they let me out.

Mary Keen

Before cars came along, there were very few accidents on the roads. If you wanted to cross the road and a cart was coming, you used to hold your hand out and everything would stop.

Miss Andrews

I had an accident in a horse and cart. My mate was driving, and we were coming along this road near St Andrew's Road in Southampton and there was a little pony trap on a side road. We were on the main road and the trap didn't pull up for us. We went on and our horse went right on top of theirs, on top of the people in the trap. Oh, they were riled – they took us to court, but we won the day.

George Perryman

We used to take the horses down to a farrier in Hobbs Place to be shoed. The streets were mostly cobblestones, so the shoes only lasted about six months before you had to get them done again. When the horses were ill, we took them to a vet in Worship Street. The only accident I ever had was just before Christmas. I was driving an open van with two horses and I'd gone down to Mount Pleasant to load up mailbags to take to the different train stations. I'd dropped some bags at Waterloo Station and as I came out into York Road, a chain came loose and one of the horses got away. It was a steep hill but I managed to pull the other horse up and stop the van. I caught the loose horse up and scolded him. I shouldn't have done really because it wasn't his fault. I reattached him and went back to Mount Pleasant, and after that we took more mailbags to Charing Cross and King's Cross. The only other accident I can remember seeing was a dray that stumbled in Kingsland Road, breaking his nearside front leg. He had to be put down.

Richard Common

I used to walk from Wallsend to North Shields, and in those days the road was just a track with hedges up each side. In the winter, there used to be an old Scotsman there, we called him 'Goosy Gander', and he used to have a big brush and he swept the mud from the centre of the road so the horses and carts could get past.

James Bowles

I remember the Yellow Perils starting in Ambleside – they were big yellow buses. Mr Jones had a little wagon that would carry fourteen, and there was always a little trip out from Little Langdale every year for the children. For this outing we went in a horse-drawn wagonette to Coniston Station and then on a train to Barrow to go to Biggarbank. The coaches used to come and stop at Mother's inn for the drink for the horses. Mother always used to give them two handsful of oatmeal in every bucket, and they had a drink of water while the men had a drink of beer. The horses only stopped coming when the war started.

Harrison Robinson

When you went out into the country, if you saw a motor car coming you used to all run out to see it. To go to Braidley in Yorkshire where my mother lived, we used to go on the train to Skipton, and that was the end of the line. Then you changed to a wagonette with four horses, which would go as far as Grassington, where they would change horses and take you to Kettlewell, where you had seven miles to walk, unless they sent a horse and trap for you.

James Bowles

The roads were kept fit for the horses, so you could get a team of five horses along them. Going downhill they had what they called a slipper, and if the lads wanted to earn a penny or two, they would go to the bottoms or the tops of the hills and put the slippers on. It was a piece of metal, shaped like a slipper, and you pushed it between the wheel and the coach at the back. The people got out and walked – the very old stayed on – but the majority of them walked. The slipper would hold one wheel so that the horses could manage, otherwise it would overrun the horses going down the hill. So the one wheel skidded downhill without turning.

Charles Whicker

Braithwaite Cannon had three MPs staying at Wall End farm, they came up for a week's rock climbing and wanted to catch the train back to London. So he set off with them in his dog cart, which was always tied up with string – old Braithwaite never had a decent cart! When he got to Slopps Bridge, part of the string broke, scattering these three MPs and their luggage out on to the road. Some friends of his quickly went and got a horse and trap, and he got them to Windermere in time to catch their train – and they gave him a sovereign for getting them there. He treasured that sovereign. From then on, it was old Braithwaite's proud boast that he was the only man in England to unseat three MPs in one day!

Harrison Robinson

I remember the electric tramcars starting, in 1901. Before that was steam cars, which I only caught a glimpse of, because I was very young. The steam cars ran from Gateshead Station to Heworth. When the electric came in, they put them along Cotesworth Road. I remember stepping over the tramlines, because I'd heard the bigger boys say the electricity would kill you.

Ronald Chamberlain

I remember seeing the first motorbus. It must have been in about 1907. Somebody shouted, 'Quick! Quick! Come and look! There's a bus without a horse!' It was a very primitive thing running along in Islington, making an awful lot of stink and noise, but everybody stood up to look.

Mary Keen

I used to travel on the Underground. I remember when the tuppenny tube was opened. You could go from Shepherds Bush to the Bank for tuppence. It was the same price, however far you went. It was very crowded because it was so popular. It was cheaper than the ordinary rail.

Nicholas Swarbrick

I used to take the train to my Catholic college. My house was next door to the railway, and you could wait until the train was actually in the station and then run out to catch it. It was a steam train in those days – and it was a journey of about twenty minutes to the station at Ribbleton, then Deepdale – a more important station, then you went under a tunnel, and out at Maudland, which was adjoining the main line which runs on that side of Preston. We more or less behaved ourselves on the train, but we had some high jinks. I'd put my head out of the window, which you lowered on a leather strap, and the ash from the smoke stack would blow into my eyes.

Mrs Kearton

Tourists were beginning to come by train. Alston was known as a quiet, clean place among the professional classes of Newcastle – some had houses here, some took rooms. There was a good livery stable, which picked people up from train and took them to their hotel or house. The wagonette which ran from Garrigill to the train took visitors there.

Going to Penrith was an expedition and required planning. It was a long journey in a brake and three, you had to be really hardy to do it in winter. At the top of Hartside, the road was very basic, with no posts or white lines, so you trusted to the horses' good sense that they could see the edge. At night you only had the candle lights on the carriage, so it was the horses that got us home.

Horse-drawn tram, Manchester, 1901.

Celebrating the opening of the Acrington Electric Tramway in 1907.

Ernest Taylor

I remember the railway accident in Crosby in 1903 – I was in the last coach of the train. Two trains used to leave Exchange Station at four-thirty – the first was a stopping train to Southport, and the second was an express to Southport. On a Wednesday afternoon, which was our holiday from school, we used to have to go back into town, and we went to Exchange Station to come home. Just for devilment, you'd get on the wrong train – the express – to get a run through to Birkdale, which was the first stop. When you got off you'd tell the fellow you got on the wrong train. Well, this Wednesday, the blessed thing came off the rails at Waterloo. Myself and my two cousins were in the last coach. We used to get in, pull the blinds down, lock the door with our stolen carriage key and get out our Woodbines. When it stopped the last carriage was quite a way out of Waterloo, nearer to the Five Lamps, and it never left the rails. When we got out on to the platform there was a bit of a commotion because somehow the engine had finished up on the platform, facing back the way it came. We carefully lifted a little girl out. She had new button boots on, and she was crying because her new boot was broken. Well, her foot was inside that boot, and it was all broken too – all crushed.

Evelina Goddard

Around the turn of the century, the hay used to go up to London by trainload. My father didn't retail it round London – that was done by various big merchants. We also sent hay up by barge. On the Deben river, nearly all those farms had quays, so barges would come up there and load from them.

Alice Smith

I remember the barges on the canal – drawn by horses. They loaded up goods in Manchester and dropped them in Castleton and then to Rochdale. Then they'd load up there, if there was anything to come back this way. We used to ride on the horses if we were allowed. When people fell in the canal, you just had to pull them out. If they had a pair of shoes on, the policeman would take the shoelace out and put the end of the lace through the person's tongue, and tie it in the buttonhole of his coat. If the tongue moved there was life in them. If not, they took them away. Lots of people did away with themselves like that. There was always someone being pulled out of the canal.

Mary Keen

I remember the first motor cars. They used to have a man with a red flag walking in front. Everyone was very excited at seeing them. They were open, with two people sitting at the back, and people used to walk and run behind them.

Mildred Ransom

Motors changed London completely, and greatly for the better. The horses on the streets had suffered terribly: it was not possible to keep the streets clean, and when horses were off the streets, every lover of them rejoiced. Motor transport also took workers further out of London and made their lives far more varied and amusing.

Evelina Goddard

As I grew older, we took to a car, which my father hated like poison. He considered it an invention of the devil! Anyway, he never drove himself, but as soon as I could drive – and I could drive quite well – I used to drive him around. The hay trade in which he had worked all his life was finished more or less, because cars were coming in, so hay wasn't needed for the horses.

Bill Elder

I can remember the first car in our area. It belonged to a man called Billy Strang Steel. The man who had been his coachman became his chauffeur – but he was only used to horses. He hadn't got the hang of steering and braking, so the car ended up in a field off the Yarrow Road.

Cecil Barnes

The first car my father had was an old Dion Singleton. You sat two each side, facing one another, a driver and a passenger in front – which made it a six. It was only about nine horsepower, and the gears were underneath the steering wheel – just one, two, three and reverse, and the clutch was also there. There was no accelerator pedal – you used a quadrant on top of the steering wheel. If I sat on the seat I couldn't reach the clutch pedal, but if I stood up I could hold on to the steering wheel, shove the clutch out, put her into gear, let the clutch in and open the throttle with this quadrant on top of the wheel. You could alter your timing, your spark as well – either advance it or retard it. We used to take it to pieces, me and my brother. We had a pulley on the stable roof and we used to lift the cylinder block off, clean all the carbon out, and grind the valves in. Cars were very rare in those days. If you saw a car go by you rushed out to see where it was going and who was driving.

Sir Geoffrey de Havilland

In Gloucester the owners of a large cycle shop had daringly bought two 3 ½-h.p. Benz cars, and a friend and I saved up and hired one, with a driver, to take us to Newbury at the end of term at Eton. It was the first time I had been in a motor car, and it was a great adventure. We had to help the car up Birdlip Hill as the leather transmission belts slipped on their pulleys, but after reaching the top we careered along the level stretches at anything up to 15 m.p.h. We eventually arrived at Newbury where we were surrounded by a crowd of excited sightseers. We felt like returning explorers.

We had scarcely, in the popular phrase, annihilated space. But after that short drive I knew that my future life lay in the world of mechanical travel. The fascination of independently powered and swift transportation from place to place that was to seize so many of the young of my generation had gained a hold which was never to relax through all my working life.

London's Piccadilly Circus in 1910 saw a remarkable array of traffic.

Henry Lansley

I carried on being a groom until I was sent to London in 1910 to learn motor driving. The first car I ever saw was about 1896 or 1897. It belonged to Lord Carnarvon. Rumour had it that he was travelling to Whatcombe, where his horses were in training. For once, rumour was right, for after some wait, along the road came a car, making a lot of noise. It was being driven by a Frenchman, who had brought it over from France to instruct the man who would become Lord Carnarvon's chauffeur.

The first car I drove was a new 16 hp Wolseley. My employer had taken a hunting box in Warwickshire. On my way a terrific snow-storm set in and, as there were no windscreen wipers, I couldn't see a thing. So I stopped at Rugby for the night, and went on next day. Luckily the car was a very heavy one – two tons, five hundredweight empty – so it gripped pretty well in the snow. Side and tail paraffin lamps were fitted and the headlamps were lit by acetylene gas, which had to be attended to daily. Also, there were no spare wheels. What we had was a Stepney, which had to be clamped to the punctured wheel. If not on very tight, it would creep and slip and you wouldn't get along at all. Only the rear wheels were braked, and as there were no self-starters, it was always necessary to swing the handle at the front.

My Wolseley could carry five people inside and two outside, as well as much luggage on the top. When fully loaded it was sometimes difficult to get up the hills without either the engine boiling, or the clutch slipping, to which those old leather-lined clutches were very prone. I have often had to get out and put pieces of hacksaw blade under the leather, to pack it up. After such treatment it would grip satisfactorily, sometimes for several weeks.

Gerald Cussons

I personally liked the old-fashioned cars with the slow revs. I took my first licence out in 1911, and I took a car from Dieppe down to St Moritz and from there over the passes down into Italy. On the way back I drove along the Riviera to Marseilles and shipped the car back to Tilbury and we came back by train. During the whole of that time I never put a spanner on that car. We'd no detachable wheels – if we had a puncture we had these Stepney wheels, which were just like a wheel, with a tyre, but they had these four clamps which fitted over the edge of the rim of the existing wheel and you tightened up the wing nuts until they were firm. It was a job in the old days to fit those Stepney wheels, you had to have it right or the boat rocked. The next invention after that was a detachable rim, but that didn't catch on – and eventually somebody had the bright idea of a detachable wheel.

Ray Head

In 1907, the police set up a 'speed trap' to catch any motorist doing more than 20 mph along the Bath Road, which was a main thoroughfare to the west. A team of three police constables went out on a Sunday morning and positioned themselves a furlong apart. The first policeman pulled out a handkerchief as a signal to the second, who estimated the speed of the driver with a stopwatch. He then waved to the third constable who intercepted the speeder. Since many drivers at the time were influential people, quite a few were let off with a warning. Others were charged at Brentford Police Station. After booking a suitable number, the three policemen used to adjourn to a pub called 'The Traveller's Friend'.

Ada Bassett

I was taught to drive in 1910, by a young man who had been at school with me. I found it very easy. He'd just turn up and change seats and off we'd go. No licence, no 'L' plates and very few cars. Wonderful time to learn. We used to drive up to London and all around. Petrol was so cheap, and I could get out and get under because the young man taught me how to change a tyre and sort out the engine.

Mrs G. Edwards

My father met his death in 1910, going round to a big house to repair a clock. He was knocked down by a motor car in Hyde Park Corner. My mother always used to say that he'd asked her to go with him that day but she hadn't gone because she had something she wanted to do. She always thought that if she'd gone, it wouldn't have happened.

Lord Brabazon of Tara

I saw my first accident at Harrow. I was coming back from the station when to my joy I saw a motor wagonette coming down Grove Hill. The driver put his brakes on too quickly and the spokes ripped right out of the wheels and the car capsized right beside me, killing the driver and knocking the four other occupants about very badly. People were afraid to come near as they thought the car would blow up – a characteristic that motors were supposed to possess in those days. I turned off the burners of the ignition and stopped the engine.

This accident impressed all the boys very much, myself included, and most them took the view that motors were very dangerous and that it was very silly to drive them. I very bravely stuck up for them, but was frowned on as being rather a half-wit for not seeing the light in the obvious way.

One day in 1900, I heard that the entrants in the great 1,000-miles motor trials were to pass by. I deliberately cut school in order to walk over and see, in a cloud of dust which somewhat spoiled the sight, those heroic figures on their fascinating machines. I can see them now and could name them all if they passed by me again.

S. F. Edge

The scene immediately before the start of the Paris–Madrid Race in 1903 is one which baffles description. As Jarrott started, the crowds gave way a little, leaving a sort of wedge-shaped space, and as each competitor started the same thing happened.

I waited until several were off before I followed, and I had not

gone far before I realised that the race was likely to become something approaching a holocaust if matters did not improve. There
had, as far as I could see, been no preparations at all to keep the
spectators in check; they were blocking the road in front and merely
gave way at the last moment. The condition of the roads, too, was
very bad, which rendered the racing even more dangerous. They
had not been treated for dust-prevention, and every car raised an
impenetrable cloud which took several minutes to subside. If a
driver wished to pass another car he simply had to await his opportunity for a bend in the road where decreased speed would render
observation possible and then take his chance of the man in front
being well over on his correct side, and so drive by well-nigh 'blind'.

The race had only been run a short distance when one of the cars
struck a woman who was crossing the unprotected road at Ablis,
near Rambouillet, and killed her. Within the first fifty miles, a
Panhard, two Mors and a Mercedes had abandoned the contest, but
one of the worst accidents of that dreadful day happened when
a Wolseley, driven by Guy Porter, crashed into the closed gates at a
level crossing. It overturned, pinned the mechanic beneath, caught
fire and roasted the unfortunate man to death.

Both Jarrott's team mates had fearful accidents; between Mont-
guyon and Libourne, one of the most dangerous stretches of road
on the whole course, Stead and another driver – Salleron on a Mors
– had a terrific struggle. It was said that they travelled side by side
for several miles, until Salleron swerved suddenly and just touched
Stead; the car turned over and over with the unfortunate Stead still
in the driver's seat, while the mechanic was thrown out a distance
of a dozen yards. Stead suffered terrible injuries. Lorraine Barrow's
accident was even worse. In trying to avoid a dog which had strayed
on to the road, his car ran full tilt into a tree. The mechanic was
pitched out and fell dead beside the remains of the car; Barrow was
flung out of the car, cleared the tree and was thrown over twenty
yards into a ditch at the side of the road, sustaining fearful injuries
which proved fatal.

Nor did Marcel Renault fare any better; he caught up Théry and

345

they, too, had a great tussle. Renault failed to notice an approaching bend in the road, and like Barrow, ran into a tree, with fatal injuries to himself. At Champniers, a Georges-Richard car upset, causing severe injuries to both the driver and mechanic. Another car collided with a wagon carrying wood just outside Bonneval. Béconnais, with whom I had often raced on motor tricycles some years previously, driving a 40-h.p. Darracq, and Jeandre, driving a 70-h.p. Mors, also came into collision, causing injuries to themselves and complete destruction of both cars. Just beyond Angoulême, Tourand on a Brouhot car ran into a woman and killed her on the spot; the car then swerved, killed two soldiers and terribly injured both the driver and mechanic.

And so this race of destruction proceeded. I could take my time and accommodate my speed to the prevailing conditions. Every few miles I came across cars smashed to pieces at the side of the road, and it came as no surprise to learn, after arriving at Bordeaux, that the race had been stopped by the French authorities. The true hero of the event was Gabriel on a Mors. He arrived first, and how he managed to pick his way through crowds of other competitors who had started before him, and without accident, is a mystery. It was one of the most brilliant pieces of driving in the history of motor racing – the sights he must have seen on the road would be sufficient to unnerve most men. In all eight people had been killed and the French immediately banned open-road racing.

A. V. Roe

After the opening ceremony an inspection of the course at Brooklands was made by all present. Mr and Mrs Locke King – Mrs King driving – led the way on their 70 h.p. Itala – made nearby at the Itala works at Byfleet – followed by Rolls on the Rolls-Royce, J. E. Hutton on his 80 h.p Berliet, the Duke of Westminster, Lord Lonsdale, and many others. There was no attempt to indulge in speed work until Mrs Locke King let her car out a little. Lord Lonsdale gave chase and within a few minutes we were all tearing round the track as hard as we could go. There were about 60 of us, all rushing along for dear life. I do not know what speed we were doing, but suddenly there appeared Warwick Wright on his racing Darracq. He passed us all as though we were standing still and we heard afterwards that he was touching 85 m.p.h. It was a most enjoyable day.

Lord Brabazon of Tara

At Cambridge I had my first motor-bicycle. I never loved anything so much. The Werner with its motor near the handlebars, which was nearly impossible to ride on a skiddy road; the Singer that had its motor inside the back wheel, a triumph of ingenuity. I knew them all. The Singer I shall never forget, for I broke its only control, which emerged from the back axle, as I was mounting outside Haywards Heath Station. I was already mounted and could do nothing but sail away through the town towards what appeared to be certain death. However, I made for the nearest hill and slowing by the brakes through the traffic, managed to stop her. But I lost about a stone in pure fear.

Annie Hartley

We had an Indian motorbike and sidecar. The sidecar in those days was at the back of the motorbike, not at the side, and a basket seat. My husband said, 'When we go over a bump, lean the way I'm going.' He left me behind many a time. I'd just pick up the cushions and get back on again.

A. V. Roe

I used to spend hours in a state of fascination watching the albatross glide majestically with motionless wings, and it was whilst at sea that I became convinced it was possible to construct an aeroplane. I asked myself, if a bird could glide like this why should not a man do likewise if he was equipped with the suitable apparatus? I built a wooden model of an albatross, much to the amusement of the crew, who used to jeer when the models had their tails behind, and there were others with equal wing areas both fore and aft. I built them as monoplanes, biplanes and even multi-planes.

It was on the 8th June 1908 that I was able to realise my dreams by making some of the first short aeroplane flights in Britain. On the occasion of the first flight I made no special arrangements for it took place during one of my routine trials.

I had been taxi-ing along the track at Brooklands when I realised I was clear off the ground, not only with my front wheels as I had been before, but with the rear ones too. I was really flying for the first time! My flight in the air was over a distance of about 150 feet and I made a very smooth landing. Several attempts were made with very much the same results each time. But as I had not arranged for official observers to be present my flight was not officially recorded. I did not even know whether anyone had seen my machine on the ground.

Lord Brabazon of Tara

It was on the Isle of Sheppey flying an Antoinette monoplane that I actually made the first recorded flight by an Englishman in this country, during the week-end of April 29th–May 2nd 1909.

This flight, which I suppose may justifiably be termed 'historic', was not a very long one nor was it very high – perhaps fifty feet. My main anxiety to begin with was not on account of the engine, which pulled extremely well, but on account of the aerodrome: it was so full of dykes and ditches that landing could be very dangerous if not made in precisely the right place.

But I had greater anxieties to follow.

While in the air I was suddenly struck by a powerful side gust of wind. The whole aircraft of course tipped sideways and the impact was so sudden that I had no time to do anything but try to correct my position in the air by heaving on the rudder control. This I did, but in my anxiety I proved a little over-zealous and suddenly discovered to my horror that the control to the rudder had broken. So there I was in mid-air and absolutely unable to control my machine.

There was nothing to be done but glide down – canted at an angle of about thirty-five degrees – and this I did. The whole thing was beyond my control. I remember seeing the pattern of ditches and dykes spreading out below me. Only a few seconds before, I had been imagining that by summoning all the skill I possessed, and with a lot of good luck added, I might be able to land without damage. Now I had only good luck to rely on.

The machine pitched forward and sideways even more, the ground span below me, and suddenly I struck the ground heavily on the tip of the left-hand wing. The impact shuddered through the machine, wires and struts snapped viciously, and with the shock of impact the engine left its moorings and came hurtling through the air from behind me – missing me by inches – and buried itself in the ground. It was a startling and disconcerting experience, but through good fortune I wasn't personally damaged. A bit bumped and bruised and dazed, and pinned down by wires, but without a scratch, I recovered to find myself being licked by my two dogs, who had chased after me during the flight.

Geoffrey de Havilland

After our first crash, back at Fulham, Frank Hearle and I took stock of our remnants and resources and made our plans for the second machine. Money was already running low, and speed and simplicity of materials and construction were essential. On the other hand, it had clearly been a mistake to economise on the propellers, shafts and gearing. We therefore did away with the troublesome twin propellers, turned the engine at right angles and mounted a single wooden propeller direct on the engine shaft, which meant we could dispose of the heavy flywheel. We also lightened and simplified the landing gear, using now two bicycle-type wheels and a rear skid, and constructed a lighter, simpler and more robust main structure. By the summer of 1910 we were ready again. We hired the same lorry, took Number Two down to Hampshire, and put her in the big shed bordering the field at Seven Barrows . . .

It was a beautiful evening in late summer, and I had already run the machine several times fast into the light breeze, feeling my way along with light touches on the rudder bar and gentle pressure

In the 1900s cars were mostly for recreational use. Motorists pose for a photograph in their cars. A Panhard is on the far right.

The start of a relay race at Brooklands racetrack in 1909.

backwards on the control stick. I pulled up alongside Frank, who had been watching the machine's behaviour keenly from the centre of the field.

'I'm going to try one more run,' I called to him above the sound of the engine. 'I'm not sure, but I think I'm almost leaving the ground. Anyway, I'm not feeling any bumps. Will you lie down as I go past and watch if you can see any daylight between the wheels and the grass?'

Frank agreed, and I took the machine back up the slight slope again, turned and took a line that would pass close beside his prostrate body. I opened the throttle and accelerated towards him. I was going faster than ever before as I approached, and eased back a little more on the stick, keeping her on a straight course with the rudder bar. I must have been travelling at 25 or 30 mph when I passed beside him, and at once eased back, coming to a halt at the bottom of the field.

A few seconds later Frank ran up alongside me. He was shouting and gesticulating and I cut off the ignition in order to hear what he was saying. 'You flew all right,' he told me excitedly. 'You were several inches off the ground for about twenty yards. Well done.'

Tommy Sopwith

On an early flight I had nothing to direct myself by, so I just kept flying on. Towns and villages passed below; I knew none of their names. Then the wind began to get more gusty. The machine swayed and lurched and the arm with which I moved the controlling lever began to ache.

Just as I was flying over a village at about 800 feet a very ugly gust caught my machine on one side and tilted it partly over. To my consternation the aeroplane refused to regain its normal position even when I exerted the full pressure of the small balancing planes fixed to the rear ends of the main planes. It was a moment I am not likely to forget. Changing hands quickly on my steering lever I leaned over as far as I could from my driving seat so as to be able to throw the weight of my body against the rising wing of my

351

Claude Graham-White risking life and limb in a Farman biplane.
In 1912 he campaigned to raise awareness of aviation in the UK
by touring the country in a Farman boxkite with lightbulbs
attached to its wings spelling out 'WAKE UP ENGLAND!'

machine. Just when I thought I should slide hopelessly down through the air the machine slowly righted itself, but another gust assailed me and I had to look out for a landing place, although I had eleven gallons of petrol left in my tanks and the engine had not misfired once. I was getting frightened. A field near a village presented itself. I planed down and sat still, quite exhausted.

Gordon Frank Hyams

Aviation was absolutely in its infancy and it thrilled me right from the start. At first, I spent a lot of my spare time making models, a few of which flew. They were driven by elastic. I used to read everything I could lay my hands on about the early flying and the men who flew. The first time I ever saw an aeroplane was during the competition for which the *Daily Mail* offered £10,000 to the first man to fly from London to Manchester. In 1910 there were two contestants, Claude Graham White and a Frenchman, Louis Polar. No one believed it was possible in 1906, as the furthest flight in Europe had only been 200 yards. Punch offered a similar sum for the first man to swim the Atlantic. One afternoon, I looked up and saw an aeroplane far away in the distance, quite low down. It turned out to be Polar who won the race.

After that, I used to cycle to Hendon at weekends. The Hendon aerodrome was in the country in those days and it was, with Brooklands, the centre of flying in England. It was large and they used to have races round the aerodrome, on a course marked out by pylons. Occasionally, they had cross country races to Stanmore and back. I remember the Frenchman, Peygout, giving an exhibition of looping the loop. I don't think it had been done in England before. After he'd done it, a lot of the Hendon pilots started trying it on machines that I would never have expected to stand the strain but there were no accidents. One day while I was there a German monoplane landed. It was of the 'Taube' type, meaning 'dove', so called because it had swept-back wingtips. It caused a lot of excitement. The exhibitions used to attract large crowds. Entrance was sixpence to stand on the ground a fair distance from the aeroplanes, a shilling to stand closer and two and six to watch from a stand.

Kenneth Cummins

I remember going to Blundell Sands to watch Graham White flying in his single-engine biplane. The plane was attached by rope to a large stake in the sand. He'd start it up and when it had worked up enough power, we boys, who'd be in charge of the rope, would release it – and he'd take off. You've heard the expression 'Pigs might fly'? Well on one occasion, Graham White took a live pig up with him and flew it over Liverpool.

William George Holbrook

I knew the first man to fly in Britain – Colonel Cody. He wore the cowboy hat and he had a beard. Just like Buffalo Bill. He had two sons and I watched one of them toss the ace of spades in the air and put a bullet through it before it touched the ground. Before he started on aircraft, Cody made man-lifting kites at Farnborough. Three big box kites were on a steel rope, fifty feet apart, and they lifted a man up. It was designed so a man could look around enemy country. From there he moved onto aircraft. He kept his plane in a big hangar on Laffins Plain and we used to pull it out for him. When parts of the airplane were loose, he tied them up with string. He used to fly up to about four or five hundred feet.

He used to give rides round the meadows at five shillings a time. I once asked him, 'What would happen if a cow got in the way?' He looked at me and said, 'I'd be very sorry for the cow.'

Frank Hedges Butler

On May 25, 1907, the 'Dolce Far Niente', carrying Captain de C. King, Lieutenant Wright, and myself, won the cup presented for competition by Mrs Assheton Harbord. The race was governed by the Aero Club International Federation rules. It was not a contest of speed, the winning balloon being that which descended nearest to a point selected by the organising committee of the Aero Club immediately before the start. Nine balloons competed. Goring in Oxfordshire was fixed as the place of descent, and it was there that we came down, 200 yards from the appointed spot. The result of the race was recorded as follows:

Mrs Hedges Butler's 'Dolce Far Niente' first. Then second, Colonel Capper's 'Pegasus'. And third, Hon. Rolls's 'Nebula'. Alas, Rolls was killed in a flying accident in 1910 and Captain King and Lieutenant Wright were both killed in the early months of the Great War.

On another occasion, we left London at nine o'clock, from the Wandsworth Gas Works, an hour and a half after the full moon had risen.

The journey was made amid the ceaseless singing of nightingales 2,000 feet below. All night, too, the peewits called and the cuckoos only rested for two short hours. Through the glorious light of the moon, so clear and shining that we could see to read the evening papers, summer lightning played continually with weird splendour. It was a night of rare delight for the naturalist. Brighton was our intended destination. We wished to escape from the shelter of London and see some new phases of the earth, particularly to see the sunrise from a height of several thousand feet. We took our supper aboard and kept a log of the journey.

The first thing that struck us as we sailed away over Surrey was the marvellous effect of the lights of London. It was a most impressive sight. Imagine millions on millions of lights, like a vast starry firmament, only upon the earth itself; with the lights of the Big Wheel at Earl's Court standing out for many miles into the heart of Surrey.

And then our own electric lights were the cause of a most interesting state of things, for at an altitude of something like 2,000 feet they attracted a host of midges or gnats. We had not thought it possible that they could fly so high. Right through the night blue lightnings vied with the silver moonlight in lighting our way; but when we lost the last of London's lights we lost all clue to our whereabouts, for we recognised no familiar landmarks in the sleeping country underneath us. If we had been able to sail a straight course, we should have kept our bearings all right; but the electric storm caused the wind to vary so much that it was only by descending now and then, and once by making inquiries, that we quite knew where we were.

It was delightfully cool, the air so soft and genial that we needed no overcoats. There was dead quiet and solemn silence and no one can realise what stillness means till he has been up in a balloon at night – and it was only broken by the songs of birds. Once we heard a mournful moaning, like the cry of a fox caught in a gin.

Half a dozen times we descended to rest, for we did not want to reach Brighton before morning. The wind was never strong, however, so our journey was as placid as we could have desired. Sometimes we dropped into gentlemen's parks, the car resting lightly on the ground, and the inhabitants of the mansions close by sleeping all unconscious of our presence. We even gently trailed our ropes over their roofs and bedrooms.

At descent we never left the car. If one of us had done so the balloon would quickly have risen to an altitude of something like 15,000 feet. We could not smoke either, but we could always read, though we much preferred watching and listening.

At about 2 a.m, just as the first lark soared singing to us, we dropped, thoroughly mystified as to our whereabouts, in a rookery close to a house. The rooks, startled out of their sleep by the sudden arrival of our car among their nests, made an extraordinary clamour. We called out, and with our noise and the increasing cawing of the rooks, a man put his head out of a bedroom window and said, 'Goodness gracious! Who are you?' 'Balloonists resting. Where are we?' 'Twelve miles from Brighton going south. Are you stuck?' 'Oh no, we're very happy. You don't mind us sitting on top of your tree, do you?' 'Not at all. Good-night.' And then the window banged.

Near Brighton Downs the wind failed. The balloon stopped dead, and a few moments actually began to sail in the opposite direction. But the change was only temporary. After making a successful descent at Portslade, just outside Brighton, at 4.30 a.m., we were back in London at 10 a.m.

Harry Eddington

Some of the old coach drivers used to stand at the Unicorn Hotel at six o'clock in the morning with their pint of beer. In those days there wasn't much tea, it was all home-brewed ale. These old chaps were that drunk they could hardly climb on top of their coaches! Old Joe McNichol used a big whip for a four-in-hand, or maybe tickled the horse under the belly with a whip stick so the horse would rear up and really frighten the people on the coach. But they could drive better when they were drunk than when they were sober, them old chaps. They could that, by jiminee, they were grand fellows.

Maurice Chapman

Every morning about ten o'clock the coach and a pair of horses with Tom Sanderson in the driver's seat would set off. 'Climb aboard!' Off they would set for a drive round the Lake District. When they came to a very steep hill all the men had to get off and walk, in fact in some cases they had to help to push the coach up the hill, but the trip was very popular.

William Keate

Once a year my sister and I spent Saturday with my uncle as my father and mother went on their outing given by the mill owner to his employees, usually to London. We would be got up early, be given a basket of food, and taken up to Banwell Hill where the village allotments were. My uncle had four or five, planted with potatoes. We had to 'pull the vilt' as they called it, which consisted of potato haulms – potato stalks, thistles, milk thistles, so my uncle could commence gardening the next day.

I think the word 'vilt' must have been a local word for filth, as I have never heard it anywhere else. After a back-breaking day and fingers full of thistles and stained with milk thistle juice, we were given a good supper, a penny and put to bed, as our parents did not get home until the early hours of Sunday morning.

Reece Elliott

The brake trip to Shields, that was an annual thing. It got the name of 'Arthur Suggett's trip' because he was the man organising it. I think about a shilling for kids and two and six for adults. We used to set away at half six in the morning, only when we got the men out the pub. We went to South Shields, for the simple reason it was easy for the horses. We went to Roker once. The kids got tired, spent all their money and wanted to get home, so they went round to the livery place and met these Sunderland lads, who started clouting horseshit at them. The first brake was stinking and full of horseshit!

Everybody ran after the brakes. We used to love Easter or Whit Monday, cos brakes was going all ways, Shields, and some from Newcastle was ganning down to Chester on the River Wear. They hoyed out ha'pennies. There were steps on the brakes, and some of the lads were clever and they would have a ride on them, on the back. One lad got fast with his trappings and it dragged him along with his feet bare. The roads were the rough flint stone, it dragged him for about a mile, all the way from the Binns, through the bridge, till it got to Arthur's Stob. His toes were red raw. Didn't stop him like!

Nina Halliday

In the summer holidays we went to Bournemouth for a month. A terrible amount of bustle in packing tin trunks and my mother's bonnet box which had a wire contraption in each side. When the bonnets were put over the wire, a long hatpin was pushed through to secure them. There was also a flat canvas holder with straps which wrapped umbrellas, sunshades, two of my father's walking sticks, one sturdy for real walking, and one elegant with a golden end like a thimble, just for show. These were all wrapped into the canvas, rolled round and strapped securely. I had my own tin trunk, painted green.

I enjoyed being at Bournemouth, because the beach was sandy and there was the excitement of so-called bathing from what seemed like a small house on wheels, which had two benches inside, and was pulled down to the sea by an old horse. When the horse stopped, you opened the door and climbed down the three steps into the sea. The 'Bathing Lady', as she was called, tied a rope firmly round your middle and proceeded to push you under the water three or four times. Then you'd go back into the machine to get rid of the sand and dry as well as you could. The 'Bathing Lady' was dressed in rusty black with her skirt pulled up and tied at the back, and a black hat – all rather forbidding until you got used to her.

My father took me for trips on the steamer which called at the pier, and we both loved it. It was no good trying to keep my floppy hat on in the wind, so my father took charge of it. This meant I could get beautifully blown, and when we got back to the pier, he did his best to tidy my hair before putting my hat on again. All too soon the tin boxes appeared and somehow got packed. It did not seem to matter how things were shaken and brushed, we always took home some sand. I was allowed to take home one piece of the broad-leaf seaweed which was supposed to foretell wet or dry weather.

Jack Hepplestone

Down the mines we never had a week's annual holiday. We had the day off at Easter and Whitsuntide and a day off here and a day off there. There was no such thing in them days as going away to the seaside for a week. If you went for a day, you were lucky. I remember the first time I went to the seaside. I went to Blackpool for the day. I paid thruppence for a row in a boat and I was seasick so I came back and lay on the sands all day.

Harrison Robinson

If you went to Blackpool, you'd pay a shilling a night for a room in a lodging house. You bought your own food, and they cooked everybody different meals. I don't know how they did it. Breakfast was bacon and egg. You cut your own bread, which you kept in your cupboard in the dining room. They'd charge you for the cruet too!

Victoria Pier, Blackpool 1904.

Women are carried to the water by horse-drawn bathing machine.

Ina Beasley

Mother would have thought it very peculiar if she hadn't gone for a holiday. Her father and mother had always gone for a holiday, so it was all part of the family custom. Grandpa said it was better than medicine, which of course is true. Oh yes, you had to go for a holiday.

We used to go to Margate because it wasn't all that distance from London. My father had an idea that the air was very pure there. He liked good, cold brisk air, and he liked fishing. We could come by train, and there used to be great excitement when you got to Whit-stable, where you had to be the right side of the carriage to get the first glimpse of the sea. Sometimes we came by boat. That was very exciting. The *Royal Sovereign* all the way down from Tower Bridge to Margate Pier. In those days they had luggage in advance, so a large trunk would be packed and sent off two or three days beforehand by van, which meant there'd be nothing to carry.

Our lodgings were not very grand, but they were clean. Mother bought the food and the landlady cooked it. I can't remember eating at a restaurant because life wasn't geared that way – you went home to meals because you weren't very far away.

My mother didn't particularly care for beach pursuits and she always kept on her shoes and stockings. She wouldn't have dreamed of paddling or bathing. Other people's mothers weren't all like that, but that was my mother – she didn't like it. So we would go down to the beach with my father and she would go and do the shopping.

We used to go down in the mornings to the beach, but not in the afternoons. We played lots of cricket on the sands with all sorts of people joining in. We dressed fairly respectably even on the beach. We always had nice cotton frocks however cold it was, and generally a pair of canvas shoes. But in the evenings and the afternoons we dressed up a bit – put a pair of stockings on – not gloves, but a nicer dress, It was just part of the set-up. You made yourself look pleasant if you were going for a walk along the promenade to listen to the band. You looked at the other people – we looked at the boys and the boys looked at us as we were getting a bit older – so we made ourselves look nice.

Florence Parker

My grandmother had to do something, so in the summer she did letting. She always reckoned her letting paid for her fire, and gas and lights – things like that. She always used to try to pay the rent up in the summer and then she hadn't got anything to worry about in the winter.

She worked hard, our old gran did. She always used to say that if she got a letting in early June, well, she was all right. She'd got the wherewithal to buy the extras she wanted to start with, all the stuff for cleaning, papering and painting – then if she got perhaps a week or fortnight towards the end of September, well, that was a bob or two for herself.

Rose Bishop

I settled down to live with my auntie in Southampton. My uncle was a deck-steward or head-barman on big liners, away seven weeks and then home for a few days. He would bring home bananas from Madeira, on a stem about three feet long. My aunt used to heat a long steel poker in the fire until it was red-hot and put it right down the hollow stem to ripen them.

Antonia Gamwell

My mother, who had taken us out to Switzerland for the winter sports, took us to Berlin on the way home. One of our school friends was the daughter of the Kaiser's Naval attaché. They thought it would interest us to go to a service in connection with the Order of the Black Eagle. The royal family and all the diplomats were present. We had a seat at the front of the balcony and we could see straight down a length of red carpet and rows of gold chairs which were filled by the German Royal Family. After the service, the Kaiser wished to thank the padre, so he marched up the carpet and stood immediately below us. I thought my sister was rather quiet and

I looked at her and realised that she was sea green. She was leaning over the balcony, about to be sick on the Kaiser, so I pulled her back swiftly and she was very sick but it landed inside. I thought, 'My Goodness! What would have happened to us if she had been sick on the Kaiser?'

Sonia Keppel

While travelling to Colombo, to stay with Sir Thomas Lipton at his tea plantation, at first each new object alarmed me – people, animals, trees. Even the fruit seemed distorted. Melons elongated, developing black pips inside; plums became rotten, and tasted of scent; bananas shrank to thumb-size, and their flesh became pink. I felt better reconciled to them all when Watty told me that the Swiss Family Robinson had lived on these fruits and, certainly, the bananas tasted delicious. Then, gradually, custom blunted my fears, and my eyes accepted the extraordinary without blinking. I saw little, humped oxen pulling wagons, like sunbonnets in shape; and black men, between shafts, pulling white men in dogcarts; and black men wearing skirts, with long hair coiled up with combs on their heads; and black women, with bare breasts, crowned by huge baskets of washing. Giant palm trees reared up on either side of the streets, and everywhere the strange sounds and smells persisted. They gave Nannie a headache, and she was revolted by the women's bare breasts. But I found them all rather exciting.

Antonia Gamwell

My mother wanted to buy me some blue fox furs, and we went to rather a famous furrier in Germany. My mother liked the pelts she was shown, so she paid for them and put my initials on the back. We went back to the hotel for lunch, and during lunch the telephone rang and the manager of the shop rang up to say that the royal yacht had come into the harbour and the Kaiser was in the shop. The manager said that the Kaiser had seen the furs that my mother had bought and he wanted them. He was told that they'd already been sold but he asked the manager to find out if my mother would

Arriving at Henley-on-Thames for the Royal Regatta.

exchange them. But my mother hadn't liked any of the other furs so she said 'No.' She was sorry, she said, but she had bought these pelts and she wasn't going to give them up to anybody. So the Kaiser went without his furs. I felt quite happy about that.

A few days later, my brother and sister nearly set fire to the Kaiserhof Hotel where were staying. Mother had rashly given my brother a toy that worked with methylated spirit which he burned. He managed to catch one of the curtains on fire while Mother and I were at the opera. There was a frightful hullabaloo when we got back.

POLITICS &
SUFFRAGETTES

Helen Bowen Pease
I was passionately pro-Irish in those days. It annoys me, the amount
of good emotional sympathy I spent on the Irish.

George Perryman
There used to be political meetings in Shoreditch near St John's
Road. I went to listen to Horatio Bottomley. He used to give a hun-
dredweight of coal to the poor people in the area. My family got coal
from him and they used to vote for him for that reason. I saw him.
He was a big fat man, always well dressed. He was a very nice chap.

Ernest Hugh Haire
In 1904, the Russo-Japanese War took place. People talked about
the 'Yellow Peril' but we stuck up for the Japanese because the
Russians sank some trawlers in the North Sea. We used to argue
about Lloyd George, Asquith and Campbell Bannerman's landslide
in 1906. We discussed politics in a free and easy way. We did our
work, we came home, we went to each other's houses, we did a little
dancing, we went to church concerts. In 1908, we were anti-German
because we were very fond of Edward VII and he didn't like his
nephew, the Kaiser. Nor did we. We were a bit unsure about Russia.
We didn't like the authority of the Tsars. My friend Jack Cross said,
'You know, the Russians are going to cause trouble some time. I'll
bet they fight the Germans.' 'The Japanese will have something to
say about it,' I replied.

Helen Bowen Pease

We always had meals with our parents, so that we always heard things talked over. I remember being passionately excited over the General Election of 1906. My father was standing as Liberal candidate for Newcastle under Lyme. The results lasted six weeks in those days because elections were declared in accordance with the times it used to take the King's messengers to get to the places on horseback. I remember distinctly moving the little pins on the map. My father was elected to Parliament and this split our family down the middle. My very splendid cousin Cecil was about to become Mayor of the Federated Potteries and he was a Conservative. He wrote to say that the Works was not behind Father. Father's father wrote to say that the great issue was free trade. It was all discussed in front of us and we hated to be regarded as moderate. When one of our aunts called us Liberals, I replied that we were Whig Radicals.

I was in the Ladies' Gallery in the House of Commons during the 1909 Budget debate. It was above the Speaker's chair and you looked right down and recognised the MPs from the bald patches on the tops of their heads. I vividly remember Winston Churchill getting up to speak. He looked very rosy and boyish.

Kitty Marion

I joined the ranks and to the stirring music of the 'Marseillaise', marched along Oakley Street, Kings Road, Sloane Street and Knightsbridge into Hyde Park. I had thought it quite funny, like a pantomime Grand March, but when I listened to the speakers, I became serious. I heard my own ideas and ideals expressed much better than I could ever express them. I heard of the injustice to women in being deprived of a voice in the government to which they were subservient; of having to pay taxes in the expenditure of which they had no voice, the inequality between the sexes before the law regarding divorce, the ownership of legitimate and so-called illegitimate children, the difference between the sexes regarding conditions and payment in the labour market, the difference in punishment for similar crimes committed, and so forth. The scales were falling from my eyes. Well, now I was awake. I was one of them and would do all I could to help and make our dream of a better world come true. So I joined the 'Militants', wore the colours, 'purple, white and green', and gradually absorbed the gospel of 'Votes for Women'.

The Women's Social and Political Union, founded by Mrs Pankhurst in 1903, pursued constitutional methods of agitation, and on October 13, 1905, when Sir Edward Grey addressed a Liberal meeting in Manchester, Christabel Pankhurst and Annie Kenney, a Trade Union Leader from Oldham, went to find out the then Liberal attitude on Woman Suffrage. At question time when men asked and received courteous replies to their questions, Annie Kenney rose and lifted a 'Votes for Women' banner, then asked, would the Liberal Government, if elected, give women the vote. Instead of receiving an answer, she was thrown out with great violence. Outside they started a protest meeting, were arrested for obstruction and the next day sentenced to a few days imprisonment. They received public receptions, which meant more publicity for the cause.

One of the first things I learned was to sell the paper *Votes for Women*, on the street. That was the 'acid' test. The first time I took my place on the island in Piccadilly Circus, I felt as if every eye that looked at me was a dagger piercing me. However, that feeling wore off and I developed into quite a champion paper-seller.

Rosamund Massy

In the suffrage days, we travelled all over England doing educational work and were at by-elections to oppose the Government candidates. I saw Emmeline Pankhurst rise magnificently to every conceivable situation. I think she preferred speaking in the North and liked large industrial centres, where people catch on to an idea so much more readily than they can in the South. I remember a by-election in Lancashire where she always received a loud ovation in the cotton factory districts. How quickly would those Northerners have discerned anything unreal in the interest shown had it not been genuine.

Mrs Pankhurst's secret was her absolute sincerity, her freedom from all cant, pose and artificiality, her freedom from vanity, from self-consciousness and her power of self-sacrifice. She was truly inspired.

Katharine Willoughby Marshall

No one hearing Emmeline Pankhurst's lovely voice could be unmoved by what she said. It was so clear that even in the Albert Hall, she never used a microphone. Her eloquence was remarkable and she talked so much common sense that it was no wonder that she had a great following of supporters. I never heard her say one word against anybody. If we abused Mr Asquith, she would wave her hand, as if dismissing him from her mind. She was a wonderful leader and a friend.

Jack Parks

Mrs Pankhurst was a daring devil. I saw her do a thing I wouldn't do myself. It was in Oxford, she was speaking, and the undergraduates released a mouse onto the platform, she went forward, picked it up in her hand and stroked it. She was the only one they allowed to speak! She got a hearing, it was an acknowledgement of the courage of the woman.

Kitty Marion

'Suffragettes' was an intended insult to the women by the *Daily Mail*, but it became a title of honour instead.

Mary Keen

I thought the suffragettes were right. They were women paying rates and taxes but with no say as to who was in Parliament. Yet an ordinary man, uneducated, ignorant, he wouldn't know what he was voting for but *he* could have a vote.

Cathleen Nesbitt

My mother was a very eager and keen suffragette. I remember coming back from America where'd I'd been on a tour with the Irish Players and when I came back to London, I found her in prison. My mother had broken a post office window with a little hammer and she'd been sent to Holloway prison. I went down to Holloway to visit her. I arrived during exercise hour. All the suffragettes were walking round the prison yard. Dame Ethel Smythe had written a women's marching song and she was conducting the women with a toothbrush from her cell window. I shall never forget that.

Kitty Marion

At a mass meeting in Caxton Hall, October 13, 1908, I volunteered to join a deputation to the Prime Minister. Our little group walked peacefully enough from Caxton Hall to the cheers and jeers of the crowd until some distance along Victoria Street, nearing Parliament Square, the police, including plain-clothes men, posing as hostile members of the crowd, broke our ranks by shouldering in and pushing us away in every direction. Two policemen, one on each side, taking us by the arm and shoulder, pinching and bruising the soft under-arm, with a third often pushing at the back, would run us along a little distance and fling us forward, causing most women to be thrown to the ground unless they were big and strong enough, like me. Of course, we realised that the brutality rested not in those poor minions in uniform, but in the Government, whose bidding they did. Aching in body and soul, I went home.

Some time later I went to a suffrage meeting in Trafalgar Square, I came face to face with a man who was turning away from it with the despairing gasp, 'What are the women coming to?' 'Their senses!' said I very emphatically. I later came across an 'anti' speaker in Hyde Park. I heckled and argued with him. At last he touched upon the badness of women and declared that bad women were much worse than bad men. 'Of course they are; women are always more thorough than men in everything,' I called out, which with a big round of applause for the women, ended his meeting.

Christabel Pankhurst gave me the opportunity of making my protest in 'deeds not words', with a stone through a government window in Newcastle on Tyne, when Lloyd George would speak there on the budget, excluding women taxpayers from his meeting. Dorothy Pethick and I were sent off to throw stones through the windows of the General Post Office. With two stones in my muff, feeling deadly sick and nervous, I made my way to the G.P.O. Without 'recognising' Miss Pethick, I joined her as she was entering, to see that no one was near the windows to get hurt by falling glass. Luckily, the coast was clear. At a given signal of the clock chiming, I shouted, 'Now for it,' and we hurled our stones. My window did not break so I hurled my second stone with lightning speed and greater force which shattered it just as a detective grabbed my arm. Wild excitement reigned while we were being taken to the police station, followed by an ever-increasing, cheering crowd, shouting 'Votes for Women!' At the police station we met the other campaigners and we celebrated our success with a supper sent from the hotel opposite.

We suffered a gratuitous insult and extra punishment by being kept in the police station without bail until the trial, a thing that was never done in London, so our friends and supporters brought blankets, pillows and other necessaries to make us comfortable. Miss Pethick and I were charged together with having 'wilfully and maliciously damaged a plate glass window, valued at £3.17.6 at the General Post Office'. Miss Pethick pleaded 'not guilty of smashing, but guilty of trying to'. I pleaded guilty to what I had done 'in the great cause of women's freedom'. The verdict was one month's hard labour for me, two weeks for Miss Pethick.

At the prison, they took our records, money and valuables, but we fought against being stripped, bathed and put in prison dress. There were eight of us, including Lady Constance Lytton, Mrs Brailsford and Emily Davison, who was later to throw herself under the King's horse at the Derby and be fatally injured. What a horrid sensation to be locked in and not able to see the sky through the high up, opaque window panes. I decided to barricade my cell with the table and bed wedged against the door. The Matron, the Chaplain, the Doctor, and even the Schoolmistress tried to persuade me to open the door, but I said, 'No, not even for Mrs Pankhurst unless she told me we had the vote.' At last, they chiselled the hinges off and lifted the door out. Then several wardresses came in, stripped me, put me into prison clothes and took me to another cell.

The next morning, my cell door was flung open and an apparently surprised wardress said, 'Aren't you up yet?' 'No!' 'Don't you want any gruel?' 'No thank you.' My hunger strike had begun. About midday, a wardress brought my dinner and strongly advised me to eat it. There was a grim note in her voice which sounded very ominous and I felt prepared for the worst. Neither food nor water had passed my lips for two days.

In the evening two wardresses asked me to come with them, I refused and, struggling all the time, they managed to put some clothes on me and drag me to the doctor's room, where three doctors, two in operating aprons, awaited me. One asked me to drink some milk. I refused and was seized and overpowered by several wardresses, forced into an arm chair, covered by a sheet, each arm held to the arm of the chair by a wardress, two others holding my shoulders back, two more holding my knees down, a doctor holding my head back. I struggled and screamed all the time. Not knowing the procedure of forcible feeding and thinking it was done through the mouth, I clenched my teeth when they had me in position and helpless. Then suddenly I felt something penetrate my right nostril which seemed to cause my head to burst and eyes to bulge. Choking and retching as the tube was forced down to the stomach and the liquid food poured in, most of which I vomited back when the tube was withdrawn. There are no words to describe the horrible revolting sensations.

I must have lost consciousness for I found myself flat on the floor. When wardresses were picking me up to carry me back to my cell, I heard one say, 'Eh, but she's heavy!' I said, 'Of course, I am, put me down, I'll walk back, they would leave work like this for you women to do.' I called the doctors a lot of dirty, cringing doormats to the government to lend themselves to such outrageous treatment of women. As I was half dragging myself and being assisted by wardresses up the stairs, I suddenly saw the prison doctor on the other side of the banister. I stopped and with all the force and venom possible I cried, 'You brute!' 'It isn't my fault, I can't help it,' he whined. 'If you had an ounce of manliness in you, you would protest against doing this,' I said and struck him in the face with the back of my hand. I regretted it at once, though it was a relief to have done it. On the way back I shouted, 'Votes for Women! Down with Tyranny!' till I was back in my cell. The wardresses tried to sympathise with and soothe me but I asked them to leave me alone and pushed them out of my cell. I flung myself on the bed and cried with rage until I heard screams and knew that someone else was going through the same torture.

That night I resolved to set fire to my cell. I pulled straw from my pillow and smashed the glass over the gas mantel. Flames shot up and filled the cell. The fire was soon spotted and I was dragged out and placed in a padded cell.

During the day, I was closely watched and visited by the Governor, Matron and Doctor. The Matron was kind and motherly and gave me milk from a feeding cup which I was by then too weak to resist. I felt I could not face the feeding tube again. She told me the other women had begun eating and that I was doing my cause no good. The Matron and everybody positively broke my spirit with kindness and coaxing, a thing I was not accustomed to, and found harder to bear than prison discipline. I refused to eat and they fed me liquids with a feeding cup. At the end of a fortnight, with the aid of a wardress, I crawled out for air and exercise.

In the past we made our protests with the intention of being arrested and sent to prison, partly to prove we were willing to suffer that in our cause. The edict now went forth to 'do all the damage possible without being caught'. After four successful fires and escapes, something went wrong with my fifth.

It happened after Emily Wilding Davison had tried to stop the King's horse in the Derby on June 4th, that someone living in the

Emmeline Pankhurst (front left) leading a suffragette parade
through London with protesters all dressed in white.

Rare footage of Degree Day at Birmingham University in 1901.

vicinity of Hurst Park race course suggested to Clara Giveen and me that the Grandstand there would make a most appropriate beacon – not only as the usual protest, but in honour of our comrade's daring deed, for which she paid with her life. Clara and I went in search of a possible entrance to the course, but found no way except to climb a fence, the spiked top of which neither of us could reach, tall as we were. About a foot above the spikes were two rows of barbed wire which looked pretty impossible for two long-skirted females to nego- tiate. However, being 'unconquerable' suffragettes, we had to get over somehow.

A piece of carpet seemed likely to smooth the way, and when I asked my landlady if she had a bit she could spare, she told me to help myself in the shed. I selected a piece, rolled and strapped it into a neat-looking piece of baggage. I also packed a wicker suitcase with a gallon of oil and fire-lighters. On Sunday night, about 9 o'clock, Clara Giveen called and we set off, going by train as far as we could, then by tram to the bridge near Hampton Court Palace, which we crossed and walked towards the racetrack. We had decided to climb over the 'unclimbable fence' as the press were to call it later, with a foothold on a tool shed. How we got over and back again beggars description. We both regretted that there was no movie camera to immortalise the comedy of it.

We carried our 'baggage' through the long grass to the grandstand at the other end of the course, where we most conveniently found an open door, leading into a pavilion. We spread our 'munition', and left a piece of candle burning, which should have lasted at least an hour to give us time to get away before igniting its oil-soaked base. However, before we reached our 'exit' the whole thing was blazing.

By the time we reached the bridge, the few people about at that hour – nearly 1 a.m. – were running towards the fire. An engine, horse-drawn, came dashing across the bridge, and others from dif- ferent directions. We strolled across, watching the blaze, trying not to look too eager to get away.

Though it had its humours, I hated the whole wretched business

– we all did, and would much rather have had the vote than do this sort of thing to get it – but we did our 'duty' as we saw it, much like soldiers on the principle of 'theirs not to reason why'.

As we walked towards Richmond and Kew, motor-cycle police came dashing along, whom we evaded each time by dodging up side streets until they had passed. We walked through Richmond, past the police station, on to Kew, nearing our destination, where Clara had arranged for us to stay, when she was uncertain of which turning to take, and a policeman offered to direct us, expressing surprise at our being out so late, to which, by way of putting him off the scent, I said, 'Oh, I am a music hall artiste and often out late.'

When we reached Dr and Mrs Casey's home, at about 3 o'clock, we found another policeman outside. It seems that as soon as the cause of the fire was discovered from the copy of the *Suffragette*, the police covered every house for miles around which they knew to be occupied by suffragettes. Clara let us in with the latchkey which Mrs Casey had given her. After breakfast, during which we related our strenuous adventures, we lay down again, Betty on a couch downstairs, I on the bed in the spare room.

At 11.30 the policeman who had followed us arrived with Detective Inspectors Pride and Pike. One came straight upstairs to tell me I was under arrest while the other 'broke the news' to Clara and brought her up to me, to read the warrant to us together, under which we were charged with being 'suspected persons found loitering in certain streets with intent to commit a felony'.

Pride fairly barked at me, 'What's your name?' Mocking his tone, I barked back, 'Kitty Marion!' 'Oh', he said. Then, in quite a pleasant, friendly manner, 'Do you know Mr Finden?' Trying to place Mr Finden in the suffrage movement, I hesitated a moment, then said, 'Mr and Mrs Harold Finden in the music halls? I've played on the same bill with them.'

'That's it,' he said. 'What a strange coincidence. I met Mr Finden at a club last night and in the course of conversation, we touched on Women's Suffrage. He said he knew a suffragette, and mentioned your name. I little dreamed I should arrest you this morning.'

Rosamund Massy

My first imprisonment was in Preston in 1909. I went on hunger-strike but unfortunately, my fine was paid by my mother at the end of the week.

Ada Wright

On Black Friday – November 18th 1910 – we were battered by the police all day long. The police rode at us with their horses, so I caught hold of the reins of one of the horses and would not let go. A policeman caught hold of my arm and twisted it round and round until I felt the bone almost break and I sank to the pavement helpless. Each time I got up and made a show of advancing to the House of Commons, I was thrown to the ground once more. The next day I found I had been photographed as I was lying on the ground where I had been flung and the photograph occupied the front page of the *Daily Mirror*. As soon as this became known to the Government, an order to have the photograph suppressed was sent to the office of the newspaper but they could not suppress the copies that had been sold.

Francis Meynell

There was a meeting at the Albert Hall of West End tradesmen to demand that the government should shave the heads of Suffragette women. I went to this meeting and I got up and opposed all the resolutions and I was the only opponent. After a while, the Chairman asked which shop I represented. 'Burns and Oates in Orchard Street' I said and there was a roar of derisive laughter. All the directors of Burns and Oates were staunch Tories. This was printed in the *Evening Standard* and the directors were utterly shocked when they read it.

Kitty Marion

On St David's Day we caught them unprepared. Volunteers for 'danger duty' were organised secretly. We were asked not to talk about what we were going to do until it was an accomplished fact, then talk about it all we liked. Each of us, separately, in a private room, was given a hammer and told which windows to break at 5.45 p.m. in the twilight and lighting-up time when people had finished shopping and were going home. I arrived at the Silversmiths' Association and Sainsbury's, 134 Regent Street, about five minutes too soon, feeling awful, and looked round for an encouraging, friendly face in the fray. But I seemed to be the only one there. Had I possibly made a mistake in the day or time? Surely not, whatever happens, I must break those windows, those two great ovals at the entrance to the Silversmith's and that huge plate glass window of Sainsbury's. I must not fail. Such and similar were my thoughts.

I walked round the block to be back just in time to see one of us a couple of shops ahead, gazing round furtively as I had done. Our eyes met in silent encouragement just as 'Big Ben' started to boom three quarters. I pushed my way between some women and the first oval and with my hammer ready, I hit it. The sound of breaking glass filled the vicinity and electrified everybody. I rushed to the other oval, broke that, then next door, Sainsbury's window filled with beautiful boxes of chocolates, then on to the next window, but before I could reach that two men rushed out of the shop, and grabbed my hammer just as a policeman, who already had a woman under arrest, came and took me too, greatly to my relief. As we were going to Vine Street a lady came up beside me and asked 'Suffragettes?' 'Rather,' I replied proudly. And she said, 'Bravo, good luck!' Our poor bobbie was deadly pale, pinched looking and speechless until, turning into Vine Street, some boys yelled 'Votes for Women', when he found his tongue and gasped, 'I've always been in favour, but after this I am against it.' We laughed, and the nervous tension was broken.

We reached the police station, where they were very busy already taking charges. We explained our action to him and told him of similar things his forefathers had done to get the vote, until we won him over again. One hundred and twenty-four women were arrested that night in Regent Street, Oxford Street, Piccadilly, Bond Street, Strand and other principal shopping centres. We were all bailed out, but next morning, we all arrived at Bow Street with baggage, ready to go to prison, for most of us were going to refuse bail since our cases were going to be referred to the London Sessions. After a long day at Bow Street Police Court, we were taken in a Black Maria to Holloway prison, where it took the officials nearly all night to book and put us in cells.

Mrs Pankhurst was already in, convicted, and we, the still unconvicted, could not exercise together for fear of the latter being corrupted. So the ground floor of our wing and staircases became a milling mass of prisoners and wardresses forcing us back into our cells, where we protested by breaking windows and banging the tin dustpans and utensils on the door to let the outside world know something unusual was happening. The Press said it sounded like a factory in full blast. I was sentenced to six months hard labour, and on the following day taken with twenty-three others to Winson Green Prison, Birmingham, where the forcible feeding had started.

Mildred Ransom

The great body of suffragists, led by Mrs Henry Fawcett, worked on reasonable and constitutional lines and there was another smaller but more vociferous body who were impatient with the attempt to gain the franchise constitutionally and tried terrorism instead. They thought 'frightfulness' would terrify MPs into granting the reform. They slashed Cabinet Ministers with dogwhips, they set churches on fire, smashed plate glass windows of shops and poured acid into pillarboxes, with the natural result that the ordinary man in the street set his teeth against granting any vote to any woman on any terms. Cabinet Ministers had to be guarded, which annoyed them extremely, and the cause was mixed up in everyone's minds with immense riots in the London streets.

During the campaign suffrage meetings were certainly lively, as the public did not discriminate then any more than now between suffragists who were constitutional and those who were militant. One result was that an Anti-Suffrage League was started which was hailed with joy by all suffragists because the League managed to attract some really good speakers and it was dull work debating with a feeble person who quivered and quaked at opposition and lost her temper when the vote went against her

I was billed to speak at a debate at Hackney Town Hall one evening and the Anti-Suffrage speaker was Mr McCallum Scott, MP. Two or three days before the meeting, an agitated secretary rang me up to ask if I had seen the literature which the Anti-Suffrage League was scattering all over Hackney, and would I be willing to cancel the meeting? I replied that I had not seen the literature, but it sounded interesting – and asked why the meeting should be cancelled. The secretary replied that the literature had just stopped short legally of inciting to violence and his Committee was of the opinion that, with the consent of the speakers, the meeting should be cancelled. Feeling ran high and they doubted if they could protect the speakers. I replied that we were billed to speak and it was the job of the Committee to protect the speakers and I should arrive as arranged.

A short time before this, the Men's Suffrage League had been founded. Their object was not so much to obtain the suffrage for women as to ensure free speech and to protect the women physically from the roughs and rowdies who thought it an admirable evening's amusement to knock the women speakers about. The League attracted hefty young men who were indignant at the behaviour of rowdy audiences and a good many of us owed it to them that we returned home whole and not in pieces.

I should say most of the roughs in Hackney were at that meeting, but we had a good chairman and Mr McCallum Scott was an excellent if slashing speaker, and between the three of us the audience miraculously became interested and threw neither cats nor cabbages. In fact, though the meeting was a great strain because the least mistake would have precipitated a storm, it passed off peaceably, to the enormous surprise of the platform and Committee. But from the first I was puzzled at the number of faces in the audience I knew – but being engrossed in the debate, I did not think much about it. But weeks after I found that my family had anxiously rung up the

Secretary of the Franchise League and asked if the Men's League would attend the meeting – which they did enthusiastically when they had perused the Anti-Suffrage Literature. Those who declaimed the theory that if women asserted their political rights they would destroy all chivalry in men had a practical answer from the members of the Men's League, and many is the time that they prevented mob violence by simply permeating an audience. The vote at Hackney was in our favour, and though I went home tired out, it was worth it.

Barbara Clark

There was something on at Jarrow at a theatre, so of course we went down. A young woman came on the stage and she sang this song, and everyone clapped her to come back and sing it again. I kept it in my mind on the walk back from Jarrow.

> Why can't the dear little girls
> Do just the same as the men?
> Why can't the dear little girls
> Have freedom now and then?
> Why have the dear little girls
> To be led about by the nose?
> And if a girl wants to marry a man
> Why can't the girl propose?
> He keeps on teasing and squeezing
> He says I'm the joy of his life.
> He keeps on teasing and squeezing
> He says I'll shortly be his wife.
> He keeps on teasing and squeezing
> He never will let me alone
> He says I shall have everything nicey nice,
> Nice when the ship comes home.

That night, when I went to bed, I said to my sister, 'I have a new song to teach you.' My mother came in after I'd sang it and said, 'Barbara, where did you learn that song, pet?' 'Oh,' I says, 'when I was with Jenny Moody down the town.' 'Well,' she says, 'you're not to sing that any more.' I says, 'Why, Mam?' She says, 'Because it's not for little girls to sing.' So she says, 'You hear what I say to you?' I says, 'Yes, I hear you Mam – I won't sing it any more.' So when my mother went in the kitchen my father says, 'What have you stopped the bairn from singing that song for?' She says, 'Tom, it's not fit for children.' 'Why,' he says, 'the bairn didn't know anything about anything like that.' But I never sang it any more.

Lillian Lenton

I went to the Suffragette Headquarters and announced that I didn't want to break any more windows, but I did want to burn some buildings, and I was told then that a girl named Olive Walley had just been in saying the same thing, so we two met, and the real serious fires in this country started.

Well, the object was to create an absolutely impossible state of affairs in the country, to prove that it was impossible to govern without the consent of the governed. The earlier militancy had consisted of mild acts which did no harm to anybody except the suffragettes themselves, and I really think people would have got tired before long of hearing of that – but no one could ignore arson, nor could they ignore young women who went about saying what I said – that whenever we saw an empty building, we would burn it. And, as I say, after that, I did burn an empty building whenever I saw one.

A few young men were very anxious to help us. But these young men only seemed to have one idea – and that was bombs. Now, I didn't like bombs – after all, the rule was that we must risk no one's lives but our own, and if you take a bomb somewhere, however great the precautions you have taken to see that it doesn't damage anybody but yourself, you can't be quite one hundred percent sure. So I didn't really approve of the use of bombs. But a young man landed two on me. After this I went to stay with some people near Edinburgh.

At that time I was wanted by the police – my description and my photograph was in every police station in the country, as was that of all the other militant suffragettes who were at the time out under what was called the Cat and Mouse Act. I used to go walking about quite openly, but people didn't suspect me. I walked up to a policeman and I asked him the way to the house I had intended to blow up. He said, 'Well, as a matter of fact, I am just going off duty myself. I'll take you.' Well, I jumped to the conclusion he had recognised me. But there was nothing to be done about it. I quite expected he would take me to a police station. So I said, 'That's very kind of you,' and walked off with him. So then he said, 'Let me carry your case for you.' I said, 'Thanks very much.' Now, had that case contained simply night things or books, I should have said, 'No thanks, it's all right,' but it struck me as such a joke to let the policeman carry the bombs. So he took it from me and he said, 'My, it is heavy.' So I said, 'Yes, isn't it?' But he wasn't taking me to a police court at all. He took me round various streets in Edinburgh and put me on the right tram, and told me where to get off. I left the trunk behind on the bus, but as I got off the conductor called out, 'You've left your case!' So of course back I had to go to get the case.

Katherine Willoughby Marshall

The second time I was arrested, in December 1910, was for throwing a potato at Mr Churchill's window – or rather the fanlight over his front door. It was a stupid thing to have done, as the glass was much stronger than ordinary window glass. The potato was well wrapped with various messages about our having justice. I chose a potato because my husband objected to my throwing a stone, in case I hurt anybody. The friend I went with, Maud Fussell, was a much braver suffragette than I and had half a brick.

The evening was dark, but we managed to hit what we aimed at. My wrapped potato made no response, but my friend's half brick had a useful smash. We were quickly arrested as all Cabinet Ministers' houses were guarded by police, and taken off to the police station, where I was charged with throwing a missile. The police station was B Division. They could not have been more civil or understanding as to why we had made the protest. They let us sit by the fire while they made out the charge sheets, etc, and we were bailed out for the night, to appear next morning at Bow Street Police Station. My friend got two months' imprisonment, while I got two weeks. We could have paid a fine had we promised not to offend again – which, of course, none of us would ever do, as we had every intention of continuing to fight.

I only wished I had known how many things I could have hidden in my long skirt with its deep hem, whereas I had nothing except a library book with four postcards in it, and a small pair of scissors. I mention these treasures, because I was able to make myself a pack of patience cards with them. I made forty-eight cards with the postcards, and with four more pieces of card out of the sides of a Thermogene box, I made the kings. The ink I got through writing to the Home Secretary and the red colour out of a book from the prison library. It was on hygiene I think. I only got it out because of its colour. With a little water and an old stick I found in the prison yard, I made the hearts and diamonds. I used my slate as a table, which I kept in my nightdress case, so that when I heard the key being turned in the prison door, I could draw the flap of the nightdress case over the cards. I usually had my prayer book open so I could escape detection. I also used toilet paper, with the help of a little milk, to cover the peephole in the door, where the wardresses looked through.

In Holloway the food was dreadful. On getting up, awful tea was brought in, with a small brownish loaf and a piece of margarine. The tea was undrinkable. I think the potatoes had been boiled in the water. For dinner we had two potatoes, boiled in their skins. They were always blue inside – I don't know why – and at the bottom of the tin plate, a piece of meat of some sort, as big as half a crown, or a bit of bacon with a small amount of carrot. One day we had what was supposed to be a suet pudding, and I swallowed a piece – but I think it must have been India rubber, for it stuck in my gullet for three days and would neither go down nor come up. Supper was greasy cocoa with a small loaf of bread and the margarine which we had left over from breakfast. No wonder we all got thinner, and of course, a hunger-strike was comparatively easy, as we got such horrid food.

The plank beds I liked better than the iron ones, which were fixed to the concrete floor. With the plank beds, one could rearrange the cell a little, though its size was only twelve feet by eight feet. I used to place my plank bed beside the hot pipe, which was the one and only joy of Holloway. For my work, I took as much sewing as I could for Borstal boys – not to sew, but to soften the hard plank. The blankets were very thin and the sheets very thick. My pair had two holes in the centre, and I said to the wardress I supposed the arrows had gone through the sheets, and even she had to laugh. Everything you used had an arrow on it.

In our cells, we had, on a corner shelf, a prayer book, a small wooden bowl for salt and a card of rules. We had a bucket for water, the lid of which we kept polished to use as a looking glass. The first morning of my prison life, I had a certain utensil which leaked, so I rang my bell for a wardress to get me another. Nobody came, so I started to bang the door with my slate until it came out of its frame. Being shut up in a small cell is pretty trying, with the window so high that you could not see out unless you tipped up a chair and stood on the top rail. However, as nobody came in response to my irate knocking, I got my tin bucket and, with the iron handle, banged it up and down against the iron door. It made a fearful row. At last a wardress appeared and asked how I dared to make such a noise. I told her I had been ringing my bell and knocking for over half an hour, and asked for what I wanted – a utensil which did not leak. The wardress really was apologetic.

The wardresses, as a whole, were quite as kind as one would expect, and later on, when they knew they could trust the suffragettes, they let us have our doors open a little for half an hour on a Sunday afternoon. We had no windows that opened and only a stuffy ventilator, so quite a number of girls had to go to hospital because their health could not stand up to the stuffy cell.

We had an hour's exercise and were supposed to walk single file around the prison yard, but later on, when there were 200 of us, this was quite impossible. We made balls from pieces of material from our undergarments, stuffed with straw out of the mattress, and played rounders and other games. Most of our suffragettes were very clever – Dame Ethel Smythe used to write our parts out on our slates for us to sing.

The bath had a small door about two feet wide, so that the wardresses could look at you to see that you were not trying to drown yourself. The sanitary arrangements had a two-foot door as well, and the chain was kept outside for the wardresses to pull. I suppose in case we hanged ourselves. Even the poker in the hospital was chained to the floor. The knife to spread our margarine on with was a piece of tin about four inches long, with a broad arrow stamped on it.

We made various things for the Government. I chose knitting and made one sock in eight weeks. I made it with red wool, stripes for the leg part and a red heel and toe. I knew it ought to have been red bands round the ankles, but anything so inartistic I could not handle. I earned 8d, which I thought quite good pay for so useless a sock.

The first Governor had to retire. He wept and told my husband that the women were nearly driving him mad. We were not allowed to go to Holy Communion for the first four weeks because we were so wicked. We were not allowed hatpins, and I had a hat which would not stick on my head when we were in chapel. It was a feather toque. I made a hole through each side of it and wore a toothbrush through it so that it kept on when my head was bowed in prayer. It caused some little interest, I am afraid, amongst the worshippers in the chapel.

We were supposed to have prison clothes, but of course it was impossible to dress two hundred of us in them, when we were all in prison together for two months. Some of the prisoners wore green wool dresses – these were the second class, and the hard labour, in the third class, wore brown dresses, but we wore our own clothes, which were a great help in getting notes out of the prison. The toilet paper that we used to write them on was so thin that it folded up in the collar bands and waistbands when the things went out to be washed. The prisoners had wonderful ideas of where to secrete notes, and in this way we heard a little of how the movement was progressing.

I got some strings out of my underclothing and tied them across the cell and hung my clothes on them, so that they should not be on the dusty floor. I hung my combinations close to the door so that the little chaplain should be shocked – and he was. I asked the Governor how he would like to have his clothes lie about an hotel floor getting all dusty, and he saw some sense in the request that we should have our cases in our cells, even if they had to be kept unlocked.

When I was taken before the magistrates, after the window-smashing, and given five days' solitary confinement and was not allowed to speak on my own behalf, I determined to make myself a nuisance, so I clung to the rail of the chair upon which a fat man was sitting. The wardresses could not undo my grip so I had to be carried out of the meeting with the chair.

On Census Night, 1901, I had to arrange transport for three caravans of suffragettes, who had decided that if they did not count in the country, neither should they be counted. Our non-law-abiding women came to where the caravans were kept and which were all ready for us, and about 8.30 p.m. we set out for Putney Heath. I had no idea that we were not allowed to camp on the Heath, but it would not have made any difference had I known, as those were our plans.

We drove quietly through London, down Trafalgar Square. I do not think anybody suspected us and we got to Putney Heath safely. The drivers had orders to take away the horses and not bring them back until 12 noon the next day, which was the hour the census ended.

We had a most amusing evening. Each caravan had a long table with all sorts of food and hot coffee going, and about 1 a.m. we tried to settle down to get some sleep. How many we were, I do not know, nor ever shall, because all through the night, parties of suffragettes kept arriving and having supper and going away, and others arriving.

About 3 a.m., there was a loud banging on the door of our caravan and a gruff voice asked who was in charge. We made no reply and pretended to be asleep, but at last I had to say I was in charge. They said we had no right to be where we were. I told them if they would push us off the Heath they could, but the horses would not be returning until noon. The forest keepers and the police and a few other officials got very tiresome and took some names and addresses whilst we prepared breakfast. In the end, the number of officials who came to interfere with our defying of the census was so large that my husband suggested that they had better call out the military.

After breakfast we hung our posters and other propaganda on the caravans and returned to the Queen's Hall for a big protest meeting. Thousands of women all over the country never were counted that census night, as we took empty houses and women slept on the floors while others were walking about the streets or stayed at our different headquarters, so that the census of women was a complete wash-out for the Government returns.

Mary Keen

I remember the suffragettes. They used to have open-air meetings in the side streets. I went in the evenings to listen. There'd be young girls standing up on a box or a table and they always had an answer to make the men look like fools. One evening, a man shouted out, 'Don't you wish you were a man?' and the girl shouted back, 'Don't you wish *you* were?'

MILITARY

William George Holbrook

The Army wasn't popular at this time. People looked upon it as something for people who couldn't get a raise. The only attraction it might have had was the smart uniform – all red and blue.

Kitty Marion

I was taken to the Tower of London, where I saw Grenadier Guards and Yeomen of the Guard. When I expressed my admiration for their smart uniforms and appearance my aunt hushed me. In England soldiers were of no account. They were lazy and only enlisted because they were good for nothing else. Nice people never took any notice of them. Nobody respected them and no nice girl would ever be seen in their company.

Jack Cotterell

I can remember being about five at the time. My father was fighting in South Africa and one particular song called 'The Boers have got my soldier Da' was popular. My mother didn't take to the song at all.

Mary Keen

I remember one night during the Boer War, I was coming home over Tower Bridge, and all at once I heard a terrible lot of shouting going on and I saw a bus with a lot of boys on top and they waved to me and I waved back and I said, 'What's the matter?' and they said, 'Mafeking's relieved!' and they said, 'Come on up!' so I ran after the bus but it wouldn't stop. When I got a bit further, everyone started going mad and they were all dancing and singing and I joined in. I danced around the Mansion House with a stockbroker until midnight. No one went to bed that night.

Don Murray

I remember the end of the Boer War. We were all allowed to go out in the playground, line the railings round the school, and we all had little Union Jacks as the soldiers were marching back from the Boer War to the barracks at the top of the road. I remember one soldier in particular had a bandage round his head and we cheered madly at him. We thought he was a wounded man. He probably had a boil or something. Still, we thought he was a hero.

Dorothy Wright

As a young girl, I was taken to York Station to see the yeomanry coming back from the Boer War. I sat on my father's shoulders and we watched my oldest brother coming off the train. There was a terrific homecoming. There were decorated arches and a carriage drawn by men of the village and a brass band and cheering crowds.

William George Holbrook

In the house where I was working, there was a gardener who had served in the Army in India. His wife worked inside the house. At dinnertime, he used to sit me down and tell me all these tales about India and the rajahs. One morning, instead of going to work, I went up to Dagenham Post Office, where I saw a sign saying recruits were wanted for the Army. So I went up to the recruiting office in East Ham and knocked on the door. A woman answered and I said, 'I want to join the Army, please.' She asked me how old I was and I told her fifteen. She said, 'You can't join the Army at fifteen! You've got to be eighteen!' but she invited me inside and made me a cup of tea.

A bit later, her husband came in. He was a smart-looking man with a badge down the side with pieces of ribbon. That showed he was a recruiting sergeant. If a recruiting sergeant picked you up in the street and gave you a shilling – the king's shilling – you were in the Army and you couldn't get out. Anyway, we talked and he said, 'When you're eighteen, I'll put you in the finest regiment in the British Army but not before.' I must have looked so disappointed that he told me to stand up. I stood. 'You're a tall boy,' he said. I was about five foot eight. 'Can you tell a white lie?' he asked. I didn't know what a white lie was. 'Can you say you're seventeen?' 'Yes,' I said. 'Right,' he said. 'Tomorrow morning, you'll come with me.' So the next morning he took me to see a doctor in Stratford. When I went in the doctor said, 'Strip!' I'd never done it in front of anyone and I was a bit nervous. The doctor said, 'Hop on your left foot and right foot alternately!' That did me! I didn't know what alternately meant! But I passed the medical and I was sent for five months' training in the Special Reserve on Hounslow Heath.

Harry Hodgson

When I was promoted to midshipman, I was appointed to the *Temeraire*, which was part of the Fourth Battle Squadron of the Home Fleet. I was very unlucky because we had a real bully for a sub-lieutenant of our gunroom. Something had gone amiss in his upbringing and he was determined to take it out on all his junior officers. He told one of the officers that he was going to beat every midshipman in the first six months. And he succeeded.

George Finch

My mother died in 1907 when I was fourteen. I was the eldest of seven children so I had to leave school and get a job, which I did as an errand boy at Simpson's shoe shop in Devonport. I got four shillings a week. One afternoon when I was out delivering, I saw a fellow coming down the road in uniform; it was Tom Carey, who was an errand boy in the chemist shop. I said to him, 'Hello, Tom! What's all this?' 'I've joined the Marines,' he said. 'How much a week do you get?' 'Seven shillings and three ha'pence and I get weekends off.' 'I'm having some of that!' I said. So I went home and

Newsboys hawking papers with stories of the surrender of
Pretoria and the end of the Boer War.

told my father. He was an ex-Marine himself and he told me to think about it. I told him I didn't want to think about it. I wanted my birth certificate so that I could join up. Eventually he gave it to me and I put it into my pocket.

I went to the barracks the next day and told them I wanted to join. They gave me a medical and then a major asked me for my birth certificate. I felt in my pocket but it wasn't there. My father had taken it out. The major was very good – he just said, 'That's all right, son. Sign here and bring it in tomorrow.' I went home and confronted my father. He gave me my certificate and said, 'You've made your bed, so you lie on it.' As soon as I'd joined up, I found out what my father meant. On my first day at Stonehouse barracks, we were given a mattress cover which we had to fill with straw, sew up the end and plump it down. So I made my bed and lay on it.

Jack Cotterell

At twelve I left school and went down the mines. Three years later, I was made redundant. I went to the Poor Law, who gave you a ticket for what you needed. No money – just a ticket for food or coal or clothes. After a few months, I found a job in a steel works, firing the coal boilers. I had to walk an hour to get to work by six a.m. and an hour home in the evening. It was a very hard life but the only one we knew; our fun was swimming in the canal and doing things that boys do. I thought, 'That's it! I've had enough of coal. I'm off to join the Navy!' I went to Bristol and signed on for seven years with the option of another five. And what job did they give me? Coal stoker!

William George Holbrook

I was on guard duty on Boxing Day night, 1908. It was the night of a big boxing match between Jack Johnson and Tommy Burns, a Canadian. Burns was only about twelve stone, Johnson was fifteen or sixteen. Burns held the championship before Johnson appeared on the scene and Johnson chased Burns everywhere across Canada and America. When Johnson caught up with him in England, Burns shot off to Australia, but Johnson finally trapped him there and they set up a fight. It took place on Boxing Day. So I was on guard duty at about three o'clock in the morning and a fellow came along half drunk. The fight had only just taken place and there was no way of knowing the result. 'Do you know who won?' asked the fellow. 'No,' I said. 'Johnson won it,' he said, 'in fourteen rounds. And Burns got paid £6,000.' When I got back to the barrack room next morning I found out the man was right. But I never found out how he could have known the result so quickly. What I did know was that Johnson had become the first black heavyweight champion of the world.

George Finch

Our day started at seven o'clock. We would exercise on the parade ground, then at eight we'd have breakfast. After that we'd go down to the cliffs to a place called the Drummer's Pit, where we'd exercise on the bugle, fife and drum. I was lucky because I'd learnt how to play the bugle with the Church Lads Brigade. I used to practise at home sitting in the lavatory. It used to wake everyone up.

Brian de Courcy-Ireland

My father accompanied me to London for my interview for the Navy. It was my first time in a big city. I was one of 360 who wanted to become a Naval cadet at Osborne; they took eighty. At the interview one member of the Board asked me how many arches Bideford Bridge had. I replied that I was astonished none of them knew! I was a bit surprised I got in, especially after they asked me to look at the clock and tell them the time in French. I simply told them the clock had stopped.

Edward Pullen

On the *Victory* they piped the boys to fall in. The whole company was assembled for the punishment. We cleared the lower deck – everybody aft, and all the boys would fall in to watch the punishment. That might go on for perhaps two hours in the morning. The *Victory* would be closed to visitors. No one was allowed aboard when punishments were taking place. They lined us up, and then the commander would read out the punishment. What they would do is pull your trousers down, lift up your flannel and then your undercarriage was showing – all bare – and that's what they used to strike at. They put canvas bags on your hands and feet so's you wouldn't wriggle away.

One boy got caught stealing – and he had to have the birch. The doctor stood by and a sick-bay steward. Then they gave the boy twelve after which the doctor said, 'Release one hand.' He took his pulse and stated, I thought rather cruelly, 'He can stick another twelve.' I saw them lift that boy off with all that part of his body bleeding. When that finished, we turned to and started cleaning the *Victory*.

You'd be caned for smoking or for the least thing. I remember seeing twenty-four birches in each tub in a tub of vinegar and others in salt water. That was in 1904. They could cane boys and they could birch boys all the time he was in his boyhood. When he was eighteen they used to give him other punishments.

Ernest George White

There was a lot of talk about sex in the seamen's mess. The married men were worse than the others. There was always talk of venereal disease, so before we went ashore we went to sick bay and asked for a tube of 'dreadnought'. You rubbed it into your penis afterwards and it was supposed to work.

If a man got venereal disease, the quicker they treated it the better. There'd be nothing said about it at all – no punishment, no criticism at all, except if you concealed the disease. Our doctor used to say, 'You've been putting your whatsname where I wouldn't put my walking stick.'

On board, if you got a dose, they'd give you a bowl and a disinfectant called Condy's Fluid. You carried on with your work just the same, with no segregation.

Edward VII and the Kaiser during the State visit to
Berlin in February, 1909. Just over five years later,
Britain and Germany would be at war.

Thomas Painting

I left school at eleven and a half, and went to work for W. H. Smith and Sons at Lichfield Trent Valley Station. My father was a ganger on the railway. During this time the Boer War was on, and I was fired with what the Army did – and not only that – I could read a magazine like *Wide World* and the *Royal* along with the *Sheffield Weekly Telegraph*. I was only fourteen and a half, but I wanted some of that excitement.

My cousin joined the South Staffordshire Regiment, fought during the South African War and was lucky he came through. He was a fighting man and only sixteen, but he put his age on to eighteen. My other hero was Bugler Dunn, who blew the charge at Tugela River. He was wounded, and when he came home Queen Victoria gave him a silver bugle. With me reading all these adventure books, I thought, 'Well, I'd like to join the Army and see the world.' I left the bookstall and went on the railway as a cartboy at Birmingham New Street and then I finished up at Coventry. I made my decision. I said to Mother, 'I'm going for a ride this morning, Mum.' Off I went to the Warwick Depot and enlisted.

They wanted me to join the Warwicks and to walk out in that red coat, but I didn't want to look like a pillar-box. So I asked, 'What's that regiment has a green jacket?' and was told it was the King's Royal Rifle Corps – four battalions, plenty of foreign service. I said, 'That's the regiment for me.' I didn't know that it marched faster than the others and had black belts and all that kind of thing. What I did know was that it was Bugler Dunn's regiment. That was enough for me. My only sadness joining up was that my mother was heartbroken when I told her I had signed up for seven years.

At Christmas in the barracks we had a jolly good meal. The barrack-room was decorated with blankets up on the wall, and our sword bayonets put on the side – and covered with white cotton wool to represent snow. We had a jolly good breakfast and a jolly fine dinner, which was attended to by the officers and the colour sergeant – the company, who served up. And we had to drink the old CO's health – and he wished us Merry Christmas – all very merry.

Frank Mason

In 1907, I was first on a draft for the West Indies, but the authorities realised that they didn't have enough men for India. India was more important so they had to revise their ideas, and so the previous drafts were cancelled and I was sent to India. I'd much rather have gone to the West Indies. I went out on the SS *Rewa*. It wasn't a comfortable journey. We had hammocks instead of bunks. You had to draw your hammock at night time and then fold it up and hand it in next morning. So many men in such confined quarters tended to get in each other's way. The food was pretty rough too. But we got through all right. I was lucky because a gunner named Hudson took me under his wing. I was seasick and in the morning, he used to push me up on deck and tell me to stop there. He took my hammock down and handed it in and in the evening he drew it out. He looked after me like a father. We passed our time playing 'Housey Housey' and gambling. There was a certain amount of boxing on board. 'Bombardier' Billy Wells, who became heavyweight champion of England in 1911, was on board with us. His talent was recognised even then.

Once we got into the warm waters on the other side of the Suez Canal, we slept on deck. I remember an Irish chap named Reardon on the ship. He'd go and sit for hours on the rail of the ship, looking across the water. This wasn't allowed of course, so he was told to move, but he kept returning to the rail. He had a dull, vacant face. When we were two days out from Aden, he took a dive over the side. We stopped the ship but we couldn't find him. Probably eaten by sharks.

Harold Thwaytes

Before we went out to India, one had a medical examination and inoculations. And every regiment had its own choice of tailors so that one's uniform was uniform. In those days, as an officer, one didn't get any allowance at all towards your clothing, your uniform, your boots or anything like that, so you had a certain amount of free choice other than the actual uniform. We took out the uniform we had in England – the red coat and the mess kit, and we took out a pattern for a khaki drill uniform. Then we arrived in India, where a native regimental tailor copied the pattern perfectly for a tenth of the price.

The weather in India was very strange to us. The climate was hot, wonderful sunshine, barren country with palm trees, coconut trees and camels. The sort of scenery we were not used to. It was strange and exciting.

There were an enormous number of servants. Each young officer was allotted a bearer. The bearer looked after your clothes, your bungalow, he saw that everything ran correctly. As a bachelor subaltern, you also had a young man of about sixteen who was being trained by the bearer, and he did all the dirty work like brushing your shoes and carrying water to fill your hip bath. The sweeper looked after the lavatory side of things. The cook went down the bazaar to do all the shopping. On the last day of the month, the bearer drew all your servants up in a line and you paid them in cash. They were always inclined to ask for advances and loans and the answer generally speaking was no. There were always people in the bazaars who lent them money and when we paid them, they went straight down the bazaar and paid it back. They were all living on tick. The servants were very trustworthy. Things were very seldom stolen. We lived to a higher standard than we would have done in England. One never thought of walking across the room to pour out one's own whisky and soda. You clapped your hands and shouted out and someone was always there to do it. There was a great deal of formality in the way of life. When I later married, my wife thought life in India was wonderful. It was less tedious than running a house in England.

Generally one called the servants by the name of their job, but one chap we had for a long time was always known as Abdul. The servants tended to pass down the regiments and they nearly all spoke English. They lived in little mud huts with no windows at the bottom of the compound. The stables were down there, too. During the hours of daylight, the servants were always doing their job at the bungalow. They were always available, even if they were sleeping on the veranda.

We had a lot of rough games when we were entertaining in the officers' mess. We used to ride piggyback on each other's backs and we'd wrestle and try to pull each other off. This we called cock fighting. Then we used to blindfold a couple of people and make them lie on the floor and hold hands and slosh each other with rolled-up newspapers. Childish sort of games, but amusing for the onlookers.

EPILOGUE:
END OF AN ERA

Sonia Keppel

Inside our house, fear for Kingy's health muted each voice, and for the first time, I was afraid to approach my stern, unsmiling mother. My father was easier, but he too was abstracted and serious. Nannie was my main help, but even she evasively answered my questions.

I was aware of some secret, but which I was considered too young to understand. This hurt me dreadfully. I could keep a secret better than my sister Violet, yet no one thought me old enough to be entrusted with this one.

The day wore on and the routine of it did nothing to alleviate my fear. I had no idea what I was afraid of, but, at every moment, I was aware of it. Too easily transmutable into the ridiculous, it remained unuttered, even to my father. And, had it been challenged, I would have been embarrassed to explain it. So, treated like a child, I acted like a child, but with an adult sense of foreboding. As far as I can remember, the day ended ordinarily, and I was put to bed. But, in the morning, Nannie broke the news to me. Kingy was dead.

A pall of darkness hung over the house. Blinds were drawn, lights were dimmed, and black clothes appeared, even for me, with black ribbons threaded through my underclothes.

Edith Turner

I can remember the death of King Edward VII: everybody in London was in mourning. We had to wear black bows in our hair and black bows on our dresses. The whole atmosphere of London was silent and mournful. People seemed very subdued.

Louis Dore

I can recall that on that day that Edward VII died, people walked about with sad looks on their faces, talked only in whispers, and the respectable wore their mourning attire. This may sound like an extravagance for people who lived in one of the worst slums in north-east London – the place where I was born – but the truth is, no one with any sense of pride would have been without mourning clothes. For men it would have been a dark blue serge suit. That evening the men and many of the women retired quietly to their local in order to console themselves. The King was dead. It was almost as if God himself had died.

Antonia Gamwell

One of my friends from Roedean lived in Lowndes Square, and she invited me to stay with them to see the funeral of the King. I was particularly pleased to do that because my uncle was marching beside the coffin. It was a magnificent procession. It was the last time so many crowned heads gathered together.

Ernest Hugh Haire

The college let us go where we liked on the day of the funeral, so five of us set out for Hyde Park. We arrived at quarter past six in the morning and the crowd lining the way was already about eight deep. The funeral procession didn't pass us until eleven, so in the meantime, we chatted with everybody. When the procession was about to come past, Alan Durban, a tall boy from Dover, went up to some girls and said to one of them, 'Could you possibly throw a faint?' 'If you like,' she said, and she dropped beautifully. Alan picked her up and shouted, 'Make way! Coming through!' and we all moved through the crowd until we were just behind the soldiers in the front row. So we were watching this marvellous procession of nine monarchs from a few yards away. We watched the Kaiser go past in his golden helmet. He was a nephew of Edward but Edward never liked him. Edward's little dog Caesar was there. The coffin was on a gun carriage and it was a quite magnificent procession. And Alan Durban ended up marrying that girl who pretended to faint.

'All the world is changing at once'
(Winston Churchill, 1911)

ACKNOWLEDGEMENTS

I would first and foremost like to thank Caroline Michel, the former Publisher of Harper Press, who conceived the idea for this book from the remarkable three-part documentary, 'The Lost World of Mitchell and Kenyon'. Caroline felt that what this silent movie footage of Lancashire during the early Edwardian period needed was the voices of the people. I hope that over the last year I have found and preserved those voices.

At Harper Collins I have had the pleasure of working with Kate Hyde, my editor, who has throughout the compiling of this book shown great enthusiasm for the project and has remained graceful, calm and patient under considerable pressure. Kate also selected the photographs for the book. I owe her a considerable debt. I would also like to thank Rachel Smyth, the Design Manager, Digby Smith, the Production Controller, Helen Ellis, the Publicity Director, and Mally Foster, the Press Officer, for their enthusiasm and expert help. Steve Cox did a tremendous job in copy editing the final draft.

Vicky Thomas and Josh Levine, who both worked with me on my last two books, put their considerable personal skills into transcribing and editing accurately and sensitively the many taped interviews. They have made this book a pleasure to compile and I profoundly thank them. I am more than delighted that Vicky is now researching her own book, *The Naga Queen*, and Josh is adding the final words to *Forgotten Voices of the Blitz and the Battle for Britain* to be published in October 2006.

I have been extremely well served by a number of curators of archives and I wish to thank them all for their courtesy and efficiency throughout the writing of *Lost Voices of the Edwardians*. The Imperial War Museum, where I am most grateful to Margaret Brooks, the Keeper of the Archive, and her always co-operative colleagues, John Stepford-Pickering and Richard McDonagh, as well as the museum's own very fine oral historian, Peter Hart. The Museum of London, where the curators Beverley Cook and Annette Day provided expert help and assistance with their fine archive. Robert Perks, the Curator of Oral History at the British Library, gave me constant support – his internationally renowned archive proved invaluable. I am absolutely indebted to Jo Bath of the Beamish Museum Sound Archive for her tireless research into the mining and industrial communities of the North East; her ear for the local dialect has much enriched this book. Jane and Paul Renouf of the Ambleside Oral History Society provided a wealth of wonderful local reminiscences from people, many of whom they had interviewed in person. Vanessa Toulmin, the Research Director of the National Fairground Archive at the University of Sheffield and joint co-ordinator of the Mitchell and Kenyon Project, contributed colourful memories of life in the Edwardian fairground and circus. She is currently compiling a land-mark collection of Edwardian images from the Mitchell and Kenyon film archive. I very much look forward to its publication in October, and thank her for her enthusiastic support for this book. Thanks, too, to Padmini Broomfield, of the Cultural Services Oral History Unit at Southampton; Andrew Schofield of the North West Sound Archive; Sheila Forster, Oral History Co-ordinator, Culture and Leisure Services, Durham; Van Wilson, York Oral History Society – to all of them I am most grateful for their co-operation and kindness.

I would particularly like to thank my friends Sir Martin and Lady Gilbert for their constant encouragement and advice and my brother, Adrian, who was always on hand to advise me on various military matters. I would also like to thank my dear friends, Don and Liz McClen, who saw me through my first book in 1983, and continue to give me their constant support, as does the broadcaster Susan Jeffreys.

ACKNOWLEDGEMENTS

In the writing of this book my very dear friend Ruth Cowen has always given me a quality of friendship that enriches my life. She gave unstintingly of her time and expertise, particularly in the editing of the first draft of the book. Her own book, *Relish: A Life of Alexis Soyer*, will be published in June 2006.

Throughout the writing of this book Lucia Corti has shown much patience, and continues to bring love and laughter into my life.

In compiling an oral history of an era so distant I was able to conduct only very few interviews in person, these men being centenarian survivors of the Great War. I had, therefore, to rely extensively on oral archives and in a few cases on published and unpublished autobiographical material. I have selected material from the following titles – I am most grateful to the publishers for their permission to use extracts:

Catching Stories – Voices from the Brighton Fishing Community (QueenSpark Publishing, 1996)

Lord Brabazon of Tara, *The Brabazon Story*, (Willliam Heinemann, 1956)

Sir Geoffrey de Havilland, *Sky Fever* (Wren's Park Publishing, 1979)

S F Edge, *My Motoring Reminiscences* (G T Foulis and Co, 1934)

George Ewart Evans, *The Days that We Have Seen* (Faber and Faber, 1975)

Frank Hedges Butler, *Fifty Years of Travel by Land, Water and Air*, (T Fisher Unwin Ltd, 1920)

Angela Hewins (ed.), *The Dillen, Memoirs of a Man of Stratford upon Avon* (Oxford University Press, 1982)

Sonia Keppel, *Edwardian Daughter*, (Hamish Hamilton, 1958)

Venetia Murray (ed.), *Where Have all the Cowslips Gone?* (Bishopsgate Press, 1985)

A V Roe, *The World of Wings and Things*, (Hurst and Blackett, 1939)

Rogan Taylor and Andrew Ward, *Kicking and Screaming, an Oral history of Football in England* (Robson Books, 1995)

Michael J Winstanley (ed.), *Life in Kent at the Turn of the Century* (William Dawson and Son Ltd, 1978)

PICTURE CREDITS

While every effort has been made to trace the owners of copyright material reproduced herein, the publishers would like to apologise for any omissions and will be pleased to incorporate missing acknowledgements in any future editions.

2. Funeral of Queen Victoria at Windsor, 1901 (TopFoto.co.uk)
6. Child with an eel and meat pie. (Kevin MacDonnell)
20. Boys and girls of St Joseph's and St Matthew's Schools, Blackburn, 1905 (bfi)
   Alfred Butterworth & Sons, Glebe Mills, Hollinwood, 1901 (bfi)
39. A boy playing with soldiers. (NMPFT – Kodak Collection)
50. A schoolgirl is checked for lice and nits. (GLC Photo Library)
65. Schoolgirls being taught to prepare food. (TopFoto.co.uk)
   Classroom scene. (GLC Photo Library)
85. Easter parade for St Joseph's School, Blackburn. (bfi)
104. Spinning in Lancashire in 1901. (TopFoto.co.uk)
   Making deliveries for the brewery Nuttall & Co, Blackburn. (bfi)
108. Tim Miners, Cornwall, 1906. (TopFoto.co.uk)
112. Workers leaving Pendlebury Colliery after their shift.(bfi)
   Women working with a recent catch: North Shields, 1901.(bfi)
132. (top and bottom) Workers leaving North Street Mill, Chorley, 1901. (bfi)
150. Parkgate Ironworks, Rotherham,1905. (bfi)

181. Policeman on duty at Hunslet vs Leeds 1901. (bfi)
    A pint of old and mild at a village alehouse, c.1906. (copyright unknown)
200. 'Cats' meat man' on a slum street, London 1905. (Top-Foto.co.uk)
    The house party at Stonor Park, Henley on Thames, gathered for a pheasant shoot. (Getty Images)
207. Bath time in a slum dwelling c.1901. (Getty Images)
    A middle-class family having tea in 1910. (Getty Images)
211. Domestic Economy School. (GLC Photo Library)
    Maids on a Cunard vessel, Liverpool 1902 (bfi)
216. Ada Wayter with her eight brothers and sisters. (Getty Images)
219. Salvation Army shelter, Medland Hall, 1901. (copyright unknown)
222. A man with a handful of pawn tickets sitting with his family in London's East End. (Getty Images)
233. Miss Lillie Langtry. (Getty Images)
238. Waiting for handouts of food in Cheapside, London 1901.
    The butcher's boy. (copyright unknown)
    The muffin man. (copyright unknown)
253. Greengrocer stall. (copyright unknown)
    Butcher stall. (copyright unknown)
262. London's Oxford Street in 1909. (Getty Images)
276. The Cup Final, 1905: Aston Villa vs Newcastle United. (copyright unknown)
    Enthusiastic crowd at Hull FC's ground, 1902. (bfi)
298. Entertainment at Hull Fair, 1902. (bfi)
    Devon and Somerset Staghounds taking lunch among the coaches. (Getty Images)
307. A music hall gallery, c.1902. (copyright unknown)
    The Whip, 1909, at Drury Lane. (Kevin MacDonnell)
318. Ballooning. (Flight International)
329. Jamaica Street, Glasgow, 1901. (bfi)
331. Wigan Fire Brigade, 1902 (bfi)
337. Horse-drawn tram, Manchester, 1901. (bfi)

Celebrating the opening of the Acrington Electric Tramway in 1907 (bfi)

341. London's Piccadilly Circus in 1910 (c) Museum of London.

350. Motorists pose for a photograph in their cars. (Getty Images) The start of a relay race at Brooklands racetrack in 1909. (Getty Images)

352. Claude Graham-White risking life and limb in a Farman biplane. (Flight International)

360. Victoria Pier, Blackpool, 1904. (bfi) Women are carried to the water by horse-drawn bathing machine. (copyright unknown)

364. Arriving at Henley-on-Thames for the Royal Regatta. (GLC Photo Library)

375. Emmeline Pankhurst (front left) leading a suffragette parade through London with protesters all dressed in white. (Getty Images) Degree Day at Birmingham University, 1901. (bfi)

394. Newsboys hawking papers with stories of the surrender of Pretoria and the end of the Boer War. (Time Life Pictures/ Getty Images)

398. Edward VII and the Kaiser during the State visit to Berlin in February, 1909.

406. Still from 'The Arrest of Goldie', dir. Mitchell & Kenyon, 1901. (bfi)

INDEX